Conversion and the Rehabilitation of the Penal System

Conversion and the Rehabilitation of the Penal System

A *Theological Rereading of Criminal Justice*

ANDREW SKOTNICKI

OXFORD
UNIVERSITY PRESS

OXFORD
UNIVERSITY PRESS

Oxford University Press is a department of the University of Oxford. It furthers
the University's objective of excellence in research, scholarship, and education
by publishing worldwide. Oxford is a registered trade mark of Oxford University
Press in the UK and certain other countries.

Published in the United States of America by Oxford University Press
198 Madison Avenue, New York, NY 10016, United States of America.

CIP data is on file at the Library of Congress
ISBN 978–0–19–088083–5

1 3 5 7 9 8 6 4 2

Printed by Sheridan Books, Inc., United States of America

Contents

Acknowledgments

THE IDEAS FROM which I draw in this book are the fruit of seeds sown in the decades that I have worked in different capacities in jails and prisons across the United States. The thousands and thousands of confined men and women as well as officers and staff with whom I have shared myself and who have shared themselves with me have in demonstrative ways made me, for better or worse, who I am. To those long ago and far away souls I send a fervent prayer of love and gratitude.

To locate the efficient causes of this book, one would need only take the 1 or the A Train downtown from where I work and reside to the 59th Street exit in Manhattan and the nearby John Jay College of Criminal Justice. That remarkable institution provided the opportunity to work on two essays and engage brilliant and supportive colleagues that led decisively to the book you are about to read. The first essay, "Religion, Conversion, and Rehabilitation," published in John Jay's *Criminal Justice Ethics* under the masterful guidance of its editor, Dr. Jonathan Jacobs, provoked a sustained reflection on the valence of conversion as a possible rudder for the correctional vessel. The second was a paper presented at the kind behest of John Jay's then-president, Jeremy Travis, at the Interdisciplinary Roundtable on Punitiveness in America. The essay, "Theological Approaches to Wrongdoing, Punishment, and Forgiveness," was a brief overview of the topic, but its richer benefit was to provide the insight that the daunting issues we confront in criminal law and policy can only be addressed substantively at the metaethical level. Finally, I was graced with the opportunity to spend a semester as a visiting scholar at John Jay in 2016 where I was supported, challenged, and befriended by two outstanding criminal justice scholars, Lila Kazemian and David Green. I cannot underestimate how large a role each of them played in assuring me that a theologian might actually have something to say to secular academicians, generally, and social scientists in particular. Lila even lent me her former office, saying that it had proved to be a fecund intellectual incubator for some of her work. I will let you decide if it did the same for me.

Introduction

THIS IS NOT meant to be a practical book. Readers hoping for a theological interpretation of the contemporary practice of criminal justice that is trimmed to fit within the movements currently active in prison reform would be wise to look to other more conciliatory accounts.[1] My intentions in this book, rhetoric aside, are more revolutionary. Revolutions, employing Harold Berman's understanding, are ruptures in consciousness, social practice, and moral self-understanding that decisively change historical precedent.[2] While the refashioning of the criminal justice system, including its legal foundation and various justifications, is not on a par with epochal events like the Papal revolution of the eleventh century; the Protestant Reformation; or the French, American, or Russian revolutions, the perspective taken in this volume could not be adopted without a large-scale transformation of penal philosophy; practice; and, indeed, worldview; or, more realistically, without an openness on the part of those who justify, operate, and reflect upon the system of criminal justice to the contributions from religious tradition and theological principle that will be presented in this volume.[3]

Specifically, I will argue that the term rehabilitation and synonyms popular among criminologists like desistance and reform are, for the most part, so hopelessly dualistic, judgmental, and in service to social ends inimical to whatever humane goals they hope to achieve that they should be stricken from the penal lexicon. I will further argue that a morally defensible, historically coherent, and effective approach to detention must manifestly reject any retributive or deterrent aims, save as latent functions of a primary focus upon conversion. This latter concept, understood as the ongoing process of overcoming subject/object duality at the intellectual, moral, and spiritual levels is, I believe, the only justification that can bear the moral and social weight and "unwanted irony" of inflicting the public violence of incarceration as a reaction to acts of private misconduct.[4] Conversion should serve as the anchor for the penal project, and if we are to be faithful to the history of confinement, it must serve as the anchor for the penal project. For it was the primary motivation for the unprecedented correctional methodology developed in the practice of penance and in the first Christian monasteries to employ time and spiritual counsel in a restricted setting as the means of shedding light upon and healing the alienation that is at the root of harm deliberately done to others. History has proven that all attempts to manipulate that penitential and monastic framework to serve other ends, including the various ideologies that vie for control of current institutional dynamics, have, in cost/benefit terms, produced too little social benefit and have cost far too much in terms of human misery.[5]

A revolution begins first of all in the imagination and requires an apocalyptic metaphor to inspire as well as sustain it, a stabilizing ideology that in the words of Mary Douglas, "sacralizes" the principles of justice by finding an analogy "in the physical world, or in the supernatural world, or in eternity, anywhere, so long as it is not seen as socially contrived."[6] In other words, to weather successfully the ravages of history, novel social experiments require a vision of the end, a teleology that guides the movement or institution to a future that is glorious (at least in the eyes of the revolutionaries). Robert Cover terms this a "nomos," a normative foundation that hallows concepts of good and evil and right and wrong. From this point of view, promulgated law, despite the claim of legal positivists, is never merely a set of contingent rules to be observed simply because they are enforced; rather, it establishes the contours and meaning of the "world in which we live."[7] Such an ultimate or transcendent foundation is needed, even in secular ideologies, to ground an institution in the heroism of its founding ideals and sustain it through the inevitable social and epistemological crises that threaten to destabilize any organization that is incapable of finding the resources within its historical memory to confront the tensions created by new social configurations and new and countervailing information.[8]

In Judeo-Christian cosmology and eschatology—the principal source for the correctional vision to be espoused in this study—the consummation of history will reveal the unity of all life in God.[9] Despite the ongoing and seductive popularity of Manichean and Gnostic mythologies among many religious adherents that pit an inherently vile, diabolical, and corrupt world against an otherworldly, celestial society populated with disembodied spirits, the Judeo-Christian proclamation is decidedly political and material or, as I will suggest shortly, participatory, in which all hierarchical, oppositional, and exclusionary divisions will be finally and decisively overcome: "The wolf will live with the lamb, the leopard will lie down with the goat. . . . The infant will play near the cobra's den, and the young child will put its hand into the viper's nest. They will neither harm nor destroy on all my holy mountain, for the earth will be filled with the knowledge of the

Lord as the waters cover the sea" (Isa 11: 6, 8–9). There will be an end of national rivalries and a reign of peace will emerge where the implements of war will be transformed into tools to feed the hungry (Isa. 2: 2–4). Jesus repeatedly employs the metaphor of the reign of God in speaking of both the meaning and goal of history; a reign that is described using social and penal metaphors: "liberty to captives," "sight for the blind," "freedom for the oppressed" (Lk. 4: 18). In fact, so insistent is Jesus upon an inclusive ethical vision that the constant theme in his preaching and parables is to begin at the margins, with those considered socially worthless and religiously scandalous, and to magnify not only their inherent sacredness but also their privileged view of reality and of the ways of God (Mt. 19: 30, 20: 16, 21: 31, 25: 31–41; Mk. 10: 31; Lk. 6: 20–26). St. Paul often repeats the theme of ontological unity and rejection of the sacred/profane dichotomy: "God has given us the wisdom to understand fully the mystery, the plan he was pleased to decree in Christ. A plan . . . to bring all things into one in him, in the heavens and on earth" (Eph. 1: 9–10); "[T]hrough [Christ] God was pleased to reconcile to himself all things, whether on earth or in heaven, by making peace through the blood of his cross" (Col. 1: 20).

The particular juridical relevance of this all-embracing vision of the meaning of history to the common practice of criminal justice is found in the Catholic concept of Purgatory. The latter, despite the distortions associated with the sale of indulgences that so rightly infuriated leaders of the Protestant Reformation, functions as a divine prison; a place where those trapped in self-preoccupation and hostility are purified through the process of penance so as to enter into loving union with God and all that God has created.[10] It is not a place of retribution but one of conversion, an immersion in the very restorative dynamics developed in the first monastic prisons to enable errant monks to once again join the common life. I have written in another context that Purgatory was the apocalyptic metaphor necessary for the normalization of the prison at the end of the thirteenth century.[11] It is no coincidence that the directive of Pope Boniface VIII, incorporated into canon law in 1298, to establish confinement in ecclesiastical prisons as the formal means to address "criminal sins" by clerics throughout the Catholic world did not occur until after the existence of Purgatory was proclaimed at the Second Council of Lyons in 1274. It provided the metaphysical horizon necessary to situate the prison within a transcendent and restorative context, the only context in which it can function correctly.[12]

The philosophical foundations that underlie current correctional practice and reflection upon that practice can be traced to a revolution of their own. Arguably, construction of that ideological edifice began at the 1870 Penal Congress in Cincinnati. It brought together the leading reformers of the day such as Enoch Wines and Zebulon Brockway and a host of national and international invitees buoyed by the optimism of new scientific theories and moral good will that would infuse the Progressive Era, and in many ways our own, with a secularized version of the Christian millennium.[13] The papers for the conference in no way belittled religious faith,[14] indeed a number of the conference participants, including Wines, were members of the clergy; rather, reminiscent of notable Christian intellectuals of an earlier time, they sought to win respect for religion by proving to their secular and skeptical counterparts that its precepts were fully coherent with enlightened reason and the canons of scientific investigation.[15] Thus, they willingly conceded that the emphasis on conversion that had played such a significant role in the motivation and configuration of the original monastic prisons, and to a substantial degree in the early American penitentiaries, had to yield precedence to the incipient social sciences, whose methods, joined primarily with education, would provide the necessary means to bring about the "moral regeneration" of prisoners through individualized treatment.[16]

Despite these decidedly secular procedural guidelines, the Progressives were not lacking their own "apocalyptic" metaphor in their blueprint for the correctional landscape. It was found in the reformatory, an institution which they were certain would not only correct the shortcomings of the penitentiary by the use of methodical, rational analysis and by adopting innovative practices from America and abroad, it would also symbolize the moral horizon, the telos, for the entire legal, institutional, and moral order.[17]

My argument will in part echo the thought of David Rothman concerning this era of reform and those that have come in its wake. He maintains that despite the genuine concern of its advocates, Progressivism failed due to its inability to perceive or pay sufficient heed to the inherent contradiction involved in willing that people suffer the pains of confinement and, at the same time, hoping that the carceral experience would make them better human beings, or at least more socially acceptable. As a result of this conceptual antinomy, generally benevolent intentions were continually stymied and then further undermined by a host of personal, political, and bureaucratic failures. In Rothman's words: "[Progressives] were convinced that their innovations could satisfy *all* goals, that the same . . . institution could at once guard and help, protect and rehabilitate, maintain custody and deliver treatment . . . [T]he Progressive effort to link them failed. In the end, when conscience and convenience met, convenience won. When treatment and coercion met, coercion won."[18]

There is little need to rehash what Rothman and other penal historians have written concerning the programmatic and instrumental errors that doomed the reformatory and, for that matter, have doomed subsequent efforts to breathe life into the moribund body of the prison. Instead, I want to highlight what I believe are the ideological and philosophical shortcomings not only of Progressivism but of virtually all current frameworks for conceptualizing and implementing the system of criminal justice. I will argue that the reforms initiated at the 1870 Congress and the consequent over-reliance upon dispassionate scientific analysis and therapeutic intervention have failed to address the "crime problem" and will continue to fail not because of the particular emphases they have championed—individualized case management, civic virtues, education, and alternatives to incarceration—but from two fundamental errors: the inability to anchor the penal project in a transcendent moral horizon and from their dualist philosophical foundations.

Concerning the first issue, the reformers and their heirs have not recognized the essential role of a moral ontology that emphasizes a natural belonging or connectedness of each to the whole of reality and a recognizable and inherently attainable goal of overcoming alienation without the need to coerce or intervene clinically in the life of the incarcerated person. Progressives and their heirs dismissed theological and metaphysical concepts and an ontology of inherent goodness as necessary to achieve the goals of fostering productive and cooperative citizenship. Instead, they took two basic approaches to criminal justice, sometimes confrontational but ultimately complementary.

One of these approaches transformed the millennial beliefs of the evangelicals who championed the Second Great Awakening and the penitentiary and, like them, maintained the erroneous and ultimately tragic vision that American institutions and its "Christian" culture were sufficient to ground the practice and, indeed, the hopes of a system of criminal accountability that could transform the lives of those under its control.[19] The residue of this unstable foundational principle is seen most forcefully in the large majority of social scientific analyses that posit the legal and social order as independent variables and measure the adjustment or adaptation of offenders to that order as the test of correctional efficiency.[20] The second expression of this organizational philosophy is seen in the mantric assurance that controlled, methodical analysis in service to a utilitarian and behaviorist conception of human development is the essential resource for programs aiming at character transformation and social adaptability. Rather than the age-old stance predicated upon a transcendent moral horizon, David Garland points out that the Progressive Era inaugurated a detention system that reflected the "rational and scientific conceptions of penal administrators and criminologists . . . These 'managerial' concerns gradually came to dominate penological discourse, turning it into a 'penitentiary science' rather than a moral philosophy."[21] Todd Clear and his colleagues similarly state that by the turn of the twentieth century, "scientific knowledge had displaced religion as a paradigm for explaining and controlling crime. Governed by the rule of empiricism, the new penal science made no accommodation for the mystical musings of religion."[22]

When the inevitable tensions and crises involved in incarceration and systemic maintenance arose, neither of these approaches had at its disposal any other recourse than the use or threat of violence to address the problem.[23] Such shallow moral foundations virtually guarantee that the current architects and administrators of criminal justice, including programs instituted to rehabilitate the confined, will continue to rely on this default, and ultimately fruitless value of power until they begin to consider an alternative: the initial correctional ethos revealed in early Christian penitential and monastic practice. Attention to this latter strategy would provoke a consideration of the functional ramifications of the assumption that all life is sacred, that people are fundamentally good—although often tragically flawed—and ultimately made whole due to their capacity for metanoia and selflessness: a process inimical to any demonstration of violence, even for the best of intentions.

The second besetting flaw in virtually all "post-religious" formulations of penal organization is dualism. That is to say they proceed from a worldview that divides reality into those with problems and those who solve their problems, or between those who need help and those who are qualified to help them, or, in the worst case, between the morally evil and the morally good. Once terms like offender or recidivist or morally maladjusted are used as synonyms for a class of people and those so characterized are defined in terms of risk or criminogenic factors, once they become "dependent variables," they are not "ends in themselves" and, from a phenomenological as well as theological perspective, they can neither be appreciated nor understood for who they are.[24] Furthermore, the ones who use the terms, whether this is intended or not, place themselves in the social and moral category of the non-offenders, somehow impervious to or having overcome the pitfalls leading to the erroneous ordering of values, or inadequate socialization, or character weakness that resulted in illegal or asocial behavior. Put another way, seeing the offender as "other" *is* the very problem that needs to be addressed if there is to be any positive future for the idea of a correctional system.

Both the default value of power and we-they, subject-object dichotomies provide the basic moral grammar of political and legal action, social scientific reports, and penal culture. They represent a "colonization by means of which the unknown is incorporated, assimilated, appropriated . . . without ever allowing its difference from the familiar to emerge."[25] In such a truncated ethical environment, as Zygmunt Bauman suggests, the "sharp knives" of order and norm become the only means to confront the human spirit that is "endemically diversified, erratic and unpredictable": "Norm is the reflection of the model of order as it is projected on human conduct. . . . 'Abnormal' stands for any departure from the favored pattern; it turns into deviation, which is an extreme case of abnormality, a conduct calling for therapeutic or penal intervention."[26] This objectification and control of those defined in terms of "criminogenic" factors must be confronted and overcome if forcible detention is to operate in a historically and ethically coherent fashion. None of this will occur without a recognition of the need for conversion, not only among those who are locked up, but also, or perhaps especially, among those who lock them up and among those who try to understand the phenomenon of criminal punishment and prescribe its institutional expression.

This call for an appreciative hermeneutic of the historical and moral origins of the prison is by no means an expression of nostalgia for theocratic intervention in the social system or for dogmatic orthodoxy. Neither is it an attempt at a surreptitious or backdoor evangelism. It is above all a call to affirm the fundamental decency of human beings qua human beings and their ability to find their way to an affirmative sociability without waving or applying the disciplinary lash. It is primarily a summons for an end to the protracted and false dualism not only within the social sciences but also between science and religion. What the theologian calls "spirit" and the scientist calls "energy" are synonymous; and both are necessarily related to matter. Just as I have criticized a scientific ideology that pays little heed to or is consciously scornful of theology and spirituality, so I am equally dismayed by what can be termed "toxic religion." The latter is ubiquitous: judgmental, legalist, and, invariably, punitive, it suffers from an elitism that is frequently quick to denigrate those who fall short of "selected" norms of sacred texts or are understood to be deviants.[27] It is associated often with a Manichean contempt for "the world" and a competitive, perverse view of conversion that divides humanity between the saved and the damned, reserving endless bliss for the former and endless misery for the latter. Such a dualist perspective dwells, oddly enough, in a space not far distant from the sort of dualism, often couched in therapeutic or social analytic language, that one finds in the decidedly areligious criminal justice literature with its methodological perspective of observational neutrality. Both tend to operate in what Owen Barfield calls "the desert of non-participation."[28]

The moral framework that utilizes conversion as its basic metaphor is one that sees participation as *the* foundational truth rather than emotional remoteness, rational analysis, and objective judgment.[29] Its roots are found in what the philosopher Karl Jaspers has termed the "Axial Age." He maintains that "the axis of history is to be found in the period around 500 BC." It was then that figures such as Confucius, Lao-Tse, the Buddha, the prophets Isaiah and Jeremiah, Plato, Aristotle, and Zoroaster, among others, lived and taught.[30] It was the birth of the unitive or integrative thinking that underlies the Eastern traditions of Hinduism, Taoism, and Buddhism and significant strains of spiritual thought in Judaism, Eastern and Western Christianity, and Sufism. It signaled the end of civilizations thousands of years old (Babylon, Egypt, Indus Valley, and the aboriginal cultures of China) and "gave rise to a common frame of historical self-comprehension for all peoples . . . for all the earth, without regard for particular articles of faith."[31] In the expansive inclusivity of its vision, wisdom and enlightenment proceed from a nonjudgmental, compassionate engagement with reality and, inevitably, with the divine or life principle that pulses within its endless manifestations. Among the people of Israel, the notion of participation was widened to include the nation as a whole in its covenantal relationship with Yahweh and, through the prophets, revealed itself in a distinct concern for the alien and the poor. The nascence of participatory religion in the Axial Age and the particular emphases of the Hebrew Scriptures anticipated the teaching of Jesus whose message of universal compassion pointed to and sought to deepen the union of all things in the force of love that created them.[32]

The theme of participation, without the conscious metaphysical touchstones, has echoes in the sociological theory of Alfred Schutz and Edward Shils, among others, and in the phenomenological tradition in Philosophy. Both Schutz and Shils argue, in different ways, that whatever knowledge can be derived from an encounter with another person can only come through a suspension of judgment and entering into a consensual relationship that Schutz described as "growing old together."[33] Edmund Husserl, and those influenced by his thought, among them, Heidegger, begin with a belief that "an appearance 'of something', does *not* mean showing-itself; it means rather the announcing-itself by something which does not show itself."[34] It is only through patient and empathic presence that "different worlds of experience . . . may still be united together through actual empirical connections into a single intersubjective world."[35]

From this religious, sociological, and phenomenological perspective, the problem that needs to be addressed for all human beings, including those who are destructive of themselves and others, is not crime; it is alienation. It is the lack of mutuality and compassionate interchange with nature, with others, and with the deepest part of the self. The solution is not punishment but a commitment to human goodness and the capacity for humans to expand their intellectual, moral, and spiritual horizons to include what was once excluded, until nothing and no one is outside the circle of care. Overcoming alienation is a problem for every human being, not simply those who have become enmeshed in the criminal justice system. Conversion is the necessary process by which that alienation is overcome and participation is either created or restored.

The chapters that follow will expand upon each of the ideas discussed thus far. Chapter 1 will discuss in greater detail the rift in historical continuity between the present and past of criminal justice regarding the practice of and justification for confinement. The moral question will be raised once again, especially what I see as the discomfort of much criminological scholarship with using moral language in anything but the most cursory and general ways, partly because, in my opinion, the ethical vocabulary is so thin conceptually that it can only be assumed within the "language games" unique to criminal theorists. The question of dualism will also be addressed in greater detail. Like the moral question, the dispassionate view of the "impartial spectator," so pertinent to the philosophical assumptions of current correctional analysis, is rooted in a deeper religious language from which it has borrowed the concept of "interiority" with its emphasis on the autonomy and integrity of individual decision making.[36] It has, however, lost its connection to a transcendent moral universe that relativizes any claims to objectivity or ontological difference between self and other. Finally, the chapter will reiterate some of the critical perspectives on the penal system that have been offered by contemporary scholars. The intent will not be to catalogue (once again) the besetting ills of the correctional body as much as to highlight the systemic dysfunction and human suffering that emerge when penal practice is organized under a logic separate from or inimical to a focus upon conversion as the most historically and morally coherent justification for the pain of confinement.

Chapter 2 will take up the critique of retribution and deterrence. While rehabilitation will be discussed in detail in Chapter 4, some of its perceived and, in my estimation, fatal shortcomings will also be raised. Proceeding from the argument concerning dualism and taking into account David Rothman's critique of the Progressive desire to detain, punish, teach, and correct at the same time, I will argue that to will the suffering of another, or to use the suffering of another to cause circumspection, if not fear, in the mind of a potential lawbreaker, or to determine not only that a person is morally deficient but also to prescribe a curative formula whose merits are judged solely by the architects of the intervention, frustrates the hopes of achieving the goal of intellectual, moral, and spiritual transformation and is indicative of a restricted and fearful consciousness that is itself in need of conversion. That is to say, punishment harms the punisher as well as the punished and is often linked to scapegoating, projection, and the most pernicious forms of religious and social ideology.

Chapter 3 will feature an analysis of the concept of conversion. As suggested earlier, I will adopt a definition of conversion as a radical shift in one's intellectual, moral, and spiritual horizons. The stages are not sequential, and one does not necessarily lead to another except in the case of the "infinite" horizon of a spiritual conversion with its panoptic compassion and its profound moral and intellectual humility. Conversion will be seen as inimical to punishment since, summarizing William James, its germination within the given person is most often initiated by a captivating moment of love and acceptance—never rejection or harsh treatment—and while it can at times be the fruit of the will of its recipient, in all cases its epiphany in the life of the convert is received as a gift.[37]

The chapter will discuss in detail each type of conversion and what the author understands to be the phenomenology of the process: a series of steps that proceed from the initial encounter or peak experience, if you will, and inevitably feature a change in one's personal narrative. At the moral and, especially, the spiritual level the subject moves into a new and interactive social identity, a heightened sense of moral accountability to the adopted community, and a progressive expansion of the circle of compassion and care. It will be my contention that conversion was the primary motivation for the practice of confining individuals for the purpose of their moral betterment; it is the principal aim of the apocalyptic metaphor of Purgatory; and failure to reexamine its moral assumptions, its methodological framework, and the specific way the penal environment was structured in order to summon and sustain it, renders the practice of penal confinement, to a substantial degree, both morally and pragmatically pointless.

Chapter 4 will present what I see as the besetting problems with the concept of rehabilitation or desistance as it is currently being discussed in criminological literature and implemented in a wide range of institutional and programmatic contexts. Once again, the problem of dualism will be discussed as well as the socially conservative assumptions that seem to flow necessarily from the attempt to avoid foundational moral commitments and allow economic productivity, "good citizenship," and, especially, staying out of jail assume the place once occupied by the traditions of ethical and spiritual wisdom tracing back to the millennium before Christ. Despite the serious nature of the critique, numerous scholars across the disciplinary terrain will be mentioned whose work echoes different aspects of the concerns being raised in this volume; scholars who, in other words, not only care deeply about society and those entwined in its legal and criminal nets, but who also decry the technocratic approach to solving social problems, the over-reliance on social control as the only "scientific" barometer of character reform, and who fashion a set of "pro-social" ends and accompanying curricular and institutional strategies to aid in their accomplishment. Like the rest of the book, the analysis of this facet of what David Garland calls "penality" is intended as an invitation to broaden and deepen the historical and moral understanding of what is currently termed rehabilitation or desistance, not to diminish the good will and care that are espoused by so many of its proponents.

Chapter 5 will discuss how the penal system might truly come to resemble a correctional system or, to restate the pun in the book's title, how it might be rehabilitated. The presentation is less the fantasy of an idealist than an archaeological investigation into penal realism; into the spiritual, moral, and structural assumptions that set the template for what the prison was meant to be: a place of conversion. Like most of the book and its use of the guiding revolutionary metaphor, the intent is to rethink virtually all of the regnant assumptions in play for those who justify, operate, and reflect upon the juridical and penal order, particularly the principles of retribution, deterrence, and rehabilitation. One concept often utilized in criminological discourse has not as yet been the subject of discussion: incapacitation. That is not due to the fact that its formulation in current thought and practice is beyond critique. Indeed, the rise of selective incapacitation and its widespread adoption as a penal strategy, thanks in no small way to the influential ideas of James Q. Wilson, has borne as much responsibility for the dramatic rise in penitentiary commitments as any of the competing strategies.[38] The reason for delaying comment upon its relative merits to this time is based on Wilson's belief that incapacitation is not predicated upon moral assumptions about the subjects of criminal prosecution.[39] While it has functioned in a way that has underscored the racial and economic inequalities that plague contemporary practice, it is the only approach that complements the use of confinement as a place of conversion.

The Conclusion will summarize the basic argument made throughout the book. In the words of Jurgen Habermas: "[A] social system has lost its identity as soon as later generations no longer recognize themselves within the once constitutive tradition."[40] I have taken this quote into consideration in framing the title for the present work. It is not a "theological reading of criminal justice" but a "theological rereading." Events in intellectual and social history, fully explicable "compromises" within their given context, led to the severing of the correctional system from its theological, ethical, and methodological roots.[41] The intent will be to show that like all institutions that have lost contact with their foundational vision, their apocalyptic horizon, and the moral ideals required to reach them, the penal complex has abandoned the one idea necessary for it to be anything other than what some writers call "a crime against humanity," or "a disgrace to the ideals of the United States."[42] That is, it has lost sight of the idea of conversion and the "pro-social," inclusive, and nonviolent assumptions that it teaches those who receive it and are necessary for those who seek to foster it. Being "scientific" cannot be anything other than an exercise in exaggerated intellectual and, ultimately, social parochialism if done at the expense of considering the motivations, the moral commitments, and the practical institutional arrangements that laid the groundwork for the practice of confinement. At the same time, being theological or religious cannot be anything other than an exercise in hubris and a disfiguring of the participatory, inclusive, and indiscriminately compassionate message of the world's major religions without respectful and grateful attention to the contributions to human knowledge and human flourishing provided by secular scholars in the sciences and the humanities. I am, paraphrasing Clifford Geertz, arguing throughout the volume for conversion to uphold the system "all the way down": conversion as non-duality and enhanced openness at the intellectual, moral, and spiritual levels; conversion as inimical to violence and forceful intervention; conversion as a necessary development in the life of every person regardless of criminal record; and conversion as the only effective justification for locking people up against their will.[43]

I

The State of Penal Ideology and Penal Affairs

ONE OF THE central arguments of this book is that much of the diffuse and largely contradictory dialogue concerning the correctional sphere and the chaotic and violent penal empire that derives from it can be traced to the lack of a life-affirming moral ontology. By this I mean an understanding of the self as radically open to and capable of self-transcendence—a view of human flourishing far more capacious and consistent than the largely subjective moral assertions of academic "experts" and the ever-shifting populist terrain that form much of the grammar for the current conversation.[1]

As stated in the Introduction, theology is at its core a meta-discourse.[2] It provides a comprehensive understanding of the meaning of history; the origin and destiny of life; and, in the present case, a vision of human betterment that locates acts of malfeasance within the domain of social and psychological alienation.[3] Furthermore, theological systems generally and, for our purposes in this volume, Christianity in particular, provide a penitential and re-integrative methodology that addresses human violence without a need for violence and creates the conditions for conversions that expand levels of tolerance, compassion, and participation. This approach, perfected and reproduced over millennia, contrasts diametrically with current positivist determinations of legal fault and justifications for punishment based upon moral suppositions that can do no other than take for granted the formal legitimacy of the legal system and the constraints it unevenly imposes on the civilian population. Put another way, the currently operative jurisprudential and penal dynamics can summon from the offender or potential offender little more than a conformity entangled in the webs of social control and the ever-present threat of the lethal power of the state.[4] I am arguing that only with the sort of anthropological and moral horizon found in theological systems (despite their dreary catalogue of organizational and operational failures) is it possible to order rightly the various emotions that arise in response to illicit behavior and interpret correctly the theories that seek to give some ethical and practical coherence to the meaning of confinement.[5]

The inability to define a good human life in terms other than personal, political, or economic pragmatism has been noted by scholars (without necessarily agreeing with the argument I am making). Michael Sandel critiques the understanding of justice advanced by John Rawls not over "whether rights are important but whether rights can be identified and justified in a way that does not presuppose any particular conception of the good life."[6] Marie Gottschalk writes that the goals of contemporary penal policy—institutional reform, successful reentry strategies, and reinvestment of some of the billions poured annually into the correctional enterprise—are repeatedly weighed in "evidence based, cost-benefit scales." She contends that this reframing of "the problem of mass incarceration in econometric terms . . . is problematic in many ways. It does little to challenge the excessively punitive rhetoric that has left such a pernicious mark on penal policy in the last half century."[7] Gottschalk emphasizes a continual theme in that policy, one with deep roots in the history of American corrections: the refusal to honor the unique dignity and untold promise of each human life as a value in and of itself. Rather, public and legislative support for funding the prison complex must, above all issues, including, by and large, those concerned with human flourishing, be linked with reduced cost and increased public security.[8] David Garland states in similar fashion that the various agencies involved in criminal justice—courts, probation, prison, and parole—are "being remodeled in ways that emulate the value and working practices of private industry." The earlier emphasis on "social work" or what he terms, "penal welfare," has given way to the most effective and least expensive ways of "monitoring" offenders and "the management of risk."[9] These neoliberal influences upon judicial procedure point to the increased "rationalization of justice." They feature "a trend toward the introduction of business methods of management and improvement of cost-effectiveness" into the courts, not to mention a vigorous emphasis on individual responsibility rather than upon the demonstrable flaws within the justice and socioeconomic systems that strongly condition practices of arrest, prosecution, and confinement.[10]

The most disturbing effect of the lack of an organizing principle that honors human life as sacred and views its careful cultivation, even in its most damaged and deranged tenants, as an end in itself is found in the millions of lives that have been harmed, some irreparably, behind the walls of its myriad facilities.[11] If we are to address in substantive fashion what James Whitman calls the operational philosophy of "degradation" and "the intoxication that comes with treating people as inferiors," moral and philosophical presuppositions, buried under the weight of generations of repetitive practice, must be brought to light.[12]

Despite the criticism to which it will be subjected in this book, the rehabilitative ideal, which went into decline in the 1970s, had provided the correctional
milieu with the mythology that had shaped its philosophical underpinnings
since the Progressive Era.[13] Although there has been a resurgence of interest in
rehabilitation as a systemic goal and, indeed, enthusiasm for some of its current
incarnations, its decentering initiated an ongoing mission or legitimation crisis
for criminal justice that, as has been emphasized, manifests itself in conflicting
discourses and institutional ennui that have in turn withered public confidence
in the justice system and, indeed, in the moral authority of law itself.[14] Tom Tyler
writes that respect for the law "is based on citizen acceptance of the legitimacy
of the legal system and its officials."[15] He notes that the most important factor
in establishing this legitimacy is the belief in the normative value of compliance: "If normative values are absent, authorities must use mechanisms of deterrence that stem from instrumental control over rewards and punishments. Such
mechanisms are costly and in many cases may be inadequate."[16] For Jeremy Travis,
the "unifying ideals" established by the Progressives (rehabilitation, parole, probation) "no longer frame our penal policy. We now live in an era resembling the
Tower of Babel—we speak no common language when we discuss the purposes
of punishment."[17] Alasdair MacIntyre perhaps summarizes best the bitter and
strife-ridden moral landscape bequeathed to us as a result of the lack of a unifying
metaethical principle: "In any society where government does not express or
represent the moral community of citizens, but is instead a set of institutional
arrangements for imposing a bureaucratized unity on a society which lacks genuine moral consensus, the nature of political obligation becomes systematically
unclear."[18]

This loss of a common ground upon which to construct a humane and socially
effective practice of detention has as its cause two issues spoken of previously that
I would like to discuss in greater detail: the first is the system's insubstantial ethical foundations that continually prove themselves incapable of inspiring respect
for others, let alone altruism, and that have no other recourse than to seek compliance by relying upon a default reserve of coercive power. The second defect is
located in dualist, writ divisive, theories of knowledge and human relations rather
than upon knowledge and insight that proceed from an "I-Thou" encounter in
which all suppositions and judgments about one's interlocutor are subordinated
in favor of openness and compassionate presence.[19]

Liberal Polities and the Ontology of Violence

The dire portrait sketched above portrays a massive arsenal of power overseeing
an equally massive penal system that has lost its ability to frame a convincing

moral justification either to those punished or to those in whose ostensible name the punishment is inflicted. As Gresham Sykes phrases this tragic lacuna: "If the policy of the prison seems to exhibit a certain inconsistency, we might do well to look at the inconsistency of the philosophical setting in which the prison rests."[20]

Oddly enough, there is one point of agreement among most of those seeking the institutional and moral Esperanto that can unite the Babel of different penal grammars, exorcise the daily horrors faced by much of the confined population, and restore some sense of public confidence in the efficacy of correctional policy: whatever role religion may have played in the origin of the prison or, to varying degrees, in the early American penitentiaries has been supplanted by superior modes of logic and practical application.[21] Shadd Maruna and his colleagues correctly note that one of the original aims of confinement was to promote religious conversion; they also correctly note that such an approach is now considered to be "anachronistic."[22]

Since the rise of the Progressive Era, the ethos of both academicians and policy makers in the domain of criminal justice has been largely dismissive of, if not antagonistic to religion in general and Christianity in particular. Zebulon Brockway, perhaps the leading voice at the Cincinnati Penal Congress and the first warden of the prototypical reformatory at Elmira, New York, sounded an oft-repeated refrain in calling religion "a failed ideology."[23] A leading rehabilitative proponent, Edgardo Rotman, similarly echoes well-worn sentiments in promoting a client-centered, therapeutic model of reform rather than reliance on "metaphysical fixations and ideologies."[24] The authors of one study frankly admit that "there is an *inclination* [emphasis my own] among psychoanalysts to conclude that various psychopathological conditions are related to religious involvement."[25] Rodney Stark and his coauthors offer their reflection on the heretofore abiding lack of scholarly interest in probing the effects of religious practice on delinquency: "The overwhelming majority of social scientists were irreligious or even anti-religious. This led them to believe that religion was a disappearing and unimportant factor in human affairs."[26] When Stark and William Bainbridge some years ago surveyed the literature on religious experience and mysticism, they found "that, although the topic had received little attention, the psychopathological interpretation was the overwhelming favorite, with conscious fraud treated as the only possible alternative."[27] One leading scholar in the sociological study of religion and deviance, Byron Johnson, was dismissed from his first tenure-track position when the department chair and dean discovered that he was a practicing Christian.[28]

It would be a fool's errand to seek to be an apologist for the historical record of the major religions. The sample of authors quoted above and the opinions they represent are correct in asserting that people of faith, like many of their irreligious contemporaries, are not immune to "psychopathological conditions." Nor can it be disputed that "metaphysical fixations and ideologies" in both individuals and entire congregations have led to violently dehumanizing judgments and the sort of righteous arrogance that so easily clusters around a dualist vision of reality.

Writing on the origins of the predilection for atheism among the cultured and educated elites, Michael Buckley notes that the aversion of Enlightenment thinkers to religion (and, by extension, the aversion to "organized religion" one finds so often in the present context) proceeded from a legitimate, even laudable, weariness with intolerance and bloodshed, either perpetrated directly by various denominations or through their influence but, either way, done in the name of God. This "abhorrence" was reinforced by "a parallel aversion to relentless dogmatic conflicts and theological argument. Europe had become weary of double predestination and the limited number of the saved, of an original sin with muted humanistic values, and of an Augustinianism which read human impotence and perversion everywhere."[29]

But the cost of emphasizing the poisonous elements in religion, Christianity in particular, has been to spread the brush of irrelevance and delusion across a canvas as broad as that of Western civilization and, more to the point of the current state of correctional policy, to dismiss the relevance, and indeed necessity, of a system (ideally) based upon the inviolable worth of human beings and their natural affinity for self-correction without the need to inflict pain.

The various philosophical systems that arose, not without good cause, in opposition to the rancor of theological polemics steered clear of one problem only to confront another even more troubling: they shrunk the moral domain to deductions drawn from the knowledge of the natural sciences, utility, subjective sensibilities, or rationally apprehensible moral imperatives. Inasmuch as each of the latter three models lacks commitment to an ethical source that transcends individual calculation, and in the case of scientific deduction, reference to moral calculation as such, the unanimous court of last resort in response to faulty social engineering, wanton hedonism, misguided emotions, or irrational behavior was some form of violence. Gibson Winter writes that the "scientific" paradigm so often invoked among academics "celebrated the collapse of traditional cosmologies, but . . . could not tolerate the historical ambiguity which this collapse brought in its wake."[30] Emmanuel Levinas, though cognizant of the need for systems of justice in the "third party" realm that exists outside the bonds of intimate care, states that these systems are characterized by "ontological alienation," where "[l]aw takes precedence over charity" and the "third party is the free being whom I can harm by exerting coercion."[31]

The animus against religion and the search for a substitute "god" to fill the vacuum created by its moral and political demotion occupied the thought of

Hobbes and Rousseau, among others. The former, in a parody of the natural law theory of the "heathen" philosopher, Thomas Aquinas, insisted that political governance must be based upon the conviction that every person is "governed . . . by his own law" derived from "a mechanistic-materialist politics" that, in turn, is derived "from a mechanistic and materialist universe."[32] Rousseau exclaimed that Hobbes saw more clearly than either his contemporaries or predecessors the danger of any faith, save a private one, and steadfastly upheld the conviction that whatever rules may apply in a celestial society have neither bearing nor authority on earth.[33] He also revived the particular distrust of Christianity found in Machiavelli: "Christian teaching does more to undermine than to promote the good health of the state . . . [This] religion of the priest . . . drives a wedge between citizenship and piety."[34]

Both Hobbes and Rousseau, as social contractarians, understood well the tension between anarchic life in the state of nature and the compromises of personal liberty necessary to maintain a secure social existence. Each relied on the power of the sovereign (Hobbes) or the general will (Rousseau) to inflict suffering upon those profiting from the sacrifices made by others while refusing to make such sacrifices themselves. Hobbes writes that punishment is "evill inflicted . . . [for] transgression of the Law . . . to the end that the will of men may thereby the better be disposed to obedience . . . the aym of Punishment is not a revenge, but terrour."[35] Rousseau adds that "nothing save the power of the state ever makes its individual members free."[36] He further notes: "Each malefactor attacks the law of the body politic. He becomes, by reason of his crimes, a rebel against and a traitor to the fatherland . . . in point of fact levies war against it. His preservation is henceforth incompatible with that of the state: one or the other must perish."[37]

Locke similarly dismissed the ancient conviction of philosophers like Aristotle and Aquinas that the human person was, by nature, oriented for a life of virtue, concern for the common good, and the practice of contemplation.[38] He asserted the "falseness" of the "supposition" that there are "certain *innate principles* . . . stamped upon the mind . . . which the soul receives in its very first being and brings into the world with it."[39] Instead, all knowledge is derived from the senses to "furnish the yet empty cabinet," stamped upon a *tabula rasa*, "white paper, void of all characters, without any ideas."[40] The implications for the penitentiary as it developed in England in the late nineteenth century, and shortly thereafter in the United States, as Michael Ignatieff, for one, took notice, were that since all human motivation is infallibly linked to the experience of socialization, it stood to reason that people could only be re-socialized by controlling sensory input in a restricted environment; an approach "tantamount to treating human beings as machines."[41]

In such a formulation, unlike the classical theories against which Enlightenment thinkers rebelled, the fundamental goodness of the human person is sacrificed for a technical intrusion upon the will of the one to be properly molded. As Charles Taylor claims: "This anti-theological objectifying view of the mind doesn't only rule out theories of knowledge which suppose an innate attunement to the truth; it is also directed against moral theories which see us tending by nature toward the good."[42]

Despite the determinist character of Locke's theory of the self, he, like most influential writers in this period, believed in God, albeit a distant and punitive rather than a loving and forgiving one: "God has given a rule whereby men should govern themselves . . . and he has power to enforce it by rewards and punishments, of infinite weight and duration, in another life."[43] Like the moral sense theorists, of whom we will speak in a moment, he maintained that each person has "light enough to lead them to the knowledge of their Maker, and the sight of their own duties" and, despite the strength of external influences, is a moral agent who calculates actions in light of the certainty of a final judgment in which the good will be rewarded and evil brought to ruin: "It will be no excuse to an idle and untoward servant, who would not attend his business by candlelight, to plead that he had not broad sunlight. The candle that is set up in us shines bright enough for all our purposes."[44] This viewpoint is, in its own way, a reflection of the Calvinist or "hyper-Augustinian" notion, not to mention the current neoliberal one, that the sinner (writ delinquent), despite, often, insurmountable odds has, in the end, no one to blame but him or herself.[45]

The Utilitarians, motivated as they were by a noble desire to eliminate the cruelty so amply demonstrated and adamantly justified under retributive principles, conceived of a penal system based upon the belief that each individual calculates action in terms of the sovereign values of pain and pleasure: pain, synonymous with unhappiness, is the only true evil; pleasure, synonymous with happiness, the only true good.[46] In this conceptualization, punishment is evil, yet, the very presuppositions upon which utilitarianism is based make its unhappy application unavoidable: "Punishment is everywhere an evil; but everywhere a necessary one . . . No punishment, no government; no government, no political society."[47]

Cesare Beccaria and Jeremy Bentham, the foremost champions of utility in matters of criminal jurisprudence, reasoned that the only way to circumvent this conceptual conundrum was to focus upon the positive consequences the affliction might render upon the malefactor and upon those who might potentially engage in similarly proscribed behavior. In other words, the fundamental impropriety of punitive sanctions can be borne due to the superior amount of happiness that will ensue in the community through the infliction of the exact amount of suffering necessary to motivate a pleasure-seeking individual from indulging in

acts contrary to what the law has determined to be the greatest good for the majority of citizens. Bentham writes: "The immediate principled end of punishment
is to control action. This action is either that of the offender, or of others: that of
the offender it controls by its influence, either on his will . . . or on his physical
power . . . that of others it can influence no otherwise than by its influence over
their wills; in which case it is said to operate in the way of example."[48] Cesare
Beccaria, whose influential volume of 1764 had such an impact on penal reform in general and the ideas of Bentham in particular, states: "It is impossible
to prevent entirely all the disorders which the passions . . . cause in society . . . In
political arithmetic, it is necessary to substitute a calculation of probabilities
to mathematical exactness. That force which continually impels us to our own
private interest . . . acts incessantly, unless it meets with an obstacle to oppose
it . . . Punishments . . . prevent the fatal effects of private interest."[49]

In conjunction with Locke's empiricism, Utilitarian thinkers paved the way
for behaviorism: all human decision making is a product of external forces. There
is no core self; there is no appeal to an inner light; no sense that the human person
has the capacity to transcend half-hearted or ill-conceived or blatantly antisocial behavior with moral and spiritual resources internal to herself.[50] Quoting
Bentham again: "When one man says 'I like this' and another says 'I don't like
it', is there—on my view—anything more for them to say?"[51] Thus, for Bentham,
Beccaria, and their host of followers, the offender can only be molded by the
proper dosage of pain. Furthermore, there is no ultimate basis for the decision
upon whom this pain should be visited and for what reason, other than the
ever-shifting moral and political consensus. The socially conformist and morally
flexible results are obvious: "The behaviorist implicitly makes the project of the
common culture . . . the criterion of value by which he judges the adjustive or
maladjustive response."[52] As we shall note as the argument unfolds in succeeding
chapters, such politically conservative behaviorist notions underlie much of the
current scholarship among not only proponents of deterrence and retribution
but also, or perhaps especially, those favoring rehabilitation.

Among the various incarnations of moral sense theorists—generally less
abrasive than Hobbes and Rousseau but equally skeptical of the public face of
religion and its inherent theocratic tendencies—there was a general avowal of
Deism, "a theology and metaphysics that banished the miracle from the world."[53]
It adopted a view of Jesus as "a Jewish ethical preacher, still illuminating the
world" despite the fact that "the Church had distorted his beliefs and maxims
beyond recognition."[54] In this theoretical stance, moral principles reside in the
sentiments that inform and judge human action. Although, as with all emotion,
they must withstand the temptation to excess, the various sentiments are directed
by disinterested reason or what Adam Smith terms the "impartial spectator." It is

this internal witness who "overcomes our selfish desires to feel unconcerned over harm done to others."[55] He adds: "the violation of justice is injury; it does real and positive hurt to some particular persons, from motives which are naturally disapproved of. It is, therefore, the proper object of resentment and of punishment."[56] This resentment, however, is "noble and generous" and "never, even in thought, attempts any greater vengeance, nor desires to inflict any greater punishment than what every indifferent person would rejoice to see executed."[57]

Since, however, there is no appeal to a mythic narrative or primordial truth that contextualizes all particular judgments nor to the tutelage necessary to perfect the emotions in the way in which one is trained to embody the virtues, the appeal to feelings such as innate benevolence becomes one without any criteria save what the bearer of the sentiment claims it to be. It is for this reason that MacIntyre argues that moral sense theories and their liberal philosophical counterparts inevitably lead to emotivism: the belief that one's immediate affective or rational grasp of the meaning of an event furnishes the sole and unimpeachable validation of its authority. As a result, one is left with no standard to judge one person's estimation of benevolence, sympathy, or resentment over that of another.[58] Perhaps Nietzsche had something akin to this in mind when he wrote "the last territory to be conquered by the spirit of justice is that of reactive sentiment!"[59]

Immanuel Kant's overall philosophical project was far more complex and more cautious regarding the human subject's ability to judge correctly than his legacy among most moral philosophers would suggest.[60] However, if one bases one's reading of Kant upon "The Metaphysics of Morals" or the "Groundwork" for that volume (which are the standard texts quoted by retributivists), one must conclude that punishment is a categorical imperative: a necessary payment in pain for the violation of law. Like the other moral formulations in Kant's system, the rational agent is cognizant of the duty to resist all hypothetical objections and obey without question what the moral law and, by extension, its appearance in the civil law requires.[61] Neglect of these canons of reason can never be tolerated lest injustice be given priority over justice: "If legal justice perishes, then it is no longer worthwhile for men to remain alive on this earth."[62]

While Kant would not decry the offender's decision to live in accord with the moral law as a result of being punished or of having undergone a compulsory program aimed at social cooperativeness, such results could never take precedence over the strict need for retributive sanctions: "[J]ustice ceases to be justice if it can be bought for any price whatever . . . Accordingly, whatever underserved evil you inflict upon another within the people, that you inflict upon yourself."[63] Thus, the one who steals undermines the security of all who legitimately hold property and, as a result, the just principle of retribution demands that such a person sacrifice his or her property; just as the same principle holds that if someone "has committed murder he must die."[64]

The theories sanctioning punishment that have been briefly outlined (and which will be further discussed in subsequent chapters) represent in large part the perspectives on penal philosophy found in the present day. Despite the differences between them, all build upon subjective foundations: each person possesses within him or herself the capacity to know and perform normative moral requirements. In each, a rational, "disengaged" self, what Charles Taylor has termed the "punctual self," seeks to control a world that in the wake of the Protestant Reformation is no longer "enchanted."[65]

This is a far different starting point than the one I am invoking that claims that a substantive transformation of character—by which I understand the meaning of conversion—while triggered by an experience or insight internal to the individual, must be sustained in a community of affective relationships to which that individual is morally accountable. In the words of the theologian Bernard Lonergan, the experience of moral growth is "intensely personal" but "not so private as to be solitary. It can happen to many and they can form a community to sustain one another in their self-transformation and to help one another in working out the implications and fulfilling the promise of their new life."[66]

It is somewhat ironic that the subjectivist stance has its roots not in the adamantly secular Enlightenment, but in the notion of interiority developed in the thought of St. Augustine.[67] For the latter, neither the external socio/legal order nor the individual will determines the content of morality; rather, each person possesses an inner light that is shared but not possessed, like "sunlight" that points the will in the proper direction: "Do not go abroad; return within yourself. In the inward man dwells truth . . . transcend yourself even as a reasoning soul. Make for the place where the light of reason is kindled."[68] At the same time, for Augustine, the created world is an external realization of God's perfect order. As humans we are called upon to respect, indeed love, that order. In fact, the entire condition of the soul is contingent upon what one loves.[69]

The difference between Augustine's understanding of the primacy of interiority and the way the idea developed during the Enlightenment is that, for Augustine, the inner life was a continual interplay between human consciousness and the presence within each of the divine. In this dynamic interchange, the believer seeks to bend his or her will to the necessarily true dictates of conscience, echoed and reinforced in the Scriptures and the teachings of the Church.[70] For the latter theorists, on the other hand, the "gap" between the pragmatic self and the core self could simply be resolved by consulting the hedonic calculus, moral reason, or the impartial spectator. In either case, rather than one's will "returned to us . . . as grace, and as restoration of a good that one can only enjoy in common," human beings came to "think of the highest good, in Stoic fashion, as that which can be self-possessed."[71]

The self that tore itself loose from religious shackles was now confronted with the need to construct a system of justice that somehow avoided the excesses of religious strife and doctrinal policing and yet reproduce the frequent ability of religious traditions to summon un-coerced consent to their foundational truths and core moral values. Jean Delumeau notes that despite these efforts, the philosophical and moral perspectives espoused by new doctrines of the self and society proved incapable of accomplishing either task: "Our era constantly speaks about liberating itself from guilt feelings without noticing that, in the history of guilt, the accusation of others has never been as strong as it is today."[72]

Marcel Gauchet has written of the dramatic social effects of importing the "divine otherness" into the human realm after the wars of religion had ravaged Europe and created an authority vacuum of literally cosmic proportions.[73] Carl Schmitt contends in like manner that modern political concepts are imported from theology even to the point that "the omnipotent God" became one with "the omnipotent lawgiver."[74]

In contrast, in medieval theology, the otherness of God was incorporated into the material realm by means of the natural law and its neo-Platonic view of hierarchy in which the Church, as a supernatural agency, functioned as the guarantor of a "natural" moral and political order that originated in God, was implanted into the human mind, and incarnated in the life of the state through promulgated law. The validity of law, indeed its very *raison d'être* was in its rootedness in a series of inviolable, rationally available, moral guidelines that were inculcated via the cardinal virtues in both micro and macro communal relationships: family, voluntary associations, church, and state.[75] All were part of the great chain of being with "none considering itself as a universal model for imitation."[76] Social control was mainly informal, carried out by the communities and associations comprising the civil order.[77] With the rejection of the medieval synthesis at the birth of the modern era and the erosion of its communal narrative, this natural order passed "imperceptibly from the level of the received to the level of the *willed*"; statutory law and its imposing reservoir of power now became the "other" and the "sameness" that holds us together.[78] Harold Berman makes a similar point: "The separation of church and state in the sense in which that phrase is understood in American constitutional law is, indeed, becoming more and more absolute, but this only means that the state itself is becoming more and more sanctified by the secular religion of the American way of life."[79]

Whatever grief resulting from religious bigotry and intolerance was circumvented by separating reason and revelation, the withdrawal of respect for ethical truths based upon theological principle within the public realm has led, as Berman suggests, to the extrication of the traditional God and the ascension of another: the state. The latter has assumed not only the monopoly over the means of coercive force; it is the last and inevitable arbiter of the endless disagreements that arise in an emotivist moral environment between multiple and competing "sovereign" wills. It is thus that John Milbank claims, even allowing for the significant advances in human rights in the modern era, that all "liberal" polities function upon an "ontology of violence."[80]

Coupled with the evanescent meanderings of the individual "pursuit of happiness," the state must take on the role not of moral adjunct to a natural order with its transcendent ethical precepts oriented to the common welfare, but as the enforcer of the norms established by legislative consent to control the bevy of inevitable conflicts that arise among the myriad seekers of bliss. This, as numerous commentators have noted, is not only an impossible task but one that has left society nowhere to turn to resolve violations of order than the threat and imposition of aggressive force.[81] The late Yale law professor Robert Cover writes that criminal jurisprudence "is either played out on the field of pain and death or it is something less (or more) than law."[82] "[J]udges deal pain and death. That is not all that they do . . . But they do deal pain and death. From John Winthrop to Warren Burger they have sat atop a pyramid of violence."[83] In like manner, Rothman's historical work into the origin and outcome of penal progressivism concluded that the institutions it spawned operated in a culture bereft of any substantive problem-solving resources save reliance on "one more sanction": "Thus, in incarceration . . . the decency of any one place rests ultimately on a coercive back-up, and that back-up in turn rests upon the presence of a still more coercive back-up."[84]

These structures of aggression that are both a model of populist notions of justice as well as a model for them create "a kind of moral circuitry" that takes on an air of "inevitability" underscoring "the necessary rightness of the status quo" and the basic assumptions governing the penal framework.[85] This gravitational energy is what Walter Wink refers to as the spiritual aspect, the internal logic or ideology that directs the perception and actions of institutions "which are not simply subject to human fiat. They possess a spirituality, an inwardness, that is highly resistant to change. The heavenly powers are *not* mere projections that mystify the real power relations. They are, quite the contrary, the real interiority of earthly institutions."[86]

In few places is this reciprocal relationship between the legal ethos and a culture that authorizes repressive measures toward a darker and poorer portrait of the deviant more pronounced than in the media and entertainment industries. According to Julian Roberts and his coauthors, most of the purveyors of what is termed "the news" pay inordinate attention to violent crime as an individual choice shorn of systemic critique that in turn both galvanizes public opinion and influences the way legislators frame anti-crime policy.[87] Speaking of the "mediated" postmodern culture saturated with investigative journalistic reports, docudramas, and daylong coverage of breaking events—typically those involving bloodshed ("if it bleeds, it leads")—William Staples calls attention to the discrepancy between falling crime rates and rising public fear of terrorists; predators; and, generally, unorthodox conduct which, notwithstanding the dates used in the quote, continues in the present day: "[D]espite the fact that the nation's crime rate, both for property and violent offenses, fell between 2004 and 2007, the percentage of Americans telling opinion pollsters that they thought that there was more crime in the United States than the year before rose from 53% in 2004 to 71% in 2007.[88]

As we have stated, this punitive spirit, shorn of any transcendent moral order against which it can be evaluated, has as its origin and terminal point society as it is presently constituted: the ever malleable collection of individual wills whose day-to-day preoccupations intrigue pollsters and ultimately politicians, and, perhaps reluctantly but ineluctably, criminal justice scholars. The penal mechanism is thus informed and re-created by a wide and morally evanescent array of personal, social, cultural, and institutional influences that determine the social reality of crime and feed the ravenous penal complex and the inevitable violence that resides like a specter at its core.[89]

Divided Hearts and Minds

Having discussed in some detail the individualist and materialist notions that have reframed the understanding of the person, having provided some remarks on the origin and content of current moral frameworks, and indicated the way both have left the public and policy makers little choice save coercive power to settle moral disputes and legal infractions, I now turn to what I see as the second of the fundamental flaws in the current approach to criminal justice. I will contend that subjective accounts of ethics and personhood are predicated upon a dualist worldview; by this I mean a set of epistemological and ethical categories that posit a divided as opposed to a unified view of reality. These categories provide for the ego and its relentless process of analysis, comparison, and judgment a clear and largely unimpeachable portrait of those outside its domain of ethical responsibility and care. Only from such a binary perspective is it possible to legitimate the marginalization; control; punishment; and, if necessary, elimination of those whom the individual ego and the collective ego find threatening.[90]

As has been mentioned, an appeal for the rehabilitation of the penal system requires some attention to the litany of such instrumental failures, but a far more important task is to direct attention to the critical need for a systemic re-conceptualization: one that is indeed a restoration of the original normative framework established to assure that confinement be an act of charity that both summons and enables a liberation from the internal confinement of a divided and alienated heart. What has been bequeathed via the liberal philosophical tradition under whose aegis we have witnessed the rise of mass incarceration (or "hyperincarceration"), its wildly disproportionate demographics, and its general tone of justifiable violence is incapable of restoring the humanism of that original blueprint in no small way because it operates with a worldview as bifurcated and parochial as that of the ones whose aberrant behavior it ostensibly seeks to address, if not correct.[91]

We have discussed the deep-seated moral ambiguity and the state of "grave disorder" that emanate from the various rationales for punishment.[92] Dualism, by its very nature, creates a world of division between the knowledgeable and the uninformed, the healthy and the contaminated, and between the morally acceptable and the reprobate. In such an oppositional world, as Dorothee Soelle relates, "the theology of neighborliness is banal because it does not include damnation and judgment."[93] It begets "a society in which we are not permitted to make a mistake . . . a society in which conversion is excluded."[94]

Thomas Mathiesen observes this dualism in what he sees as the ideological functions of the contemporary prison: the expurgatory, the diverting, and the symbolic. In the first, persons drawn from "the unproductive population of late capitalist societies" are "housed, controlled, and conveniently forgotten." The diverting function enables those who sentence and approve the detention of the above to direct their attention to the faults of the imprisoned and ignore the legal and moral infractions for which they (the punishers) are responsible. The symbolic function operates on the principle that painting those entrapped in the system, at least metaphorically "black," enables those outside the grip of the legal system to image themselves as its opposite.[95]

There is nothing novel about this tendency to allow thought at a distance about others to substitute for a primary experience that brackets all but compassion as the goal of human relationships and the knowledge we derive from them. As Richard Rohr suggests, humans are "hardwired" to think dualistically: "the ego desperately wants to feel pure, saved, moral, significant, and superior" and thus continually divides the experiential field according to a host of predetermined mental constructs: comparison; analysis; categorization; and, inevitably, moral judgment, granting itself, in virtually all cases, a place of unassailable privilege in determining the content of those categories.[96] This is not a secular/religious observation but an eminently human one. For instance, in spite of Jesus's clear example and teaching that people should condemn no one, judge no one, and will harm upon no one (Mt 5: 21-26, 38-48; Lk 6: 27-42) Christians, particularly after Christianity was established as the official religion of the Roman Empire in the early fourth century, duplicated the same divisive and violent policies that had been directed against them when their faith was subject to sudden and virulent persecution; a pattern that it and its members, as well as the congregants of other religious traditions, have duplicated innumerable times over the centuries.[97] Similarly, there are strong sacred/profane and material/spirit dualities in much religious thought, despite, as noted in the Introduction, the overarching vision of cosmic unity that was advanced in the Axial Age and the Eastern and Western religious that emerged in its wake.[98]

In terms of the origins of dualism in modern thought and institutions, once again, religion played a leading role. While they can be traced to Platonic and neo-Platonic thinkers as well the welter of Gnostic sects that sprang up early in the Christian era, arguably, the launch point of systematic dualism in the West emerged in the late eleventh century when Pope Gregory VII declared the full independence of the Catholic Church from all state intrusion. This sea-change event ushered in a "legal revolution" that not only resulted in a universal code of (canon) law, the first law school (Bologna), the origins of the legal and judicial professions, and the modern "inquisitorial" method of juridical investigation, it also led to the church-state dichotomy and the decision of the former to allow the law to determine the punishment a given offender had to suffer as a separate category from the penitential discipline imposed by the priest in the confessional.[99]

Influential thinkers such as St. Anselm of Canterbury (1033–1109) complemented this trend toward a radical separation between the divine and human as well as between the sacred and the secular by promoting an interpretation of the suffering and death of Jesus as a compensatory sacrifice to appease a God enraged over human consort with evil; God's justice in effect only satisfied by the shedding of blood.[100] His work, arising at the dawn of the construction of canon law, helped solidify, according to many scholars, a default retributive component into the ground water not only of Christian theology but that of the Western legal systems that were being compiled in response to their new found "official" separation from the Church.[101]

In the wake of this change in the perception of the world and the human soul, seminal intellectual voices such as Descartes, whose method of radical skepticism, despite his rather pious intentions, withered what was left of the organic relation between church and state and between the person and God.[102] Taylor notes that Descartes is the progenitor of modern philosophy and speaks of the implications of the stance he assumes: "The thesis is not that I gain knowledge when turned towards God in faith . . . What has happened is rather that God's existence has become a stage in *my* progress towards science through the methodical ordering of relevant insight. God's existence is a theorem in *my* system of perfect science."[103] The resulting emphasis on the moral and epistemological autonomy of the individual and the gradual evolution into ethical relativism has led to an ideology of separation between subject and object that we wear in the West like we do our own skin: "To come to live by this definition—as we cannot fail to do, since it permeates and rationalizes so many of the ways and practices of modern life—is to be transformed: to the point where we see this way of being as normal, as anchored in perennial human nature in the way our physical organs are."[104] Harold Berman, for one, believes that it is this dualism that is primarily responsible for the steady decline of the humanity of our social, economic, and political institutions.[105]

Radical skepticism and its pronounced dualist starting point, regardless of one's opinion on its justification, need not subsume all scientific inquiry but, if Taylor and Berman are right, it has unfailingly become the dominant methodological stance governing the collection and evaluation of data, one in which, employing Husserl's terminology, there is a "hostility" to the notion of transcendent "ideas" or essences that "must eventually prove dangerous to the empirical sciences themselves."[106]

George Herbert Mead is a noteworthy exemplar of the positivist belief that the detached, scientific viewpoint surpasses all previous attempts to understand and overcome the challenges to social cohesion caused by illicit activity. He states that the social problem of aberrant behavior was always assumed to be addressed successfully by religion, "through a change in the heart of the individual." But religion, he states, is capable only of reaching that goal "in the world to come, not in this one." He then adds: "scientific method is, after all, only the evolutionary method grown self-conscious" and thus "science comes in to aid society in getting a method of progress. It understands the background of these problems" and "it has a method for attacking them."[107]

Few, if any, domains are more emblematic of this chasm between a moral ontology based upon participation and the inherent dualism of the materialist worldview than the philosophy and practice of criminal justice.[108] The quantitative, technical approach to data gathering in which the independent variables are typically the current social and legal structures is the extension of the liberal philosophical tradition tracing back to the Age of Science and to thinkers like Descartes and Locke. It has all but silenced the objections to those conservative foundations, particularly those proceeding from a theological perspective. As Garland states, the regnant dualist methodology (not his vocabulary) has been able "to dominate the field and to limit the range of questions which appeared appropriate or worthwhile."[109] Since "situational" variables such as culture and economic class are far more slippery in measuring human motivation and moral analysis, the emphasis in most social scientific programs with regard to illegal behavior is on "dispositional" variables such as character or personality traits in which it can be assumed that crime or a return to criminality are posited and measured as an antisocial gesture.[110] In this sense, the category of deviance emerges to be as much a moral fault as a legal one: "Penal signs and symbols . . . provide a continuous, repetitive set of instructions as to how we should think about good and evil, normal and pathological, legitimate and illegitimate, order and disorder."[111]

Despite the historical evidence of dualism as a human phenomenon, one deeply interwoven into individual reflection and institutional practice, including religious practice, it is central to my argument for the rehabilitation of the penal system that it exists as an anomaly within the predominant ideology of ontological unity displayed in the "wisdom" traditions. A similar stance of non-duality is assumed by the phenomenological tradition wherein one is directed to overcome the stance of difference and separation by bracketing prejudicial comparison and judgment through a "second naïvete" of compassionate participation.[112] In addition, insofar as the origins of psychiatry and, to a significant degree, psychology can be traced to Freud's and Jung's appropriation of archetypal myths and symbols, there is, in the origins of these disciplines, an inherent connection to the revolutionary change of religious metaphors that commenced during the Axial Age. It was at that historical juncture that mystical union first came to be conceived no longer as an ascent into the heavens but a descent into the depths of the psyche.[113]

Systemic Results of Ideological Disorientation

Kant believed that each person seeking to manage the undue influence of sensory stimuli on proper behavioral calculation possessed an innate rational capacity to ascertain and affirm a consistent kingdom of moral ends.[114] Far from this optimistic projection and the theory of retributive justice that proceeds from it, the ethical consequences of generations of reflection upon the phenomenon of crime and the legislative and policy initiatives that have accompanied it have resulted in a justice system repeatedly implicated in charges of moral bias based upon race, class, and the elastic determination of what counts as a crime and who counts as a criminal.[115]

These determinations of criminal culpability have been augmented by aggravated mechanisms of surveillance and social control emblematic of the "new penology" that have, in turn, accelerated the targeting, apprehension, and detention of racial minorities to a level never duplicated in the national record. Norval Morris writes: "Yes, there is measurable racial discrimination in our police practices, in our prosecutorial practices and in our sentencing, but the bulk of the discrimination generating crime lies elsewhere . . . the whole law and order movement that we have heard so much about is, in operation, though not in intent, anti-black and anti-underclass—not in plan, not in desire, not in intent, but in operation."[116] Troy Duster noted this trend some decades ago but suggests that what is procedurally new is not the consignment of blacks "to the bottom rung of the American economic and political order. What is new is the currently emerging sense of the 'permanency' of that condition."[117]

Among the most convincing explanations for this unprecedented development is the resurgence of Social Darwinism in the 1980s and the resultant neoliberal economic policies that have removed a wide array of national and international controls on the acquisition of profit by the financial and corporate sectors. At the same time, the ideological function of this relentless reconfiguring of income distribution places a sharp emphasis on personal responsibility in reaction to the actions of undesirable populations: the swelling multitudes of either domestic poor or those uprooted from their homelands by the desperate search for labor and social stability.[118] Wacquant expresses these paradoxical foci of neoliberal penality: "the state stridently reasserts its responsibility, potency, and efficiency in the narrow register of crime management at the very moment when it proclaims and organizes its own impotence on the economic front, thereby revealing the twin historical-cum-scholarly myth of the efficient police and the free market."[119]

Scholars have noted this intense emphasis on the infractions committed by the poor, the restricted moral options open to them that result from it— particularly given the severe social and economic constraints placed upon the hundreds of thousands released from captivity each year—and absolution of the economic and political structures from all responsibility for their penury.[120] Thomas Mathiesen writes, reflecting the thought of Nils Christie: "The law is equal for everybody, but to the extent that our society is a class society, the law will also have this characteristic: the law threatens neither private capital nor international exploitation of weak nations! The law threatens, on the other hand, theft and related acts, typically committed by people from the lowest strata of the working class."[121]

The "new penology" and its capacity to utilize an expansive net of surveillance to peer, as Foucault suggested, into the "interstices" of individual and social life to detect "the slightest illegality" and enfold its perpetrator in the cloak of delinquency has utilized that capacity to manage "a permanent offender population" consisting of perpetually "at risk" members of the underclass.[122]

The carceral network not only serves a disciplinary function, it selectively incapacitates the members of populations made dispensable both by their criminal history and, increasingly, their inability to cope psychologically with the constraints of poverty, systemic violence, and/or with their own particular genetic and organic susceptibility to mental illness.[123] The well-documented argument that the traditional role of the jail has been to impound undesirables such as "the public nuisance, the sick and the poor, the morally deviant, and the merely troublesome and neglected" has found an added function in the era of mass incarceration: a low cost form of "waste management" providing a "repository" for those "for whom the depleted social services no longer provide adequate accommodation."[124]

What I think is safe to say is that all of this reinforces with a wallop the point made earlier that the dignity and sacredness of the persons under surveillance and confinement has never been a primary focus of the justice system. Diana Gordon states that the overarching concern of the "umbrella model" of criminal procedure is to involve "the largest number of possible miscreants . . . in the justice process . . . Comprehensive coverage, whether achieved by the clear cut contacts of arrest, indictment, or conviction or through the shadow of the criminal record or curfew is the aim, not structuring a relationship between the state and citizen."[125]

A theological perspective maintaining the ontological worth, indeed irreplaceability, of each person and his or her capacity for, longing for, and susceptibility to participation, transcendence, and conversion looms in silent, critical witness—"despite the policing of the sublime"—to the distorted practices of arrest and conviction and the ever-present need to secure order with the barrel of a gun.[126] It is a theological perspective, grounded in the early Christian approach to asocial comportment that refuses any sort of dualist reduction of the offender to fit the contours of either the current systems management approach or, for that matter, to fit the contours of any system that separates those in the grip of the justice system from an a priori communion with all others, including those empowered to intervene, evaluate, and detain them. It is an approach, in the terminology of Emmanuel Levinas, in which "the relationship with a *being* is an invocation of a face." In such a relation "the infinite resistance" of a being to the power of violence is affirmed.[127]

The perspective of which I speak has a spokesperson in Pope Francis who announced the "Year of Mercy" in 2015. In his inaugural speech he said: "How much wrong we do to God and his grace when we speak of sins being punished by his judgment before we speak of their being forgiven by his mercy. We have to put mercy before judgment, and in any event, God's judgment will always be in the light of his mercy."[128] A complementary view, sans religious sentiment, is espoused by Bryan Stephenson: "It is when mercy is least expected that it is most potent—strong enough to break the cycle of victimization, victimhood, retribution and suffering. It has the power to 'heal psychic harm', injuries that lead to aggression and violence, abuse of power and mass incarceration."[129]

"I-Thou" relations are the foundation of human personhood: relations predicated upon the overcoming of any radical distinction between consciousness and reality.[130] The ontological primacy of these relations is affirmed in the theological interpretation that I am offering but also within the phenomenological tradition in both philosophy and sociology. One of the most important representatives of the latter is Alfred Schutz: "Insofar as each of us can experience each other's thoughts and acts in the vivid present . . . I know more of the Other and he knows more of me than either knows of his own stream of consciousness. This present, common to both of us, is the pure sphere of the 'we.' And if we accept this definition, we can agree with Scheler's tenet that the sphere of the 'we' is pre-given to the sphere of the self."[131]

The theological, ethical, and systemic rudiments of the approach that is necessary to rehabilitate the penal system require much further elaboration. At this point, however, I have argued in this chapter that the contemporary system of criminal justice and its ethical justifications are in critical need of a wider narrative arc that includes their initial formation in a moral formula that addresses human destructiveness not by punishment or violence but through a methodology of penance capable of creating the conditions for conversions in persons naturally oriented to transcendence and participation. Until this once prominent, now forgotten, focus of the meaning of confinement is to some degree recovered, the penal system will continue to wound but not heal due to its insupportable ethical foundations and a fundamental attitude of separation rather than union with those whose comportment it is charged to address.

2

It Is Wrong to Punish Anyone for Any Reason

AS THE CHAPTER title implies,[1] refashioning the penal system with atten-tiveness to its ancient justification, structure, and meaning requires abandoning, among other things, the moral sanction to bring willful harm upon those found guilty of crime. This chapter will begin with a brief overview of a cor-rectional system based upon patient accompaniment and benevolence as opposed to violence. It will then critique the principal justifications for punish-ment: retributivism, deterrence, and the way incapacitation is generally under-stood in the current context.

Criminal Justice as Inclusion

For purposes of clarity, let us begin with the understanding of punishment that informs this volume. Thomas Aquinas suggested that punishment must have three foci: it must be for a fault; it must be contrary to the will; and it must be painful.[2] While it can be argued that any form of detention meets these criteria, including confinement in a facility whose aim is conversion or an expanded and inclusive consciousness, an important distinction exists between pain that is intended by the state as a manifest function of the penal environment and a penal environment that is manifestly based upon care and accompaniment of the offender (but in which the one confined will undoubtedly suffer). The former is the operative understanding of the meaning of criminal justice as we know it. In the words of Edward Sutherland and Donald Cressey: "Control of criminal behavior by criminal law is control by deliberately inflicting pain and suffering on those who do not conform."[3] This entrenched ideological require-ment took on an even more exaggerated punitive focus when the philosophy of rehabilitation fell out of favor in the wake of the social upheaval of the 1960s. At that point, as Craig Haney surmises, "infliction of pain appeared to become an end in itself."[4]

In contrast, I argue that the only pain that the guilty should suffer is that which they bring upon themselves as a result of recognizing the alienation and internal suffering at the root of asocial conduct.[5] This latter suffering, not externally imposed, is best understood as repentance or contrition. Using Aquinas again, ideally, the penal process fulfills a medicinal function, "not only healing the past sin, but also preserving from future sin."[6]

While it is commonplace to assume that those culpable of harmful actions can only be addressed legitimately by inducing a measure of duress somehow comparable to the offenses they committed, this was not always the case. Not that history has yet witnessed nonviolent social systems; violence has been endemic to human social organization ever since the development of agriculture.[7] That said, Christianity introduced a new concept into Western thought concerning criminal misbehavior, particularly after its official recognition in the wake of Constantine's Edict of Milan in 313. That concept was mercy: an unprecedented emphasis on the plight of the poor and, by extension, the prisoner with an attendant sense of compassion and solicitude. Peter Brown writes that "in a sense, it was the Christian bishops who invented the poor . . . bringing [them] into ever sharper focus."[8] Alex Tuckness and John Parrish maintain in their study on the topic that Christian bishops in the post-Constantinian period "acquired the influence necessary to encourage public officials to show mercy to those convicted of crimes . . . In contrast to the ancient philosophers, these early Christian writers did not emphasize deterrence, prevention, or protection as the primary purposes of punishment, although their importance was acknowledged. Instead, the early Christians held that the essence of punishment is that it aims at 'correction of the soul.'"[9]

What is lacking in current criminological theory and operation is the intellectual resolve, indeed the imagination, to consider the substantial reconfiguration of legal and penal dynamics that would result from a type of "post-Constantinian" recognition of the value of such premodern influences on the societal response to proscribed behavior. Such a recognition, among other things, would open the possibility to re-conceptualize the prevailing oppositional notion of justice in favor of one that is relational.[10] It would furthermore allow for and, in fact, necessitate a critique of the anthropology of the autonomous individual of philosophical liberalism—virtually unknowable to prior generations as they grappled with the problem of human destructiveness—from which proceeds an "objective" view of justice that under the banner of fairness often objectifies those whose actions are subject to prosecution and punishment.

The point here is not that our premodern predecessors treated their captives kindly or humanely; but they did so against a markedly different ethical horizon than that of the "invulnerable" modern or postmodern individual, untethered from fundamental ties to a tradition, who, due to that very moral isolation, is more easily susceptible to "judge or ignore without feeling the pain of others."[11] James Whitman has forcefully and eloquently argued this point in his survey into the origins of the legal concept of "reasonable doubt." He contends that for our early medieval ancestors, there was normally little confusion concerning the identity of the guilty party in a serious infraction. The hesitation in the execution of justice had to do with the moral justification to bring violence upon that person for his or her misdeed: "The best lesson to draw from the history of reasonable doubt is not a lesson about how to apply reasonable doubt correctly . . . The real root of our confusion about reasonable doubt has to do with the fact that we have lost the old conviction that judging and punishing others are morally fearsome acts. We have a far weaker sense than our ancestors that we should doubt our moral authority when judging other human beings."[12]

Criticism of the current philosophical approach notwithstanding, it is important that a rigid dichotomy not be fashioned between the two perspectives. The worldview of modernity, or late modernity, despite its fundamental epistemological and ethical belief that agents can be separated from their actions, is hardly impervious to the moral issues raised in willing that others suffer. It was precisely that worldview, as Pieter Spierenburg, among others, has noted, that was so instrumental in banning public humiliation, torture, and public executions.[13] As stated in the last chapter, despite the criticism directed to Moral Sense Theory and Utilitarianism, the leading figures in these pivotal movements were committed to minimizing the agony inflicted on wrongdoers and, in fact, horrified at the thought that anything but concern for the good of both victim and offender be the principal justification for the imposition of punishment. For them, and the countless others who draw inspiration from them, any use of violence to curb the unruly must be predicated upon the belief that pain is legitimate only in as much as it is both rational and freed from vindictive emotion.[14]

Despite this laudable reticence, my argument throughout this volume is a summons for those concerned about and involved in the planning and operation of criminal justice to take a further step: namely, not only to place firm constraints upon the punitive response but to will harm upon no one, regardless of what they have done.[15] This commitment is central to the concept of conversion and will be addressed in detail in the next chapter, but at this juncture some explanation is necessary.

The principal issue for those guilty of harming others and for those responsible for addressing their misdeeds is not the application of an abstract conception of justice; it is the very real phenomenon of participation or inclusion. The question should not be what a given offender deserves, but how can that person be enabled to broaden the intellectual, moral, and spiritual imagination to puncture the barriers of antagonism. I am not arguing that remorse and suffering have no place in social policy or in a criminal court of law; I am arguing that neither can they be imposed without, normally, creating further dis-integration.[16] They can only be summoned by carefully attending to the methodological guidelines that the history of confinement and the resources of the wisdom traditions have long provided. And, for those who suppose this approach somehow avoids the rough side of justice, I suggest that no level of misfortune can be inflicted upon another for his or her malicious behavior that is not already causing acute torment within the heart. A person confronting his or her loneliness, cruelty, and shame—without the state deflecting that self-incrimination due to institutional callousness or neglect—will endure great suffering.[17] Pascal writes: "Nothing is so insufferable to man as to be completely at rest, without passions, without business, without diversion, without study. He then feels his nothingness, his forlornness, his insufficiency, his dependence, his weakness, his emptiness."[18] It was precisely for this reason that St. Benedict, in his sixth-century Rule, always assigned a wise older monk to visit regularly and counsel the incarcerated brother, "so that he be not devoured by too much sorrow."[19]

In like manner, a rehabilitated penal system would reconsider the impact of jettisoning a moral ontology of fundamental human goodness and susceptibility to re-biographing a troubled narrative from the understanding of human malevolence.[20] Liberal theorists, whether consequentialist or deontological, are often shielded by the constraints of their philosophical understanding of the person from allowing their natural compassion to envision a justice system opposed to painful punishment, or punishment masked as benevolence. Arthur Shuster phrases this constraint as follows: "Most prominent strands of contemporary liberalism . . . insist on maintaining a strict neutrality toward the various conflicting views of the human good, as a result of their skepticism regarding that good. Constrained by this neutrality, liberals can impose 'penalties' . . . which are intended to deter crime and to compensate victims for their losses, since this can be accomplished without requiring individuals to obey the law for what some might hold to be the morally right reasons."[21]

The phrase "morally right reasons" is, of course, ambiguous. For while one can interpret it, as I do, as a justification to incapacitate those who have seriously harmed others and provide compassionate accompaniment as they confront the horror of what they have done, retributivists, including many drawing upon theological resources, interpret this phrase as a responsibility to assure that malefactors suffer for their deliberate neglect of statutory law.

Outline of the Retributive Position

What justification is sufficient to enable one to conclude that another must be made to suffer for violation of a legal ordinance? As Ronald Dworkin phrases it: "Day in and day out we send people to jail, or take money away from them, or make them do things they do not want to do, under coercion of force, and we justify all of this by speaking of such persons as having broken the law ... Even in clear cases ... we are not able to give a satisfactory account of what that means, or why that entitles the state to punish or coerce."[22] Assuredly, the history of retributivism begs to differ with Dworkin's claim (and my own). A number of validations have been offered across the centuries for the retributive impulse, among which one finds reestablishing the balance of justice, just deserts, the *lex talionis*, a negation of the negation, addressing unfair advantage, moral education, satisfaction for the victim, and communal solidarity.[23]

Since the literature on the subject is so vast and the position being advanced in this volume (hopefully) so apparent, I do not see a need to try to dissect the discreet theories but to summarize areas of commonality among them. The retributive position will thus be encapsulated in what appear to be four constitutive claims. I am not suggesting that they are exhaustive of all of the parallel and symmetrical arguments offered by proponents, but I believe they are sufficient to portray with acceptable scholarly accuracy the retributive position. The common threads are responsibility, desert, emphasis on the action itself rather than the person performing it, and support for other punitive justifications as long as they are secondary aims. A fifth defense is found among all theological accounts and some, but not all, secular accounts, namely, that the offender must suffer because what he or she did was morally wrong.

First, philosophical positions defending the idea of retributive punishment are united in that they presume that the perpetrator is the one who bears primary responsibility for the unwarranted action and must therefore bear the painful consequences. In the words of Daniel Dennett: "If no one else is responsible for you being in state A, you are."[24] In like manner, H. L. A. Hart states: "If an individual breaks the law when none of the excusing conditions are present [unconsciousness, lack of muscular control, threat of coercion], he is ordinarily said to have acted of 'his own free will', 'of his own accord', 'voluntarily', or it might be said 'He could have helped doing what he did.' "[25] The reader will recall that the notion of responsibility lies at the heart of the neoliberal ethos with its fusion of free market dynamics and individual liability for legal transgressions. This is not to suggest that all advocates of retributivism are in accord with the neoliberal agenda, but neither can the coherence of the former with the capitalist focus on personal accountability be dismissed out of hand. For, like the consumer in the free market, the legal deviant shares the fate that befalls those who of their own volition make unwise or unfortunate choices.[26] This is yet another indication of the power of the anthropological assumptions underlying liberal conceptions of human agency; that is to say, the guilty mind is also a coldly calculating mind (mens rea) capable of standing aloof from its own history: "The core of criminal law doctrine, centered around the concept of mens rea and the variety of criminal excuses, probably comes closer than any other set of social practices to an instantiation of the Kantian conception of the responsible human subject as the noumenal self, characterized exclusively by a rational free will unencumbered by character, temperament, or circumstance."[27]

The second of the common characteristics of retributive theory is the notion of desert. In the words of Andrew Von Hirsch, "someone who is responsible for wrongdoing is *blameworthy* and hence may justly be blamed."[28] One might think of Hegel's claim or, later, Dostoevsky's portrait of Raskolnikov in *Crime and Punishment*, that the criminal desires to be punished ("it is . . . his implicit will"); he or she knows that the offense was a nullity of right which, when "annulled by coercion" is an "annihilation of the infringement."[29] In the thought of Nicholas Wollerstorff, liberalism is incorrectly associated with solipsistic projection; rather, he argues, human rights and those who bear them are inherently social. This sociability, in turn, makes people accountable for transgressing the legally established privilege of another for purely selfish motives, at which point the "person who was wronged . . . acquires certain retributive rights."[30] Anthony Duff has a large corpus of work dedicated to communicative theories of punishment. Proceeding from a Kantian background, but rejecting the latter's absolute sense of merited affliction, he defends the inherent rationality of offenders and the need to instruct them on the nature of the social obligations ignored by their conduct and encourage them to take upon themselves without ire the judicial sentence as a form of penitential exculpation.[31] Even the mildest of retributivists, such as Joel Feinberg, insist that punishments must be distinguished from penalties (e.g., a parking ticket) and while they need not result in "hard treatment," the proscribed action must at least be addressed by a form of public denunciation, a "disapproval and reprobation."[32] What these perspectives and their numerous affiliates share in common is the moral requirement that the perpetrator endure a measure of legally sanctioned torment "because he [or she] deserves it."[33]

The third mutually held principle is that vindictive justice is focused on the negligent act—an act that violates a normative obligation to do what is right—rather than upon the person performing it. It falls, therefore, under the moral stance of deontology.[34] It brackets the action freely chosen from any mitigating circumstances that might tempt a consequentialist to take a more conciliatory view of the actor's motivations and intentions. Michael Sandel's summary of the position is that "society, being composed of a plurality of persons, each with his own aims, interests, and conceptions of the good is best arranged when it is governed by principles that do not *themselves* presuppose any particular conception of the good; what justifies these regulative principles above all is . . . they conform to the concept of *right*, a moral category given prior to the good and independent of it."[35] Kant is probably the most quoted and emulated proponent of the deontological stance. Concerning the choice to do evil, he claims: "For whatever his previous behavior may have been, whatever natural causes influencing him . . . his action is yet free and not determined by any of these causes; hence the action can and must always be judged as an *original* exercise of his power of choice."[36]

Fourth, despite the primary emphasis on an act-centered notion of desert, retributivists are clear in their support for deterrence, incapacitation, rehabilitation or, for that matter, conversion as long as they are secondary effects of having made the convicted person suffer for his or her misdeed. Ernest van den Haag insists that retribution is primarily meant "to enforce the law and to vindicate the 'legal order' "; he adds, however, that retribution and utility "do not exclude each other," that criminal prosecution induces legal compliance among eligible wrongdoers, and that there is some warrant for selective incapacitation.[37] Although Von Hirsch believes it possible that "the threat and imposition of punishment induces more compliance than if there is no punishment," this fact could only render deterrence a beneficial result, not the compelling reason to inflict harm upon the guilty."[38] Kant argues that violations of the freedom of others or of property rights must be punished because they violate the universal law, but he is quick to add that a favorable result of the repressive order is to enhance the conditions under which those freedoms and rights can be enjoyed.[39]

So, to summarize, persons deserve to be punished for no other primary reason than they are responsible for having voluntarily chosen to undertake a proscribed action. But by whom is the action proscribed? The first answer is the nation, state, or legal community. For Anthony Duff, reminiscent of the thought of Durkheim, "the wrong flouts the defining values of our polity."[40] The grounding principles of all democratic societies, whether one views them from a republican, contractarian, or positivist framework, assume the legitimacy of promulgated law and the sworn duty of all citizens to uphold it, regardless of the added value a belief in the deeper moral significance of those legal claims might add to their compliance. In the words of Joseph Raz: "It may be a necessary truth that all legal systems conform to some moral values and that a system which violates those values cannot be a legal system. My claim is merely that if this is indeed the case then these necessary moral features of law are derivative characteristics of law."[41] The authority of the state, then, is the necessary condition for law's legitimacy, but it is not the only source that retributivists may rely upon to uphold their belief in punishment.

Religious Defenses of Retributivism

Thus far we have seen that secular defenses of retributive justice need not rely on moral reasons to support their claim that criminals be punished. It is enough that the action is reprehensible simply because it was prohibited. Yet some secular positions do rely upon a moral argument: that an act is punishable because it is in itself evil.[42] In Chapter 1, some of the philosophical positions based upon such ethical commitments were commented upon and critiqued. What needs significant attention, however, are those sources espousing punishment that rest fully upon theological or religious beliefs, especially ones that insist that the divine or cosmic forces demand vindictive punishments upon the unruly.[43] Since, as Leibniz noted, Christian theology has had an "astonishing" impact on the development of jurisprudence in the West, most of my attention in this section will be directed to an exposition and critique of Christian belief in a God who wills not only the unavoidable internal suffering that results from sinful behavior but also that fallible human beings act in God's stead to bring violence upon other fallible human beings who have committed those proscribed actions.[44]

Fallibility, indeed, is very much at play in the discussion about punishment. Every major religious tradition maintains the belief that "sin," understood here as willful alienation from others, from nature, from one's core self, and from a given tradition's understanding of divine revelation, is what the prominent Catholic theologian Karl Rahner calls a "permanent existential."[45] The core self of each person is grounded in freedom and self-transcendence yet, as Heidegger notes, is always "thrown" into the lifeworld or what Rahner terms the "categorical" milieu of social existence wherein the self can never achieve an absolute sense of its transcendental center nor full awareness of the motivations and repercussions of its discrete actions. Thus, each regularly uses her freedom poorly and often harms herself and others.[46] Jesus was hardly being diffident or ironic when he stated: "Why do you call me good? No one is good but God alone" (Mk 10: 18).

Although Rahner speaks of human weakness in terms of twentieth-century phenomenology, the reflection upon fallibility echoes across ages of theological speculation. Moses Maimonides wrote of the inevitable propensity to blindness in "the apprehension of the true realities" due, among other things, to natural aptitudes. Concerning the latter, he argued that one who is hot-tempered "cannot refrain from anger even if he subject his soul to very stringent training."[47] In similar fashion, the revered Sufi mystic, Al-Ghazzali, envisioned the interior life as an interplay between appetite, intellect, and will. He noted that since appetite precedes the capacity to think and desire, it frequently overpowers the intellect and fuses with desire to grasp the object of its devotion. He maintained that this craving for carnal satisfaction can only be thwarted through the discipline of prayer but, even then, remains compelling and surrender in some form to its demands inevitable: "In every human being passion prevails over intellect; the impulse which is a device of Satan prevails over the impulse which is an instrument of the angels."[48]

Given this magnetic attraction to selfish preoccupation and disregard for the moral law inscribed into the pattern of human development, all of the major religions now believe in what Alan Bernstein calls a "moral death." Gone is the ancient neutrality of the nether world where the departed abide in a gloomy but non-punitive realm that the Hebrew Scriptures named "sheol." Beginning with the "Coffin Texts" in Egypt's Middle Kingdom, each religion, invoking the cry of Job against "a pallid half-life without either reward or punishment," has come to affirm that justice unfulfilled in this life is justice denied if not enforced in the life to come.[49] In the monotheistic faiths and, for the most part, the Eastern traditions, existence is patterned upon an exitus/reditus (going forth and returning) theme. All life comes from a transcendent source and it is to that source that all life returns.[50] For our interests, the question is what does the return mean in terms of sin/crime and a painful reckoning.

Simply put, for the theological retributivist, the reditus is a rendezvous with a just God who rewards the good and punishes those who are evil. This punishment is meted out at the end of life for crimes unaccounted for in the earthly realm. While earthbound, however, the ruling authorities, "God's jailers and hangmen," according to Luther, operate, for better or worse, as divine regents.[51] Augustine exhorted Christians to endure political violence, even if innocent of direct involvement in the events precipitating it, since the punishment can be considered as one's due for past sins.[52] Calvin took up the same theme: "We need not labour to prove that an impious king is a mark of the Lord's anger, since I presume no one will deny it . . . [I]f invested with public authority, [the ruler] receives that illustrious divine power which the Lord has by his word devolved on the ministers of his justice and judgment, and that, accordingly, in so far as public obedience is concerned, he is to be held in the same honour and reverence as the best of kings."[53] As John Neville Figgis summarizes the divine right of kings, subjects are responsible to both God and king, but the latter responsible to God alone: "[Resistance] to a king is a sin, and ensures damnation. Whenever the king issues a command directly contrary to God's law, God is to be obeyed rather than man, but . . . all penalties . . . are to be patiently endured."[54] To a large degree, Christian evangelicals, who dominate the prison chaplaincies in the United States and the numerous programs offered to captives, operate under this theological paradigm. According to a study by Tanya Erzen: "Many faith-based ministries support imprisonment itself because they operate under the assumption that grace and transformation are possible because punishment is ordained by God and manifested in incarceration."[55]

The Gospels reveal that Jesus made occasional direct reference to a God of judgment (e.g., Mt. 25: 31–46; Mt 5: 21–30; Lk 6: 24–25) and also invoked retributive sentiments in a number of parables. One of these latter instances is found in his adaptation of a popular folktale, probably originating in Egypt, about a rich person unmoved by the suffering of another who goes to hell after he dies (Lk 16: 19–31). Retributive themes are also contained in the Parable of the Tenants (Mt 21: 33–46, Mk 12: 1–12, Lk 20: 9–19); The Wedding Feast (Mt 22: 1–14; Lk 14: 15–24); and the Ten Virgins (Mt 25: 1–13).[56]

It would be impossible given the scope of this book to attempt a biblical exegesis of the passages just quoted, let alone all the retributive references in the Hebrew Scriptures. What is important for the origins of retributivism in the West, however, is that powerful and authoritative stories such as those just referenced have had a substantive impact on the social, political, and moral imagination of Christians through the centuries. For instance, "The Last Judgment" in Matthew 25 formed the backdrop for the Florentine criminal court in the Middle Ages where, according to Samuel Edgerton, hell "was often portrayed as a system of dark caverns . . . looking not unlike the dank jail cells of the old podesta's palace."[57] Edgerton notes that medieval artists were frequently commissioned to produce works "depicting images in public places intended to encourage respect for communal laws and customs" in such a way that "the public punishment of criminals took on the stylized form of a morality play."[58]

Despite its use by temporal authorities to bolster support for their punitive policies, it is worth noting, not to mention both ironic and disconcerting, that in his depiction of the final judgment, Jesus is not addressing individuals at all. The lesson is directed to the nations. It is not only the lack of sympathy of entire societies to the needs of the poor and, specifically, to the imprisoned that provokes God's ire, but it is also the inability of those collective bodies to recognize that Christ self-identifies in the passage with everyone who suffers want or the pains of imprisonment. It is also noteworthy that Edgerton maintains that for the faithful, tutored in the images of mercy for the poor and the captive alluded to at the beginning of this chapter, the works of art, carefully crafted to evoke justifiable rage at those in the local prison or on the gallows, often invoked feelings of sympathy and compassion for the ones forced to bear state-sanctioned violence.[59]

The Bible has, of course, been invoked often over the centuries and has provided more than enough kindling to fuel the ire of governors and their loyal subjects upon those who have violated the law. But an important point that needs further elaboration is that, for the most part, theological justifications for punishment either ignore the Bible completely (especially the Gospels) or they summon common (and somewhat anomalous) references from the New Testament— typically a passage in Romans (13: 1–4) and some parallel verses in Peter (I Pt 2: 13–14)—as well as select references from the Hebrew Scriptures.

The verses from Romans and Peter have been called upon often to induce Christians to see the righteous hand of God in the use of state-sanctioned aggression against its enemies. Luther follows Augustine in claiming that Christians have no need of the "sword" since they mirror in their personal lives the nonviolence of Jesus, but he often refers to the two biblical passages above to insist that a Christian must support its necessary use: "Because the sword is a very great benefit and necessary to the whole world, to preserve peace, to punish sin and to prevent evil, he submits most willingly to the rule of the sword, pays tax, honors those in authority, serves, helps, and does all he can to further the government, that it may be held in honor and fear."[60] In fact, Luther also states that, if needed, Christians should take up the weapon of vengeance themselves out of love for the victims and potential victims of crime: "Therefore, should you see that there is a lack of hangmen, beadles, judges, lords, or princes, and find that you are qualified, you should offer your services and seek the place, that necessary government may by no means be despised and become inefficient or perish."[61]

Scholars have long debated the meaning of the passage from Romans and whether it is simply an anomaly in Paul whose letters so often contrasted the life-giving Spirit of God and the unnecessary constraints imposed upon Christians by attentiveness to the law.[62] Luke Timothy Johnson, for instance, argues that the verses are not only incongruous in light of the sweep of Pauline ethics but also do not refer to civil government at all, only to the ethics incumbent upon members of a household. In spite of this, Johnson argues that the passage has been magnified to suit "reactionary" and "totalitarian" political interests.[63] Similarly, Ernst Kasemann states that the text is "an alien body" in the Pauline corpus, has opened the door "not only to conservative but also to reactionary views even to the point of political fanaticism," and addresses not submission to the state but "functions ranging from the tax collector, to the police, magistrates, and Roman officials."[64]

Concerning the use of the Hebrew Bible to support repressive policies to lawbreakers, it is important to remember that imprisonment was unheard of in Israel until the Assyrian king imposed the practice upon the post-exilic community; the death penalty was rarely, if ever, practiced after the exile; and justice (mishpat), according to numerous scholars, was understood as the means to insure the protection of the innocent rather than condemnation of the guilty.[65]

I accept that certain readers are now crying "unfair." They may rightfully claim that there are just as many New Testament scholars who disagree with the sources just utilized and maintain the authenticity of the Pauline (and Petrine) claim that God does, and Christians should, give support to the political regime in all save intrusion upon matters of faith.[66] Furthermore, they might also insist that the theme of retributive justice in the Hebrew Scriptures is far more integral than the passing comments I have registered. A noted Christian retributivist, Oliver O'Donovan, for one, would claim that to reject the right of the state to punish, and indeed, if deemed necessary, inflict the death penalty, is to defy the repeated biblical analogy between sin and death.[67]

There is no disavowal that I am arguing that *any* willful act of violence is a denial of grace and a transgression against a primal ontology of care and participation—whether the violence is committed by a criminal offender or agents of the state—and that such acts contradict what I see as the unitive and merciful message of the Bible. Undoubtedly, the reader has already formed his or her mind on the matter and, with a little research, can easily summon well-respected biblical scholars to sustain or refute my position against the legitimacy of punishment.

Let's call it even, then. What we have done, at least, is to portray the contours of the biblical argument and points of possible contention. What I would like to do now is turn the matter in another direction by looking in some detail not so much at the question of biblical exegesis but the position that, by and large, theological defenses of retributivism are not based predominantly in Scripture at all. Rather, biblical citations have been used in the role of providing "proof texts" to lend credence to three theological notions, containing *some* Scriptural basis. These concepts have provided much of the ideological muscle that upholds the organized vengeance of legal systems and many, if not all, retributive justifications. Those conceptual frameworks are predestination, atonement, and the sacrificial victim.

In several works, Augustine introduces the notion of predestination into the vocabulary of Christian theology: that God selects a certain number of "elect" from each generation upon whom the grace of salvation is bestowed while the rest of humanity is allowed to pursue deliberate acts of rebellion leading to eternal punishment: "Faith, then, as well in its beginning as in its completion, is God's gift; and let no one have any doubt whatever, unless he desires to resist the plainest sacred writings, that this gift is given to some, while to some it is not given."[68]

This theme, found in the more peripheral "anti-Pelagian" Augustinian texts,[69] was taken up anew and given central prominence by John Calvin in the sixteenth century: "By predestination we mean the eternal decree of God by which he determined with himself whatever he wished to happen with regard to every man. All are not created on equal terms, but some are preordained to eternal life, others to eternal damnation."[70] Predestination reached the shores of America— on the *Mayflower*, to be exact—and found its way into the national ethos with the first Puritan settlers.[71]

From this dualist cosmic perspective, the ethics of punishment for the Puritans was quite elementary: those lacking the grace of salvation give witness to their unruly natures, and their need for physical repression, by the unrighteous acts in which they indulge. The punitive justification was further abetted by the belief that those who were divinely favored were aware of their redemptive destiny and, more to the point, that Puritan "divines" could perceive the state of the human soul, especially regarding those to whom election was denied. Perry Miller comments upon this: "Puritans contended that regeneration was usually an ascertainable experience, that men could tell whether they were or not in a state of grace. With this conclusion they went beyond Augustine, for he would have never said point-blank . . . that a man himself could possibly know whether he had it or not, much less that a set of impartial examiners could discover the true state of his soul."[72] Kai Erikson sums up the positon: "The truth as seen by the Puritans was wholly clear. God had chosen an elite to represent Him on earth and to join Him in Heaven. People who belonged to this elite learned of their appointment through a deep conversion experience, giving them a special responsibility and a special competence to control the destinies of others."[73]

This divisive anthropology of grace and corruption, and the surety that the "saints" knew the difference, attests to the belief that the inculcation of virtues into the vice-ridden destined by God for eternal punishment was more than "madness and folly . . . a chasing after the wind" (Eccl 1: 17); it was doubting the wisdom of God's infallible wisdom: "Puritan attitudes toward punishment had a fairly simple logic. If a culprit standing before the bench is scheduled to spend eternity in hell, it does not matter very much how severely the judges treat him."[74] Thus, only through repressive means can the delinquent be corralled and forced into some degree of compliance with the law.[75]

The Puritans helped lay the foundation for one of the dominant paths of moral reflection with regard to criminal justice: that the juridical process was meant to be a painful means of teaching a lesson in the hopes of containing a rebellious spirit and dis-incentivizing the seduction of aberrant behavior. According to T. Richard Snyder, such a theological conclusion is a regrettable diversion from the common belief in the Protestant ethical tradition of an abundance of grace available to all. In his words, this interpretation affirms that "[w]hatever grace creation once possessed has been lost with the fall. Only in redemption is grace restored. That being the case . . . those whose condition is less than favorable

(such as criminals, the sick, the poor) are reaping the just deserts of their unre-
deemed state. It is then but a short step to dismissing them as less than fully
human."[76]

There can be no doubt that the Puritan spirit of self-confident judgment
upon the moral and legal status of those "known" to be outside the boundaries of
the elect remains very much in the American subconscious. Alan Hunt reflects
upon the manner in which contemporary moral discourse revives early colonial
patterns: "The changes in the regimes of self-governance did not simply replace
some earlier version, but rather injected . . . new forms of authority and expertise . . . with the shift from 'vice' and 'sin' to contemporary concerns with 'addiction' and 'abuse.' "[77]

Another theological justification for repressive punishment upon those who
are socially disruptive has been linked to the early medieval Christian theologian, St. Anselm. Drawing upon Augustinian influences, not unlike Luther and
Calvin, Anselm exhibited both a pious submission to the ineffable mystery of divine mercy and justice and a rather pitiless theological account of the meaning of
the Incarnation (God taking on human flesh). Early works, such as the *Proslogion*
(1078), were penned while living as a monk—before becoming embroiled in political intrigues after being named the Archbishop of Canterbury. In that early work
he stands in awe of God's inscrutable goodness: "[D]o You with justice in one
way punish the wicked and with justice in another way spare the wicked? . . . For
in sparing the wicked You are just in relation to Yourself and not in relation to us,
even as You are merciful in relation to us and not in relation to Yourself."[78] Yet it
is not for such pious restraint that Anselm is most remembered. It was his later
position on the matter that extends its shadow quite formidably over the history
of retributive justice.

It was as a more world weary archbishop that Anselm penned his most important work, *Cur Deus Homo* or *Why God Became Man* (c. 1098). Here, he
ponders the question of why Jesus had to die such a cruel death (what is known in
Christian theology as the atonement). The answer he provides is that humans had
dishonored God by rebelling against the perfect order that God had created, one
in which, had they not allowed themselves to be seduced by the devil, they would
have flourished in both earthly life and eternity. This egregious offense required
that there be recompense: "The will of every rational creature must be subject to
the will of God . . . This is the debt that angel and man owe to God, so that no
one sins if he pays it and anyone who does not pay it, sins. A person who does
not render God this honor due Him takes from God what is His and dishonors
God . . . Now as long as he does not pay back what he has plundered, he remains at
fault."[79] And in a blunt retraction of the meek resignation before the mysterious
ways of God in the *Proslogion*, he goes on to say: "One who has not paid the debt

is uselessly crying 'Pardon.' One who has paid, is paying because this very act is the point of payment."[80] Put simply, Anselm argued that, though liable to punishment, no human expression of remorse and restitution could satisfy an affront of infinite proportions: "[N]o one but God can make this satisfaction . . . But no one ought to make it but man," therefore, Jesus, the divine offspring, was born to die and offer, through his painful death, the necessary antidote for human malfeasance and to reopen the road to salvation for sinful humanity.[81]

The smoke and fury of Reformation polemics aside, Anselm was deftly repackaged by Luther and Calvin, and to some degree by Aquinas, and bequeathed to generations of their followers. Note Calvin's restatement of the satisfaction theory in his discussion of the Lord's prayer: "To sins [Jesus] gives the name of *debts*, because we owe the punishment due to them, a debt which we could not possibly pay were we not discharged by this remission, the result of his free mercy, when he freely expunges the debt, accepting nothing in return; but of his own mercy receiving satisfaction in Christ, who gave himself a ransom for us" (Rom 3: 24).[82]

A number of theologians have centered both their analysis and their critique of contemporary criminal justice upon the ongoing salience of the belief, which they trace to Anselm, in a vengeful God who cannot be appeased by anything but human blood.[83] David Burrell argues that Anselm reduces the polyvalent symbol of the cross and the inscrutable God to a single explanation.[84] Timothy Gorringe paints his critique in more colorful terms. Anselm's logic of the atonement "reeks of cruelty" and offers a "mysticism of pain": "[He] makes God the one who *insists* on debt. The debt humanity has incurred must be paid with human blood." He then adds: "The penal consequences of this theory were grim indeed. As it entered the cultural bloodstream, was imaged in crucifixions . . . recited at each celebration of the Eucharist, or hymned, so it created its own structure of affect, one in which earthly punishment was demanded because God himself had demanded the death of his Son."[85]

Gorringe has his critics who insist that his interpretation of Anselm is too narrow and ignores the Trinitarian nature of God.[86] These criticisms have some merit, in my opinion, from a viewpoint based in systematic theology, but Gorringe and other detractors of Anselm are correct in their observation concerning the influence that "satisfaction theory" has had on the understanding of retributive punishment as a quantum of pain owed to an offended deity. Many Christians across the centuries have been tutored in a narrative of the Passion that maintains that Jesus came to earth in order "to die for our sins," despite the fact that there is scant evidence for this belief in the New Testament generally, and the gospels in particular.[87] The residual influence of this theology on the way justice is perceived, especially criminal justice, cannot be overlooked.

The work of Rene Girard is also important in locating another cultural resource that provides an important basis for contemporary retributive theory. Girard has traced the origin of religion to the need to use violence in ritual fashion to destroy a "surrogate victim": a person sacrificed to appease an angry god; a death which temporarily purges the social tensions created by internecine conflicts triggered by "mimetic rivalry" for mutually desired objects.[88] The key to the longevity and consistency of the practice of finding and persecuting the scapegoat is that the irate "god," paralleling the thought of Durkheim, was a reification of the needs for order and solidarity within the chronically unstable community.[89] Scapegoat theory can only function in an environment of moral self-absolution. The participants in the sacrificial death must be unaware that the victim is the innocent projection of their own divisive and narcissistic rivalries.[90] Interesting also for current penal demographics is Girard's insistence that the victims must bear a physical resemblance to their executioners, and yet cannot be from the privileged sectors of the community for fear of a vendetta-like reprisal from the families of the slain. Therefore, the scapegoats must be people who are either outside of or on the fringes of society: typically, prisoners of war or slaves.[91] The reverberations of Girard's theory are resounding not only in creating a lens to view the narcissism at the root of the retributive impulse but also in uncovering the hidden prejudices that sanction the isolation and sacrifice of those outside a narrowly parochial, and privileged sector of society.

It is essential to add that, in Girard's opinion, the Bible generally and the New Testament in particular overturn the need for sacrificial victims to assuage an enraged deity. Stories such as Cain and Abel, Abraham and Isaac, and Joseph in the Hebrew Bible reveal both the innocence of sacrificial victims and the favor God bestows upon them. While in his passion and death, "Jesus . . . provides the scapegoat par excellence—he is the most arbitrary of victims because he is also the least violent. At the same time, he is the least arbitrary and the most meaningful . . . in whom the previous history of mankind is summed up, concluded, and transcended."[92] In short, he argues that there can no longer be a coherent theological justification to harm or kill a supposed malefactor in the name of God.

Yet, despite this, Girard does not part company with Gorringe, not in regard to the influence of Anselm's atonement doctrine, but in his observation that modern legal systems, despite their efficiency in transmuting sacrificial violence into a sober, rational, bureaucratic procedure are extensions of a society in which victimizing the other has been taken to an unprecedented level: "Victimage is still present among us, of course, but in degenerate forms that do not produce the type of mythical reconciliation and ritual practice exemplified by primitive cults. This lack of efficiency often means that there are more rather than fewer victims."[93]

It is my contention that the above influences, rather than Scripture, have had the most decisive impact upon a theological portrait of criminal justice as a dispensation of pain and, through that medium, upon the way justice has been imagined and institutionalized in secular polities. Thomas Aquinas, for example, reprised Anselm's concept of a violated order of justice whose repair demands some form of administered suffering: "Now it is evident that in all actual sins, when the act of sin has ceased, the guilt remains; because the act of sin makes man deserving of punishment, in so far as he transgresses the order of Divine justice, to which he cannot return except he pay some sort of penal compensation which restores him to the equality of justice."[94]

Aquinas has a richer sense of the Catholic tradition's commitment to use confinement as a means of healing the soul and instilling virtue than does Anselm, but it is revelatory that the Catholic Church, in its official documents, focuses significantly upon the retributive sentiments in St. Thomas while, at the same time, reproducing the irreversible conundrum between punishment and reform. The Catechism thus reads: "Punishment has the primary aim of redressing the disorder introduced by the offense. When it is willingly accepted by the guilty party, it assumes the value of expiation. Punishment then, in addition to defending public order and protecting people's safety, has a medicinal purpose: as far as possible, it must contribute to the correction of the guilty party."[95]

My position on the religious (specifically Christian) defenses of retribution is twofold: one historical and one, for lack of a better word, evangelical.

Historically, a commitment to retributivism largely ignores the first thousand years of Christian practice in which a solution to human alienation was crafted through its sacramental system (especially the practice of penance) and its monastic system (especially in its development of the idea of the prison as a place of conversion/moral transformation). It would take far too long to explain in detail the source of this rupture with the past, but the short answer has to do with the official separation of the Church from secular influence in the eleventh century, the consequent need to develop a comprehensive system of orderly operation, and the rapid emergence of the first universal code of law (canon law), the first law school (and university, Bologna), the legal and judicial professions, case law, and, at the same time, ecclesiastical prisons in every diocese in the Catholic world to punish those found guilty of "criminal sins."[96] In an unprecedented development that tainted the waters of legal justice at their very inception, this legal revolution divided acts of human mischief into an external and internal forum; only the latter could be forgiven outright in the sacrament of penance. The former required adjudication in an ecclesiastical tribunal and, if culpability was determined, punishment in an ecclesiastical prison.[97] As Remi Brague notes, for the first time in Christian history, people came in contact with God through contact with the law.[98]

An example of this massive shift in social and moral understanding is found in the way Jesus's directions on how to approach disruptive members of the community in the Gospel of Matthew (Mt 18: 15–18) are interpreted in one example before and one after the eleventh century. For St. Benedict, Jesus's counsel on seeking reconciliation with a disruptive person by repeated and ever-widening communal interventions prior to excommunication resulted in a patient approach (admittedly with the threat of corporal punishment in some cases) that culminated, as mentioned previously, in a confinement accompanied by communal prayer for the absent brother, accompaniment by an older and respected member of the community, and overseen by an abbot who saw himself in the same relation with the offender as Christ with the lost sheep who embraces it and carries it back to the community.[99] John of Paris, writing at the end of the thirteen century, states that among the powers granted by Christ to the apostles is the judicial, the "power to coerce in the external forum by which sins are corrected through fear of punishment, especially sins in scandal to the church. The concession of this power is in Matthew 18: 15–18."[100]

The evangelical critique is simply that no justification for treating human weakness and sinfulness with the infliction of pain is in any way consistent with the portrait of Jesus in the Gospels; half the content of which reveal Jesus being moved to remedial action by human suffering and alienation. He never asks for repentance as a condition of bringing health and reconciliation to anyone. He wants to heal and the healing is meant to reconnect the leper, the blind, the handicapped, the prisoner, the prostitute, the traitor, the widow to the community that at best tepidly accepts their condition or, worse, isolates and ignores them altogether. Jesus is neither surprised nor angered at human weakness and sinfulness; the only instances in which he appears perturbed are in describing "religious" people who arrogantly believe that they are better than the ones they exclude and look down upon. This gracious portrait of unconditional concern is what is referred to as the "kerygma" (the proclamation and core content of the gospel) that always calls for an active response on the part of the hearer.

Dorothee Soelle, following Rudolf Bultmann, explains the kerygma as the "absolute" in Christian faith "that accosts each individual."[101] She contrasts it with "pure" theology in its critical evaluative role without "suppositions, content, or consequences"; an epistemological approach that "encourages the dualistic bifurcation of reality into two hierarchically arranged realms—faith above, politics below."[102] It is her correct contention, given the absence of "kerygma" in the ecclesiastical defenses of punishment, that the "hierarchies of the large churches could not have been interested in the what and how of Jesus's life, because this interest would have called them radically into question . . . The official church uses the kerygmatic Christ as a means of discipline. . . In other words, the Christ who rules in the church and who has supplanted the biblical Christ is the Christ of the rulers."[103]

These brief statements opposing a theological warrant for punishment will have to do for now as I want to reconnect our narrative with a wider critique of retribution and deterrence.

Critique of Retributivism

While retributive arguments cohere given their premises and the careful steps their authors take to assure their rational consistency, it is in the practice of criminal justice, the task of seeking to measure the level of foreknowledge, consent, and responsibility in a given legal subject—fulfilling the retributive requirement that punishment fit the crime—that their Achilles heel is exposed and shadows of doubt begin to cloud their conceptual logic. One can (and should) legitimately question the ability of anyone empowered to judge and to punish to discern correctly the internal state of an individual and the degree to which that person's action is truly malevolent. For Robert Cover, we "construct meaning in our normative world by using the irony of jurisdiction, the comedy of manners that is *malum prohibitum*, the surreal epistemology of due process."[104] Thomas Aquinas may lack Cover's rhetorical flourish but makes the same point: "[M]an can make laws in those matters of which he is competent to judge. But man is not competent to judge interior movements, that are hidden, but only of exterior acts which appear; and yet for the perfection of virtue it is necessary for man to conduct himself aright in both kinds of acts."[105]

The notion being re-orchestrated here is that of human fallibility, whether that of the offender or the judge, or, for that matter, the victim,[106] especially when the host of educational, experiential, emotional, and psychological factors that affect human action come into play. This state of fallibility has been discussed by scholars across the intellectual terrain, not as a means to dismiss the grave consequences of harming the innocent, not as a means to shun the need of the offender to take responsibility for the harm caused, but as a challenge to the veracity of the claim that the perpetrator is somehow different, perhaps even ontologically different than the rest of us who regularly fail to honor the sacredness of the lives of those with whom we live.

The existential doubt raised about the capacity of rational calculation (by consciously detached observers, no less) to discern the internal degree of moral responsibility of another and the amount of suffering to which he or she can rightly be subjected should give pause to the judgmental. It not only resurrects the arrogance of the Puritan divines who thought that their "election" provided infallible knowledge of the state of another's soul, it should also lend a degree of credence to the notion that defenders of retributive punishment are not appealing primarily to our reason at all, but rather to our emotions. Bruce Waller, for example, claims that the concept of moral responsibility originates not in rational analysis but "in the harsh and undiscriminatory strike-back reaction we feel when we suffer harm."[107]

Part and parcel of the phenomenon of mass incarceration is a vibrant populist sentiment that is so much a part of the American political tradition and, to be sure, a consistent factor in the shaping of criminal policy.[108] The current face of this dogmatic artifact is revealed in an anthropology of inherent evil assigned to a subgroup of the citizenry considered to be outside the pale of human sensibility; an anthropology fueled by a mélange of daily images of domestic and international horror drawn from the robust electronic and media sectors to which so many willingly subject themselves.[109] Such a base ideology "obstructs the possibility of conversion," is predicated upon "isolation of [people] from each other," the "inability to communicate," and is "characteristic of a society in which we are not permitted to make a mistake."[110]

In contrasting the largely discredited "penal welfare" approach to the confined population with the one presently employed, Garland notes that in the first strategy, the interests of the prisoner and the common citizen were seen to be remarkably alike, whereas in the current volatile cultural atmosphere—one in which people are routinely startled, repelled, and terrified by the randomness and finality of violence—the interests of the convicted and the collective body are seen to be in fundamental opposition.[111] Haney's argument is similar: "Claims that prison rehabilitation programs everywhere were failing badly were used to support an antiquated and unfounded argument that criminality was an intractable trait and the predisposition to offend would not yield even in the face of the most powerful and well-designed correctional programs."[112]

The conviction that passion or resentment, not rational deduction, provides the lifeblood of the punisher has been emphasized by many commentators, none more influential than Durkheim: "It would indeed be mistaken to believe that vengeance is mere wanton cruelty. It may very possibly constitute by itself an automatic, purposeless reaction, an emotional and senseless impulse, and an unreasoned compulsion to destroy. But in fact what it tends to destroy was a threat to us. Therefore in reality it constitutes a veritable act of defense, albeit instinctive and unreflecting. We wreak vengeance only upon what has done us harm, and what has done us harm is always dangerous. The instinct for revenge is, after all, merely a heightened instinct of self-preservation in the face of danger."[113] This same theme is taken up by Joel Feinberg who speaks of punishment as "legitimatized vengefulness": "[I]t can be said that punishment expresses the judgment . . . of the community that what the offender did was wrong. I think it is fair to say . . . however, that punishment generally expresses more than judgment of disapproval; it is also a symbolic way of getting back at the criminal, of expressing vindictive resentment."[114]

Not to be dissuaded, defenders of retributivism, especially those working from a Kantian perspective, maintain the integrity of reason over the sweep of the powerful vengeful emotions described by Durkheim and Feinberg. To whatever degree these defenses may be convincing to those who enable and command the penal apparatus, they take away with one hand what they bestow with the other: the very mastery over the emotions being heralded fosters, of necessity, an inability to take compassionate account of those made to suffer under its rubrics. Elaine Scary writes one must make a deliberate effort to overcome such aloofness; otherwise it only augments the endemic enigma of pain: that for the sufferer, being in pain is the nearest thing to "having certainty," while, for those outside its grip, it is a primary example of what it means to have "doubt."[115] And this doubt is immeasurably enhanced by the fact that the institutions wherein that cauldron of suffering is fueled are purposely designed and administered to assure that the cries of the afflicted are muffled to all but the community of the afflicted: "How does one record and comment on an absent presence that no inflicter wants known and most victims fear to reveal?"[116]

It is, I suspect, for this reason that the mode of pain delivery (imprisonment) does not strike most outside the walls as excessively cruel, if cruel at all: "The crucial difference between corporal punishments which are banned, and other punishments—such as imprisonment—which are commonly used, is not a matter of the intrinsic levels of pain and brutality involved. It is a matter of the *form* which that violence takes, and the extent to which it impinges upon public sensibilities . . . Consequently, routine violence and suffering can be tolerated on condition that it be discreet, disguised, or somehow removed from view."[117]

But are we all really unaware or is it, perhaps, that we just do not care? The dualist mind that seeks shelter in objectification and rationalization is haunted by the sense of its "thrownness" (Heidegger) of having been "launched" (Levinas) into a world where one's mind, body, and spirit cannot be dissected from one's temporality, one's historicity, one's personhood, and from the primary responsibility of care for the other. Thus Levinas states: "To think is . . . to be engaged, merged with what we think, launched—the dramatic event of being in the world"; while Heidegger insists that the "phenomenon of care in its totality is essentially something that cannot be torn asunder."[118]

Were this not enough, despite the (presumed) good intentions of most prison personnel, legislators, and retributive theorists, punishment tends to further alienate offenders. In a meta-analysis of programs aimed at curbing recidivism, MacKenzie and Farrington conclude: "Interventions that emphasize deterrence or control have not shown evidence of effectively reducing recidivism and some appear to actually increase later criminal activity."[119] Sykes states that in order to "endure psychologically" in a lifeworld wherein the prisoner is constantly reminded that he is "contaminated" and must be sealed off from people who are "decent," he must find a way "to reject his rejectors."[120] In their work on motivational interviewing, the psychologists, Miller and Rollnick, insist that coercion retards moral development: "Many of the clients we see have no dearth of suffering. Humiliation, shame, guilt, and angst are not the primary engines of change. Ironically, such experiences can even immobilize the person, rendering change more remote. Instead, constructive behavior change seems to arise when the person connects it with something of intrinsic value, something important, something cherished."[121]

Finally, retributivism has substituted violence for a far more rooted human need: compassion. What Marie Gottschalk calls "the carceral state" has engendered "a highly distinct political and legal universe" inhabited by "partial citizens" and "internal exiles."[122] It has failed to see that to will painful suffering upon another says more about the lack of moral self-knowledge of the punisher than it does about justice.[123] John Lofland points to the fact that the concept of the "degenerate" not only precedes but also conditions the way those in that category are treated, especially in relation to the law: "Without a conception of deviant types of persons . . . how effectively might the boundaries be drawn between the 'good life' and the 'bad life'? How effectively might the limits of acceptable behavior be dramatized and communicated without a continuing supply of 'degenerate' sorts who personify all that which is to be avoided?"[124] There is but a short step, according to Whitman, from such negative social categories to applying the status of inferiority and the practice of "degradation" upon those who populate them.[125]

From a theological perspective, inasmuch as persons will the punishment of others, they have forgotten a primal rootedness in a universe infused by grace at every pore, one wherein the role of Providence is to bind "the wounds of the world."[126] As Linda Meyer states: "If we think of mercy as undeserved leniency for one who is guilty . . . then mercy describes the human condition."[127]

Much of the critique that has been directed to retributivism is applicable to another of the principal justifications for the infliction of suffering on the culpable, deterrence. I will therefore offer only brief remarks.

Outline and Critique of Deterrence

As discussed in the last chapter, deterrence views the offender not simply in terms of what he or she did but in a wider sociopolitical vision of how the punitive response can be a tool to deflate the appeal of illegal conduct both by the offender and the wider populace. While some commentators observe a general decline in the theoretical lure of deterrence in recent decades, it is impossible to ignore as an adjunct, if not architect, of penal strategy since there is a constant monitoring of crime rates across the social and political continuum and at least an implicit assumption that those figures have something to do with the amount of punishment that is being imposed on the guilty.[128] For Stanley Cohen, the implicit link between deterrence and utilitarianism makes the former unavoidable since, in his view, "crime-control systems are utilitarian by definition."[129]

While there are those who maintain that punishing someone in order that someone else thinks twice about committing a proscribed action has some empirical grounding, the theory is both morally and practically troubling.[130] The obvious moral objection of using the offender as a pawn in a strategy of inflicting suffering as a means of inducing fear and legal compliance has been raised by classical retributivists such as Kant and Hegel, and their more contemporary associates like Herbert Morris and Anthony Duff.[131]

In the empirical dimension, deterrence proceeds from what Sykes calls "a complicated cause and effect relationship" between punishment and desistance.[132] This suggests a flaw, impossible to disguise with legal jargon, in the application of strict causality to any human action given the multiple layers of intellectual, emotional, and psychological motivation. Or, perhaps better to say, such a reduction is *only* conceivable when an equally impossible *reductio ad absurdum* is posited that there *are* no other motivations in the psyche than the momentary emotive deductions of the hedonic calculus or, for that matter, the rule-based utility of Mill.[133] In short, calibrating the relation between the amount of pain delivered and the subsequent history both of those punished and those for whom the punishment serves a pedagogical lesson ignores the question of the false positive.[134]

As mentioned in the last chapter, the theory is directly correlated to behaviorism: there is no core self to which a moral appeal can be made or a self that can be transformed through internal enlightenment. The individual is a product of social engineering and the controlled application of external stimuli. The socially conservative implications are disturbingly apparent as the regnant distribution of power becomes the baseline against which proper and improper action is determined and regulated.[135] Furthermore, and here we see how the theory pairs with rehabilitation, it "has an alarmingly paternalistic tendency. Utilitarian punishment theories tend to view crime as analogous to disease . . . From this point of view, the special expertise of criminologists, psychologists, and bureaucratic administrators entitles them . . . to dictate the nature and direction of treatment (punishment) that offenders should receive, according to the experts' calculation of maximum social utility."[136]

Regardless of the shallowness and callousness of its moral roots, the belief that human behavior can be manipulated in the interests of social control has appeared consistently throughout penal history, including early in the second millennium. Richard Fraher has traced the development of the legal culture in the twelfth and thirteenth centuries and maintains that deterrence was very much in evidence as a determinant of judicial policy. He reveals that practices of criminal prosecution were adopted from the *Corpus Iuris Civilis* of the Roman emperor Justinian and its twin belief in punishment in the service of public interest and the use of punishment as a deterrent. Concerning the latter, Innocent III wrote that the failure of the Church to punish crimes "creates an audacity of impunity, through which those who were bad become worse."[137] In his defense of the aim of deterrence, three passages were quoted from Justinian's *Digest*. The first states that deterrence is the *magna ratio* (predominant reason) to prosecute crimes; second, the person who has done wrong should suffer public indigence; and third, deterrence is fostered through something resembling an aesthetics of terror in which notorious bandits are hung publicly in the neighborhoods most affected by their crimes.[138]

Whether one looks at the concept historically or in its present iteration, it falls into the same trap into which Progressives ensnared themselves: the same trap that eventually proves fatal to any theory that seeks to coerce human beings into being more socially responsible than they presently are. In the words of Rusche and Kirchheimer, anticipating Rothman, it ignores "the insoluble contradiction" between moral betterment and the imposition of pain.[139]

Thoughts on Incapacitation

The dissonance created by seeking fruitlessly to construct a penal system that admirably serves all the possible meanings in the current methodological vocabulary also includes the belief in incapacitating the once and future offender while, at the same time, hoping that it might serve other goals (retribution, deterrence, and rehabilitation).

Even though incapacitation, due to its morally agnostic starting point, does not fall into the metaethical problem of basing condemnation and suffering on unsupportable moral grounds, it revives Justinian's aim of punishing in the service of public interest and shares in the general consensus that correctional pragmatism (positivism) does no disservice to other systemic goals. Von Hirsch maintains that positivism has long been a "prevailing" notion in American penal ideology, "in the sense used by writers in the Italian positivist school." Its goal is "to prevent future crimes by convicted offenders. When those crimes might be forestalled through rehabilitative efforts, treatment programs should be tried.

But to the extent that the success of such programs was uncertain, the offenders who were bad risks could always be restrained."[140] Thus, the justifications for incapacitation are reminiscent of the logic of deterrence in as much as the intent is the reduction of acts foreseen to be in the detainee's future. It therefore exists in a double moral darkness wherein there is an infliction of suffering but the suffering is enforced for actions that the offender not only has not committed but also that he or she might never commit.

To be sure, proponents of selective incapacitation object to this categorization. The success of Wilson's (correct) determination that there is little social value in punishing the person for whom the shame and fear of a conviction itself (sans imprisonment) will result in a lifetime of compliance was paired with the equally correct assumption that crime rates (in their social construction) will recede by focusing upon the small percentage of the population who commit a significantly high percentage of the offenses reported annually.[141]

The reader will recall that my position is that incapacitation is the only justifiable reason to place someone in custody. I thus affirm that social control is a relevant consideration in the determination that, say, violent offenders must be quarantined because actions that bring grievous harm upon others are the expression of misanthropic feelings that normally have a long prehistory; one that cannot be assuaged or made benevolent by sheer force of the will. I also agree with proponents of incapacitation that an assessment of the character of the potential detainee is not a sufficient condition for his or her incarceration. Where my own thought differs, however, is that the suspension of judgment is *not* in order to sanction a positivist outlook in which control, security, and the prevailing juridical climate are the only legal tender in the economy of justice. Rather, one is incapacitated because that person has lost contact with her own natural sociability and capacity for self-transcendence: because she has resisted the natural outward flow of care and is, metaphorically, already imprisoned in a space of fear and anger.

Concluding Thoughts

In a culture where policy grows out of the shallow soil of expediency, the public hunger for security, political opportunism, and the fear of violence, an equally violent penal system is the only certain operational variable in judicial and penal ethics. Ruth Wilson Gilmore writes that in contemporary culture, "punishment has become as industrialized as making cars, clothes, missiles, or growing cotton."[142] There is simply no deeper moral or theoretical well from which to draw. In Garland's words, all other conceivable systemic options are "minor considerations."[143]

The pragmatics of allegiance to the current distribution and imposition of power also serves an academic function. It provides a stable basis of scientific variables for criminologists and legal scholars to measure the effects of punishment on desistance (however selective the determination may be as to who the criminals are). The circle is complete when the citizenry can be reassured that when crime rates are lowered, no serious objection need be raised to the "justice juggernaut."[144]

I have argued in this chapter that it is morally wrong to punish anyone for any reason, regardless of the theological, philosophical, or practical justifications offered by its advocates. Punishment accomplishes a double victory for violence. As Nietzsche claims, "it makes men harder and colder."[145] No matter how much one tries to dull the harm done to others and to oneself in the name of due process by hiding behind the barrier of objective distance or "the mathematical manipulation of data," vengeance is a two-edged sword that exists in the heart before it is unleashed upon others and wounds the assailant as much as the victim.[146] I repeat Girard's claim that human rage over unattained material and psychic desires can either be assuaged through patient restraint and detachment or projected upon a scapegoat under the banner of appeasing the bloodthirsty "god" of justice.

The only reason why anyone should be deprived of their freedom of movement and association is to seek to create the conditions for a conversion as a means of reclaiming one's inherent and virtually limitless reservoir of compassion. It is to that subject that we now turn.

3

Conversion as Inclusion

"THEY" ARE NOT THE PROBLEM ... I AM

THUS FAR, IT has been argued that the conceptual and methodological vocabulary of criminal justice is riddled with contradictions and unsupportable justifications stemming from historical amnesia, shallow moral foundations that can do no other than result in violence, and a prevailing dualist (writ divisive and oppositional) worldview. Of course, slinging arrows of critique at a target as massive, visible, and vulnerable as the penal complex is easy to do; and, more to the point, has been done with admirable sagacity by a legion of talented scholars. This volume, however, has far more on its mind than to offer another indictment. The first two chapters were necessary to provide a radical and terminal diagnosis, but they are prefatory to the real object of this study: First, to cast the entire human project as one of inherent and comprehensive sociability; and the entire drama of human destructiveness as one in which all are villains.[1] Second, to affirm that to come to full personhood, conversion is a necessary and ongoing process for everyone, not just the men and women in our jails and prisons. Each person must find the means to overcome the judgmental, and, ultimately, violent dualism that, without a fundamental shift in the "natural attitude," functions by erecting barriers of separation and hostility with unknown or unwanted sectors of experience.[2] Third, to reject any justification for confinement save to create the conditions for a continued broadening of the horizon of one's participation in and care for the world.

This chapter will first discuss conversion as a key element in moral growth and the role that penal solitude plays in stimulating a reconnection with the internal and inexhaustible reservoir of compassion. It will then discuss the basic rudiments of what a conversion is and what it is not. This will be followed by a step-by-step phenomenology of the conversion process. Finally, I will offer some thoughts on what the ideas presented suggest concerning the current status of criminal justice policy and the assumptions upon which that policy is based.

The Prison as Metaphor for Introspection

Although the ancient concept of forced incarceration that has morphed into the modern prison has lost its initial justification as a place of conversion; and despite the aimlessness, violence, and anomie that haunt its cell blocks, the experience of penal solitude, fashioned to invite concerted moral and spiritual reflection, continues to do so despite institutional obstacles. The atmosphere of negation stimulates a self-inventory, and that process of internal review is the first step in recovering the only humane meaning correctional confinement can offer. Irene Becci writes that in prison, "individuals are confronted with existential questions in a particularly intensive way. The conditions of detention and everyday struggles for freedom in relation to space, time and body create a situation in which religion gains particular meaning."[3] This susceptibility to the transcendent is reiterated in a study by Todd Clear and his colleagues: "[For some] the attack against the self, represented by the prison term, is too real to be denied. A certain truth about their lives must be confronted: the final failure of their choices. Religion, in its substance, holds possible routes out of the dilemma, for it not only explains the cause of the failure, it also prescribes the solution."[4]

These quotes suggest that the human heart is oriented to participate in a reality that far exceeds one framed by narcissistic pursuits. Yet, as has been discussed, immersion in the lifeworld does not make that ontological orientation necessarily apparent. In the deliberate climate of deprivation and idle time that is the prison, however, individuals trapped in the shackles of self-preoccupation and anger become acutely aware of their painful isolation and, ideally, if the conditions are carefully fostered, begin to recognize and embrace their internal yearning to live harmoniously in and with the world.

Let me quickly add, lest the reader think that one must become "religious" in order to be led to such introspection, that the longing to overcome loneliness, fear, and hostility is universal and the process by which that isolation is overcome at ever-expansive levels is what I am referring to as conversion. Maslow insightfully emphasizes the needless dualism between science and religion in confronting the joys and sorrows of human life: "I want to demonstrate that spiritual values have naturalistic meaning, that they are not the exclusive possession of organized churches, that they do not need superior concepts to validate them, that they are well within the jurisdiction of a suitably enlarged science, and that, therefore, they are the general responsibility of *all*."[5]

Many well-respected secular scholars recognize this orientation to see be-yond the empirical self and connect to a larger conception of life and moral ac-countability. Shadd Maruna speaks of substantive character change "coming from within . . . freeing one's 'real me' from . . . external constraints."[6] A study by Kent Kerley speaks of some of the prisoners he interviewed discovering their "true self" as a result of their spiritual awakening.[7] John Braithwaite states: "The cultural as-sumption of basic goodness and belief in each individual's capacity for eventual self-correction means that 'nurturant acceptance' is the appropriate response to deviance."[8] Katherine Becket notes the lack of such an affirmative anthropology in her appraisal of some penal conservatives whose desire to control what they perceive as "a threatening and undeserving underclass" rests upon a "pessimistic vision of human nature" and the belief that "the causes of crime lie in the 'human propensity to evil.'"[9]

One can also consult classic texts in cognitive psychology and philosophy that speak of the innate capacity for and the normal human development of successive levels of ethical awareness, responsibility, and concern for others. Lawrence Kohlberg writes that "children often generate their own moral values and maintain them in the face of cultural training . . . these values have universal root."[10] As many readers know, Kohlberg posits six levels of moral development characterized by a growing sense of personal integrity and other-directedness. At the sixth level, in many ways consonant with what will be presented concerning conversion, the person adopts a "self-chosen, comprehensive, and consistent" worldview that mirrors the "Golden Rule" (Do unto others as you would have them do unto you).[11] For Jean Piaget, cognitive development at each stage of life is identical to a "Copernican revolution" of moving from self-preoccupation to self-transcendence made possible by a process of decentering the ego that he calls "decentration."[12] In the thought of Josef Pieper, taking issue with Kant's distrust of the instinctual, "virtue perfects us so we can *follow* our natural inclinations in the right way."[13]

Recalling, once again, the notion of fallibility, there is an unavoidable dis-sonance between the experiential and the transcendent self, or between what Heidegger calls the "they self" as opposed to the "authentic self."[14] That is to say, there is an inherent tension between the freedom and intersubjectivity that de-fine the person at the core of her being and the daily reality of making life-altering (and sometimes life-denying) choices relying solely on the ego and its necessary perspective of difference and separation. This existential dilemma leads inevitably to conflict, alienation, guilt, and, eventually, lack of meaning on one hand, while often stimulating a longing for repentance and inner healing on the other. The study by Clear and his co-authors notes that many of the incarcerated "refused to adopt an exculpatory view of their guilt. Instead, they seemed to accept a profound personal responsibility for their crimes and for the wrongfulness of their conduct."[15] In one study of conversion, the authors note that at the psychological level, the movement to conversion "may be seen as a response to the individual sense of either his personal condition of finiteness or the finiteness of whatever gives him his fundamental identity."[16]

I have been using the word alienation to describe this inner conflict between the "I" as radically relational in its basic orientation to experience and the "I" or ego in its bifurcated and oppositional stance vis-à-vis reality. For Levinas, this alienation is "the first injustice," the condition in which ones being "is radically separated from a totality of which it is a part."[17] To live in such a narrow lifeworld is to exist in what Gibson Winter calls "bad faith," a condition in which "the harmony of the self and other to which the 'I' belongs is sacrificed for a lesser reality of the 'I's' choice, and the basic relatedness of the self and other is denied."[18] Jacques Lacan addresses this loss of the true self in its isolation from the "Word" (*verbe*) which is the source of creation and creativity: "The . . . paradox of relation of language to the Word is that of the subject who loses his meaning and direction in the objectification of discourse . . . for here is the most profound alienation of the subject in our scientific civilization, and it is this alienation that we encounter first of all when the subject begins to talk about himself . . . the '*ce suis je*'. . . has become reversed in the '*c'est moi*' of modern man . . . the *belle aime* who does not recognize his very own raison d'etre in the disorder he denounces in the world."[19]

Although the experience of incarceration tends to accentuate the process of self-analysis, what is being described here is the *human* condition: not simply the condition of the men and women under lock and key. The "best practices" for overcoming this destructive alienation are no different for the bureaucrat and the day nurse as for the thief in the police lockup or the murderer on death row. The question concerns what it will take for each of us to recognize the radical distanciation between who we truly are in our profound inner relation to being and who we think we are immersed in the warp and woof of daily existence. For many, hitting rock bottom, coming to one's senses at last (Lk 15: 17), occurs after a great catastrophe; for others, the precipitating event is less dramatic; but one thing is certain: nothing in one's largely unconscious and repetitive framework for marking the meaning of life changes until things begin to fall apart.

The Meaning of Conversion

I understand that in choosing conversion as the principal theme of this volume, many readers may feel wary of some hidden proselytization or attempt to revive some lost artifact of theological orthodoxy. Admittedly, like virtually all terms common to theological discourse, the concept is ambiguous, perhaps especially to those who are irreligious or whose religious vocabulary does not include a term that is most commonly utilized in Christian parlance. To be sure, there are a host of other synonyms for the sort of substantive character amendment to which I am referring. Karl Barth mentions "alteration" and a "new life"; Tanya Erzen speaks of "heart change"; Peggy Giordano and her co-authors describe it as "cognitive transformation"; Maslow calls the phenomenon a "peak experience"; William Miller, "quantum change"; evangelical Christians say it is being "born again."[20] While some of these terms have considerable merit, I am using conversion because it is the one theological notion, perhaps the only one, that is a standard concept in the social sciences; albeit, not always presented in the same light that will be cast upon it in this study. Put differently, the databases and bibliographic codes that provide the bulk of the literature on a profound change in one's life course are typically filed under "conversion." That said, it is my hope that the interpretation being offered here (what I, obviously, believe to be the correct one) will not only be fully transparent and understandable to a wide audience, but also one whose merits will be appealing as a penal strategy, if not also a personal one.

So let us begin with a few basics. All forms of perception, from a phenomenological perspective, take place within a horizon.[21] Conversion is the process by which the intellectual, moral, and spiritual horizons against which one measures one's place in the world and the meaning of events are fundamentally altered and, eventually, expanded until they are all-inclusive. As Henri Bergson claims in describing mystical experience, conversion creates not simply an elongation of the borders of one's participative consciousness since the dualism of the social instinct "at the basis of social obligation always has in view . . . a closed society, however large."[22] Rather, the change is "one of kind not simply one of degree"[23] Like the "burst [of] a dam," it sweeps its recipients "into a vast current of life."[24] Bernard Lonergan calls it an "about face . . . that can keep revealing greater depth."[25] William Miller nicely sums up the shift in perspective as one of "quantum change" in which the "experience of unity is common . . . an ineffable oneness with all of humankind, with nature, or the universe."[26] It leads to a state of wonder "that shatters our ordinary world and gives access to a literally unlimited horizon. In doing so, it awakens inexhaustible longing."[27]

Conversion always begins with what Maslow calls a "peak experience," an "ecstatic" moment in which, true to the etymology of the word, one is carried outside the self as presently constituted to a realm beyond any prior knowledge or state of being. Heidegger speaks of a "rapture," "an ecstasis," a "moment of vision."[28]

Each conversion features self-transcendence: an openness to the present moment in which one, minimally, brackets the urge to judge; maximally, is possessed by an affirmative sociability. In the experience that constitutes its initial stage, one is "self-forgetful, egoless, unselfish" and the world is seen "only as beautiful, good, desirable, worthwhile."[29] Merleau-Ponty (commenting on Husserl) writes that in this state I communicate "from the center of my being with a pre-personal thought . . . to express the internal structure of the world as it is for a universal thinker."[30] For Lonergan, such transcendence does not dismiss one's experience; rather, "it includes it, preserves all its proper features and properties and carries them forward to a fuller realization within a richer context."[31] Winter calls it a "thrust toward wholeness," and "a passion for unity."[32] In Heidegger's schema, the visionary moment leads one to view the phenomena in each situation as "objects of care."[33] In summarizing the cognitive psychology of Erik Erikson, James Fowler, Lawrence Kohlberg, and Jean Piaget, Walter Conn concludes that for each of them, "[p]ersonal development is the ever greater realization of the radical drive for self-transcendence, for reaching out beyond oneself affectively and cognitively."[34] For one former captive, the conversion is, above all things, a call to love: "And in order to walk in love, I have to love you regardless, like He loved me regardless. So if you come up to me and cuss me out, that does not give me the right to cuss you out."[35]

Put negatively, conversion is the antithesis of alienation or, as it might be described in theological terms, living in a state of sin. Edgardo Rotman has a similar insight: "[S]in can be regarded as a precedent of the modern socio-psychological notion of alienation."[36] Yet, whether viewed through the lens of religion or psychology, the issue of the greatest importance for human flourishing is to overcome the barriers erected by the self in isolation. This "sinful" tendency is found not only in the criminal class, but in each member of every social and economic class. All are called to recognize, despite the exaggerated and expanding levels of self-seclusion in the world, that "basic human needs can *only* be fulfilled by and through other human beings . . . Loneliness, isolation, ostracism, rejection by the group—these are not only painful but pathogenic as well."[37]

In affirming the centrality of the groundbreaking moment and the shattering of horizons that are its trademark, I am not suggesting that the precipitative event accelerates the relational and integrative speedometer of the converted from zero to sixty in a matter of moments. It is, indeed, quite the opposite. As we will see, the implications of a conversion experience take a lifetime to unfold and embrace. In other words, regardless of how appealing and dynamic the portrait of the world once hidden behind the "dam" of fear and prejudice appears to be, the person affected is still receiving and interpreting the event with the same linguistic, cultural, social, and psychological constraints she possessed in the moment before she awakened into a new world.

Having said that, although only the preface to a possible new life, the initial unveiling of a reality that transcends the artificial boundaries and constraints that imprison the true self is the sine qua non of the conversion process. It is an elevating moment that, in the words of Husserl, enables the recipient to glimpse the "worlds" beyond the phenomenal world. It is the "eidetic" point of view—that of things in themselves. At that moment, "the *real world* . . . the correlate of our factual experience, then presents itself as *a special case of various possible worlds and non-worlds*."[38] For Thomas Merton, the unifying perspective is not the result of a cognitive affirmation but from an encounter with the source of life that overwhelms any sense of the self as isolated or separate: "Underlying the subjective experience of the individual self, there is an immediate experience of Being. This is totally different from an experience of self-consciousness . . . It has in it none of the split and alienation that occur when the subject becomes aware of itself as a quasi-object. The consciousness of Being . . . is an immediate experience that goes beyond reflexive awareness. It is not 'consciousness *of*' but *pure consciousness,* in which the subject as such 'disappears.'"[39]

William James is most helpful here as he wisely distinguishes between religious experience and conversion. The former is the necessary first step in the movement toward unitive consciousness but it lacks the communal and disciplinary context necessary to free the self from its ideological and characterological captivity.[40] Its importance lies in the fact that it is a gratuitous encounter; one that is immediately "luminous," "reasonable" in the noetic message that the recipient gleans from it, and "morally helpful."[41] Following E. D. Starbuck, James believed that such decentering moments are "normal adolescent phenomena" (which may help explain the seemingly random and easily replaceable infatuations of the young) and, for our purposes, always the manifest aim of any correctional or personal strategy that seeks to broaden the limits of care within the heart.[42]

The third element that typifies a religious experience—the resultant growth in moral awareness and responsibility—is particularly important because it helps solidify the difference between the new allegiances often stimulated by a "born again" encounter and the ever-expansive horizon that characterizes the meaning I am assigning to conversion. Put differently, the moral meaning of a conversion, or, if you prefer, its proof is the adoption of a worldview that is always inclusive and never exclusive. It continually creates a both/and as opposed to an either/or perspective. This defining trait places the interpretation being offered here in sharp contrast with the way many researchers and, perhaps more cogently, many self-proclaimed converts often decipher the meaning of the luminous and destabilizing event. As the authors of one study note, "it has often been difficult for sociologists to distinguish between conversion and commitment."[43] Peggy Giordano and her co-authors make the same contention; one that, incidentally, gives *some* credence to the shallowness of what is often referred to sarcastically as "jailhouse religion": "It is important to distinguish between fleeting situational use of spirituality in some trying circumstances from spiritual transformations that seem to have long-term impact on offenders' lifestyles."[44] Clear and his co-authors also point out that "conversion" in the pejorative sense I am critiquing can lead simply to the rejection of one form of intolerance by the adoption of another. They write: "[W]hen inmates discuss their religious views they often take a literal interpretation of the teachings of their faith ... Thus, when inmates seem to experience religion as a basic truth that is presented without complexity or nuance ... the rhetoric of religious fervor can take on the quality of intolerance."[45]

In his classic study, A. D. Nock takes pains to distinguish the radical reordering of the self, "the reorientation of the soul" that is synonymous with a conversion from "adhesion," which he depicts as a change from a preexisting commitment or lack thereof to a state of group affiliation.[46] Despite this crucial distinction, most accounts of conversion reduce the phenomenon either to the adoption of new social arrangements (denominational switching in the religious context) or to the movement from a state of unbelief to one of religious commitment. Arthur Greil provides evidence of this thin understanding of the concept so prevalent in the literature: "I have argued ... that it is theoretically possible for an individual to become converted from just about anything, regardless of previous dispositions, provided he orients himself to significant others who share a new perspective."[47] While Lofland and Stark are more precise in their analysis of the phenomenon, they still insist that a conversion has to do with the adoption of a new worldview—regardless of its ideological, social, and moral content.[48] This is corroborated in Rodney Stark's most recent work: "Conversion is a shift across a religious boundary," while "reaffiliation" is a shift within a religious boundary.[49] He goes on to say: "People convert to a religious group only when their interpersonal attachments to members overbalance their attachments to nonmembers."[50]

This false positive of narrowing conversion to group or denominational association is a pitfall to which sociologists of religion and criminologists are particularly susceptible, as they require a predetermined set of operational variables and, normally, a pre-test, post-test, control group model to track "scientifically" the "salience" of a change in the lifestyle of the self-proclaimed convert. As some respected scholars have pointed out, the time may have come to "blame the messenger": "Although social scientists have recently made some progress in distinguishing conversion from related phenomena, most conceptualizations remain ambiguous and not explicitly presented."[51] Byron Johnson states: "There is little documentation on the prevalence of conversions and even less on the way conversions or spiritual transformations influence behavioral change."[52]

This methodological shortcoming is particularly problematic, from my perspective, in the correctional context. It not only collapses the unrestricted compassion that marks a true conversion into the restricted perspective just spoken of but also easily accommodates itself with the conservative, positivist model of behavioral change in which "adjustment" to institutional rules and staying out of jail are the only viable (writ measurable) options to denote what a conversion is and does. Religion is reduced to an "epiphenomeon" whose value resides in its ability to control the rambunctious.[53] As Snow and Machalek phrase it, "authentic enduring inner change" is the issue, not "compliance with the demands of intense normative pressure."[54] Johnson writes that "when discussing prosocial behavior there is much more involved than merely obeying the law and desisting from criminal behavior. We need to know why people do admirable things or altruistic acts."[55]

This reductionist tendency is exacerbated in the literature by an "empirically and theoretically misguided" approach to data collection wherein the self-report of a conversion experience is accepted at face value: "Following the customary sociological practice of treating verbal accounts as objective reports that speak for themselves, most researchers who have studied conversion tend to accept converts' statements as valid and reliable records of past events and experiences."[56]

These methodological deficiencies have not only produced a euphemistic understanding of conversion but have also been adopted in much of the rehabilitation literature (which will be critiqued in the next chapter), whose authors are ever anxious to uncover the programmatic silver bullet that "works" to make "them" more law-abiding.[57] A great amount of ink has been spilt on whether regular attendance at religious services leads to "conversion" which, in turn, leads to "desistance." In these typically shallow analyses, acquiescence to the prevailing legal and socioeconomic continuum is the measure of religious devotion and rehabilitation. A strategy, I might add, that consigns both to irrelevance. Byron Johnson, for one, has noticed this superficial comparison: "[I]t is not hyperbole to suggest that a religious conversion—often referred to as a 'born again' experience—has been viewed as synonymous with prisoner rehabilitation."[58]

There are undoubtedly other important ideas in the effort to provide the broad contours of the meaning of conversion, but I hope that many of them will be answered in the phenomenological analysis to which we now turn.

Phenomenology of Conversion

There are five elements essential to the understanding of conversion being offered here. While I number them sequentially, all save the first two are interrelated, mutually dependent, and open to ever-greater depths.[59] First, there has to be a crisis of meaning in the life of the convert. Second, in the midst of the darkness and, often, despair that accompany the crisis he or she experiences a benevolent and reassuring "moment of clarity" that is both unprovoked and life affirming. Third, this experience triggers a questioning of identity, life course, narrative, and community: the recipient cannot go back and, yet, cannot go forward without a new symbolic and social framework. Fourth, the ethos and discourse of the new community echo the "noetic" quality of the transformative event and serve as an authoritative source of knowledge, discipline, and accountability. Finally, the experience is always progressively life affirming and inclusive. Stated differently, the authenticity of the conversion is tested in the expansion of humility at the intellectual level, compassion at the moral level, and non-duality at the spiritual level.

The Crisis

Conversion cannot happen until the structures of meaning in the world one inhabits are in a state of flux, if not ruin. The illusion that things are well, more or less, is often sufficient to ward off, at least temporarily, the nagging doubts that they are not. After all, there are, within easy reach, the panoply of distractions, not to mention, medications, of an "attentional economy" that bombards and stimulates the senses at every turn and serves to dull the condition of "bad faith" or the "injustice" of a lonely, disconnected existence.[60] The psychologists William Miller and Stephen Rollnick utilize the terms "ambivalence" and "discrepancy" to depict the lives of those mired in such a state of discontent. The ambivalent are at least implicitly aware of the social and moral impoverishment of their existence yet unsure of the way forward or of the possibilities that lie just beyond their grasp. Yet, no change can come without a sense of discrepancy and "the larger the discrepancy, the greater the importance of change."[61]

The person poised for a life-altering experience is thus in what Victor Turner calls a "liminal" space, a precarious condition of unknowing that lies in between the old and new structures of existence.[62] For Lonergan, the operative term preceding the liberating event is "dialectic." This denotes a conflictual state so profound that no amount of new information or variation in perspective can rid the recipient of its shadow.[63]

This liminal condition of ambivalence, discrepancy, and dialectic faced by so many offenders and non-offenders is analogous to what William James calls the "divided self," a poignant recognition of "incompleteness" and "inner discord."[64] He further states that those in the grip of this malaise often possess a "sick soul" with a "morbid" fixation upon conflict and malevolence. For them, "the evil aspects of life" have become "its very essence."[65]

For not a few, this environment of deprivation, isolation, and sorrow is how life is lived and it is how life comes to an end. Many criminologists now view such an alienated and lonely life as the seedbed of destructive behavior. D. A. Andrews and James Bonta, who have had a decided impact on the re-emergence of rehabilitation as a viable organizational principle, conclude that an antisocial personality "is one of the best predictors of criminal behavior." They see its origins in what they call "a difficult temperament . . . [T]his personality constellation appears central in the makeup of life-course-persistent, high-risk offenders."[66]

For a conversion to occur, the barriers that magnify the sense of incompleteness and isolation and restrict the outward flow of compassion and the desire for community must be punctured. As Reinhold Niebuhr remarks, the self in "a state of preoccupation with itself" cannot chart a different life course until the former one is "broken" and "shattered."[67] Similarly, Lofland and Stark note that the liberating event only comes when people are at a point where all seems lost.[68]

We know that the pains of confinement often bring people to such a level of visceral despair, yet it is precisely there that conversions so often occur. Kent Kerley discovered that most of the conversions reported by his interviewees occurred "in prison or a half-way house, and they occurred in the midst of major troubles and low points in their lives, or what most call 'rock bottom.' "[69]

Those at the brink of conversion, typically, are undergoing a "dark night of the soul."[70] In the language of Alcoholics Anonymous, they have come to realize their "powerlessness" and that their lives have "become unmanageable."[71] Life has thrust them to the point of "surrender," either after trying to change their patterns of behavior and failing (prelude to a voluntary conversion) or, simply, just repeatedly failing (prelude to an involuntary conversion).[72] They have like Jonah or Jack Abbott entered the "belly of the beast."[73] In his study of conversion, Arthur Greil suggests an important insight: the remorse of loss can only exist when one has truly lost something of inordinate value. What is most valuable of all, he suggests, is meaning: "[The person] is a meaning seeking animal who cannot endure the sense of being bereft of a viable worldview . . . those whose identities have become spoiled become 'seekers' who search for a perspective that can restore meaning to the world."[74]

One author suggests that this movement from chaos to capitulation, from emptiness to inner satisfaction is at the root of all Western notions of conversion. They can be viewed either through a Platonic/Augustinian lens in which, in a sudden event, the soul "attains perfection by turning away from the images and shadows of temporal life toward eternal and unchanging realities," or from an Aristotelian/Thomist approach in which "completion and fruition" come in a "process of ordered stages."[75]

The key point in all descriptions is that "the last step must be left to other forces." At the impactful moment, as James writes, "self-surrender becomes . . . indispensable."[76] One might say that in order to ascend on a new, life-affirming path, one must have traveled the downward path of despairing the excuses and justifications that enabled the fractured existence to continue so long and with such devastating results.

Yet the shattering of the false self under the weight of failure proves to be completely counterintuitive. Although the next step in the path of descent would seem according to all empirical evidence and imaginative forecast to be a definitive confirmation of the uselessness of one's time on earth, like Jonah, the moment of utter defeat results in a reclaiming of purpose, an experience of overwhelming compassion, and the promise of liberation to the captive spirit.

An Experience of Undeserved Compassion

The process of "hitting bottom" does indeed produce a shattering; but it is a shattering of the barriers that entrapped the true self. The experience is a singular, uncanny, unexpected, and, for lack of a better word, gracious event in which "one is swept into the vast current of life" of which Bergson speaks. It is a confirmation of one's existence; so much so that fully half of the seventy women Kerley interviewed after having completed their time in the penitentiary spoke of their conversion as their "second birth."[77] Tanya Erzen relates the recovery of meaning amidst the wreckage of a sundered life: "One undergoes a conversion and becomes a new creation through an intimate and accountable relationship with God. After reaching a nadir in one's life, faith initiates a heart change, softens the inner worlds of the most hardened, incorrigible criminal in order for the redeemed person to blossom."[78] In their study of the topic, Joe and Mary Ellen Barnhart recall James's insistence that feelings of inferiority and helplessness often unconsciously create the psychological conditions for a "self-surrender" that clears the way for the convert to receive a life-affirming message and to offer a life-affirming response: "At an unconscious level, various new expectations have been coming into existence and new alignments have been formulated, when suddenly the process breaks forth at the level of conscious feeling. And it comes as something of a surprise. The convert . . . is surprised by joy!"[79]

Religious literature is, of course, replete with conversion stories in which a person living an aimless or destructive existence is overwhelmed by a revelation that not only radically alters the life trajectory but also directs him or her to live fully aware of and reliant upon the inner workings of the divine spirit. The conversion of St. Paul is legendary and, while unique in its dramatic circumstances, follows the arc of all such luminous and destabilizing encounters. Traveling to Damascus to arrest and prosecute members of the nascent sect of Christianity, he is suddenly bathed in a blinding light from which the voice of Jesus emerges asking Paul why he is persecuting him. It is not so much an accusation as an invitation to become a messenger of "the way," a summons that produced not a shred of hesitancy in Paul who, left sightless for three days (in the belly of the beast, if you will), joined the very community that he had vowed to destroy (Acts: 9: 122).[80]

One author speaks of the frequency with which the "signification phenomena" of conversion accounts result from "direct communication" with a "transcendent agency."[81] Nock also points to the "miraculous" nature of so many of these epiphanies, linking such healing encounters with the rapid growth and spread of Christianity.[82]

It is noteworthy that criminologists who, by and large, still view the criminal justice enterprise in the constricted, dualist language of punishment, social control, and desistance tend to affirm that experiences of human affirmation and falling in love often stimulate former offenders to chart a socially cooperative life course. Robert Sampson and John Laub initiated an influential research track in emphasizing the importance of viewing crime in the context of the entire life course and the empirically demonstrative influence of "turning points" often produced by "marital attachment and adult commitment to educational/occupational goals": "The idea of a turning point is closely linked to role transitions ... [T]urning points are helpful in understanding stability and change in human behavior over the life course."[83]

A turning point is an apt synonym for conversion. A new perspective on life has come into view. The old way and the old associations, at least for now, have been forsaken. A light-filled road lies ahead, the destination promising but unclear, and, whatever the condition of her prior existence, like St. Paul, she is not the same person she was an hour ago.

A New Identity in a New Community

The moment of awakening—alluding to a foundational concept in Eastern and Western spirituality—that so significantly alters one's self-understanding leads, of necessity, to a questioning of identity.[84] One is forced to ask and address with the utmost seriousness the basic questions of who am I and why am I here.[85] The affirmation and solace that accompany the awakening initialize a restructuring of the personality inasmuch as there is a reconfiguration of what James calls the "habitual center of personal energy," or, paraphrasing George Herbert Mead, one moves a "universe of discourse" from the periphery of one's life to its center.[86]

This shift of self-consciousness leads not only to "serious and drastic changes" in one's vocabulary but a new understanding of past, present, and future.[87] As Paul Ricoeur phrases it, "life is an activity in search of a narrative."[88] One's sense of self can neither be a series of random and unrelated events nor "an immutable substance incapable of becoming;" rather, the human experience invariably summons "exactly the kind of identity which narrative composition alone ... can create."[89] A conceptual and symbolic vocabulary is needed to interpret the life-altering event in story form.[90] The convert is compelled to initiate a reflection that explicitly explores the change he or she has undergone in terms of its "origins, developments, purposes, achievements, and failures."[91]

Consistent with the dynamics of conversion, the urgency for a narrative reconsideration of the meaning of one's existence arises normally not as a result of successful accomplishments or fortunate circumstances but from the often surprising and always painful recognition of how difficult and capricious life can be, regardless of social and economic conditions. What one expects and what one receives are always fitfully conjoined, and the difference between the two, what might be termed the unforeseen, is precisely the impetus for the autobiographical impulse, as Aristotle stated long ago.[92] This retelling can be suffused with bitterness and self-loathing that, if turned inward, often result in acts of masochism; or, if projected outward, of hostility or even violence toward those perceived as enemies. In the case of the converted, however, despite "expectations gone awry," the narration points to the very problems that caused so much pain as the necessary preparation and catalyst for a life of civic engagement no longer dominated by isolation and anger.[93] In his noted work on the ethics of character, Stanley Hauerwas states that the narratives of the converted tend to feature a consistent set of touchstones. Typically, one finds the commitment to avoid self-destructive solutions when faced with hardship, to see through current distortions, to discover in moments of misfortune a way to transcend the powerful urge to control, and to develop the practices necessary to keep one from having to resort to violence.[94]

The way Hauerwas conveys his ideas on the moral essence of a renewed character reminds us that plot is not only essential in fiction. Every life must be able to be synthesized in such a manner that the vast panoply of disparate details can be situated in metaphorical and temporal relation to the outcomes that endure, that are central to the truth of the account, and that consist of the "message" or didactic lesson the narrator is trying to convey in telling her story. This analytical engagement with one's history gives the entire chronology, in the words of Emil Brunner, "a title to reality."[95] Events become far more than mere occurrences, "something that just happens." Rather each contributes "to the progress of the story . . . to its beginning and its end."[96]

It goes without saying that men and women enduring the frequently life-shattering trauma of a penitentiary experience and being suddenly enveloped in the assurance and elation of conversion would, with uncommon vigor, emulate this rewriting of the life script. The perpetrator of a crime is always "entangled in the stories that happen to him" and seeks that "irreducible dimension" that leads to a deeper sense of human fulfillment.[97]

These accounts of transformation are not only powerful in themselves, they point to the reality of narrative intelligence in the analysis of the criminal justice enterprise. If the primary way that the meaning of a human life can be communicated is though narration, then these conversion reports are a surer vehicle to communicate the meaning of the penal experience—its sorrow, shame, and potential healing function—than the amassing of empirical data aimed at controlling the millions and millions with criminal records. Ricoeur states that the veracity of these narratives is "much closer to practical wisdom and moral judgement than to science or the theoretical use of reason."[98]

Although I am not comfortable with much of the rehabilitative vocabulary, Maruna clearly understands that biographical revision is not only part of the proof of someone in the process of "making good" but is also a requirement to diminish the destructive behavior that led to incarceration. He says that "to successfully maintain their abstinence from crime, ex-offenders need to *make sense* of their lives. This sense making commonly takes the form of a life story or self-narrative."[99] He utilizes religious vocabulary in calling this act of rewriting "a shameful past into a necessary prelude to a productive and worthy life" a "redemption script."[100] In similar fashion, Erzen writes that the "heart change" that occurs among the imprisoned can only be actuated effectively by a "narrative vehicle."[101]

The personal chronicle of "redemption," regardless of the beneficence of the intervening moment and the desire to redirect the life course, has little or no meaning lodged in the inner world of the convert who is, after all, a social being. A conversion always begins as an intensely personal moment but it can never be "purely private."[102] Wittgenstein tells us that there is no such thing as a personal language.[103] The conversion sequence must be made intelligible to conversation partners. It must be "signified and communicated through the patterns of expression that are shared with the community."[104] This necessarily raises the question to whom exactly might the story be related in a manner that is not only intelligible, but also in a way that is understood, embraced, and correctly interpreted. Here, we encounter the irreplaceable role of community in the conversion process.

Communal life is held together by a common memory and a common history. This is as true for a nation or a business enterprise as it is for a religion. The only difference between the latter and former examples is that for the members of a religious denomination, the story functions as a metanarrative, helping one to "understand everything."[105] In either case, what is essential to the cohesion of any given institution is dependent upon the location of the events of the present in an ongoing conversation with the past. Jerome Bruner states that human culture cannot operate without some means of interpreting "the foreseeable or unforeseeable imbalances inherent in communal living."[106]

In terms of conversion, the convert enters into a social unit and culture both synchronically and diachronically. To hear the communal narrative or, in religious traditions, the archetypal myth is to be issued "an invitation not to be as the story is but to see the world as embodied in the story. In time, the sharing of common stories creates an interpretive community, a matter of great moment not only for creating cultural cohesion but for developing a body of law."[107] Speaking similarly but in theological terms, Milbank writes that for the Christian, the stories related in the Gospels "are not situated in the world . . . the world is situated within these stories."[108] Maruna and his co-authors note that the Christian convert learns "to adopt the lexicon of the Christian community . . . The framework of Christianity provides the master story that allows the individual to 'read' the world again."[109] Snow and Machalek speak of "rhetorical indicators of a conversion," among which they include "biographical reconstruction," "adoption of a master attribution scheme" that "informs all casual attributions," a suspension of analogical reasoning since "the new view is unique and incomparable," and an embracing of the new identity.[110]

The community of memory provides the new convert an echo of the epiphanic event in its group discourse, ethics, symbols, and rituals. Sociologists often call this process of immersion in a new community "encapsulation."[111] Max Heirich states that such a cultural and social transition plays "a striking role" for the religious convert seeking to sustain the positive energy of the conversion, while Lofland and Stark add that the new convert seeking to absorb and emulate the language and ethos of an adopted community requires contact with members on a daily or even hourly basis.[112] In the Barnhart study, the authors suggest that St. Paul's injunction "to put on Christ" (Rm 13: 14) is more than a sartorial metaphor. It is rather the process "of being immersed into a new cultural framework and becoming united with a new sub-society."[113]

An apt metaphor for the temporal movement of the community, and that of the convert within it, is the pilgrimage. The term denotes "neither progress according to a recognizable blueprint nor a random and ineffective wander."[114] Kerley speaks of the women converts he interviewed often viewing their new life story in a way suggestive of a pilgrimage motif: "They believed that the adventures they experienced were part of God's master plan for their lives and had meaning . . . Attempting to find God's purpose in their adversities allowed the women to be reflective and to reevaluate their criminal past."[115]

The convert thus finds in the communal association the necessary intellectual, moral, and spiritual foundation upon which a life of expansive sociability and concern for others can be constructed. Overcoming a binary worldview, however, is no easy task. After all, as Jesus quips, no physician can heal himself (Lk 4: 23).

Accountability and Character Reform

Not only does the new convert find the support and affirmation of the community essential to sustaining the first fervor of a major redirection of the life course, but, of equal bearing, he or she is also made accountable to the community. As one whose life seeks to emulate the communal narrative and, especially in religious contexts, the noble ideals of its founder, the novice or apprentice must learn more than creedal orthodoxy and the highlights of the tradition; he or she must acquire the skill to enact distinguishing aspects of the narrative in thought, speech, and action. To quote Hauerwas: "The language the agent uses to describe his behavior to others, is not uniquely his; it is *ours* . . . An agent cannot make his behavior mean anything he wants, since at the very least it must make sense within his own story, as well as be compatible with the narrative embodied in the language he uses."[116] One of the women converts in the Kerley study reflected on adopting a new and, in terms of her past, counterintuitive lifestyle amid the pressures of confinement: "Sometimes your flesh speaks out before your religious part does . . . You have to practice staying focused on certain things. Because it's not just something you are going to do, it's a learning process."[117] For many of the other women, resisting the temptation to revert to their former way of living was accomplished only because "the women routinely set very strict standards for conduct, attire, language and relationships."[118]

The notion of learning a craft or trade is a perfect analogue. One must be taught not only the language of the trade, but its core set of skills and the subtleties of their practice that only a master craftsperson can provide.[119] Lindbeck extends the craft metaphor to religion: "Religion cannot be pictured . . . as primarily a matter of deliberately choosing to believe or follow explicitly known propositions or directives. Rather, to become religious . . . is to interiorize a set of skills by practice and training."[120] For MacIntyre, the precondition of the integrity of a narrative is that for the entire duration of one's affiliation with a given community, one seeks to inculcate the virtues expressive of its highest ideals. Accountability for one's actions is the sign of and testimony to the truthfulness of the tradition.[121] Barth writes that "conversion . . . is neither exhausted in a one-for-all act, nor is it accomplished in a series of such acts . . . It becomes and is the content and character of . . . life as such."[122]

It is in community that converts are able to reconstruct the meaning of life by an honest accounting of the evil that they have willfully done to others—the "little [or big] murders" in which they have participated.[123] As Heidegger insists, guilt is the first cry that our inner being utters when the doors of self-absolution and inattentiveness that kept it silent for so long are finally flung open.[124] This is precisely why there is never a need to will that another suffer. What is required, as we have stressed, is the accompaniment of the penitent/convert as she learns what Heidegger calls "resoluteness" in facing her past and "anticipation" as she looks honestly at the prospect of her own death.[125] In his research, Maruna found that all of his interviewees had to pass through a daunting period of shame and guilt and he highlights the role played by other-centered (generative) activities in the healing process.[126]

It is also in the community that the convert is able to place the events of his or her life within a liturgical and spiritual framework. Put simply, the tradition provides novices with the resources to stay in contact with the benevolent ap-parition or experience that favored them in their moment of despair. Whether one calls it prayer, meditation, or contemplation, a discipline is involved not only in learning the rubrics of worship but also the practice of ego control that is essential to meditative practice. To progress from a life of self-preoccupation to one of restraint and accountability normally features the adoption of a spiritual regimen. Nock observes the frequency with which converts turn "from luxury and self-indulgence . . . to a life of discipline and sometimes to a life of con-templation, scientific or mystic."[127] Contemplation here means a compassionate openness to the moment without judgment or analysis, both in the flow of daily events and in regular periods of silence and solitude. Such practices are not only for those self-defined as religious or spiritual. Joseph Pieper believes that they lie at the heart of the meaning of "leisure" in its classical sense. They comprise "a form of stillness that is the necessary preparation for accepting reality; only the person who is still can hear . . . Leisure is the disposition of receptive un-derstanding of contemplative beholding and immersion—in the real."[128] For Heidegger, meditation or contemplation is expressed in the state of "hearkening" to the voiceless communication from one's depths that can only be received in the hush of a quiet heart.[129] Teilhard de Chardin beautifully states the move-ment into the core of one's inner being that characterizes this life-altering prac-tice: "And so, for the first time in my life perhaps . . . I took the lamp and leaving the zone of everyday occupations . . . where everything seems clear. I went down into my inmost self, to the deep abyss whence I feel dimly that my power of ac-tion emanates . . . At each step of the descent a new person was disclosed within me . . . And when . . . the path faded from beneath my steps, I found a bottomless abyss at my feet, and out of it came—arising I know not from where—the cur-rent which I dare to call *my* life."[130]

The particular valence of the need for ritual and communal solidarity can also be seen in the loneliness and isolation that a conversion can cause for the person who has no framework of interpretation, no personal mentoring, and no wider community in which he or she can find solace and meaning. The emptiness and violence of the prison environment is thus a doubly wasted opportunity: not only in the lives that are shattered in its punitive culture, but also in the incoherence of an institution without a life-affirming moral center that is, by that very fact, ignorant, inattentive, and even hostile to the frequency with which confined men and women discover that the splintering of their former self-understanding often produces an opening that, paraphrasing Leonard Cohen, allows the light to come in.[131] Rodney Stark and his co-authors insist that "religiousness alone" seems incapable of sustaining a life-affirming desire in one enmeshed in the criminal justice system: "Only within a significantly religious social climate—a moral community—does the individual's faith generate this power."[132] A prisoner in Mississippi gave this testimony: "Well, since coming to Parchman, I've had to change the folks I hang with cause . . . they mostly run around with gangs . . . So I had to just break away and just start hanging with Christian brothers."[133] Byron Johnson summarizes this perspective succinctly in claiming that the failure of an offender to connect with a supportive community subsequent to a conversion experience is "a recipe for disaster."[134]

This lack of a wraparound network of conversation, support, and challenge can easily derail the inspirational impetus to restructure one's existence. Lonergan attests to the continual possibility of such a relapse: "Besides conversion there are breakdowns. What has been built up slowly and laboriously by the individual, society, and culture can collapse. Cognitional self-transcendence is neither an easy notion to grasp nor a readily accessible datum of consciousness to be verified."[135] He adds that it is one thing to honor values, "but can they keep outweighing carnal pleasure, wealth, power?"[136] Maslow balances the "peak experience" that propels the conversion process with the possibility of a "nadir-experience" while James speak of the risk of "backsliding."[137] While it is true that James's investigations reveal the permanence of most conversions and the "shallow" quality of those who tend to view converts as pathological, the convert, especially at the beginning of her journey toward wholeness, is vulnerable and verbal commitments made in the euphoria of the primal experience can easily dissipate once the difficulties involved in shedding one's moral skin become disturbingly apparent.[138]

James also accurately perceived that men and women who experience conversion in an institution unable to appreciate its power or communicate sympathetically with its recipient are invisible, voiceless, and easily dismissed as unstable or as "hysterics."[139] Becci quotes one such convert: "Some do take me seriously in what I do, but others, mainly my old mates who are still strongly rooted in their milieu . . . they say, 'Roland has been up too long . . . he has built himself an altar and prays to the Buddha, they got him.' "[140] Kerley's interviewees testified to the essential role of a kindred community to cushion the convert in the negative air of the penitentiary: "[I]nmates claimed that they had to be diligent about their new faith-based identities, or else they would easily be consumed by the negativity of prison life. To stay positive, they needed strong ties to prosocial people on a regular basis."[141]

The community is central to guiding and sustaining the life of the convert. Irving Goffman speaks of the need of "islands of civility" in "total institutions" like the prison.[142] And it is this idea of civility that is emblematic of conversion at its mature level—not just civility to the groups of whom one is a member, or to those to whom one is bound by kinship, but to everyone.

A Process of Progressive Participation

To repeat again: the criticism being made in this volume of the penal system and the various theories that vie to provide its organizational drive shaft is that they suffer from two tragic lacunae: (1) the lack of a life-affirming moral ontology; and (2) a set of binary dualities that have no recourse than to objectify and, by that objectification, demean the purported recipients of justice despite the admirable intentions of many legal and penal professionals.

While most literature on conversion centers upon its religious dimension, I want to re-emphasize that although the understanding of conversion offered here does indeed acknowledge the frequency with which it is orchestrated in religious terms, the necessary development that characterizes all conversions is overcoming dualism and embracing ever-broader levels of participation, regardless of one's religious orientation or lack thereof. In their highly regarded study on this topic, Snow and Machalek correctly state that "the notion of radical change remains at the core of all conceptions of conversion, whether theological or social scientific."[143]

The radical change that determines the veracity of a conversion is an ever-expanding openness to life in its pluriform manifestations.[144] Conversion "is not a terminal act . . . the new convert now works to make conversion behaviorally and experientially real to self and others."[145] Making a conversion real is to carry to completion Whitehead's ontological principle: each being is "positively somewhere" but, "in potency everywhere . . . [He or she] "has a perfectly definite bond with each item in the universe."[146] The fulfillment of one's ontological potency takes place at the intellectual, moral, and spiritual levels.

One experiences an intellectual conversion to the degree that one continually challenges the automatic epistemological conclusions to which repeated practice clings. Every socially mediated identity, without a conversion, to employ the thought of Berger and Luckmann, performs actions within the context of its own biographical blueprint. This narrative "locates all collective events in a cohesive unity" in which "discrete actions are thought of not as isolated events, but as related parts in a subjectively meaningful universe whose meanings are socially articulated and shared."[147]

This is the natural attitude to which Arnold Gehlen, among others, refers: the taken-for-granted mindset that the inner coordination of countless structural arrangements makes possible.[148] When the related parts in one's "subjectively meaningful universe" are working properly, one need not pay attention in anything more than the most elementary way, for instance, to the various appliances and utilities in the household. Indeed, the more privileged and comfortable one is, the more the structural arrangements of the social world beyond the home also function in such harmonious fashion that they appear to be natural. Kohlberg uses the term "cognitions" to describe the mental function of processing and connecting information and events that, in turn, establish the causal logic by which future experiences will be evaluated. The key point is that such patterns of interpretation will persist until a crisis in the lifeworld disrupts their predictable outcome and creates a cognitive change.[149]

The natural attitude or cognitive template also has a moral dimension. Let us assume that a given individual "naturally" feels violent impulses when confronted by a given situation. Repeated experiences in that person's past have created a patterned neurological and emotional response that results in the inability to envision, let alone practice, a solution to the obstacle in a patient, if not compassionate manner. What is needed in such a person is not that he or she be judged as a deviant or shocked through pain into docility. In the latter case, the person who judges suffers from the same moral and epistemological shortcoming as the one being judged—the only difference being that between politically sanctioned or legitimate violence on the part of judge and punisher, as opposed to the politically proscribed or illegitimate violence of the miscreant. Violence is always the wrong response to human error, regardless of whether the state and the populace approve of its use. What the given "offender" requires—on either side of the prison walls—are the conditions wherein that person can regain his or her native desire for self-transcendence and overcome the "naïve realism," or the "myth . . . that knowing is like looking."[150]

Robert Cover stresses the importance of this cognitive humility for those in the judicial (or, in his words, "jurispathic") profession, seeking to judge, under a "positivist hermeneutic," how much pain people from racial, ethnic, and religious backgrounds other than that of the judge ought to suffer without a concerted effort to appreciate the substantive ways language and culture recast the meaning of legal proscriptions. Such "jurispathic" logic is evidenced when judges, "confronting the luxuriant growth of a hundred legal traditions" assert "that this *one* is law and destroy or try to destroy the rest."[151]

One undergoing intellectual conversion acknowledges that "the world mediated by meaning" can only be known by an "integrated and communal process of understanding and judging . . . that is proper to fully human knowing."[152] For Kohlberg, it is the process of stage transition that, with proper nurturance, leads to a thought progression that is universal, impersonal, consistent, and rooted in a commitment to the dignity of the human person.[153]

Human beings do not need to be excoriated, or made examples of, or even made the objects of therapeutic intervention to be liberated from the "blunder" that the imperial prompts of the ego have any factual relation to reality.[154] They, like each one of us, must "discover the self-transcendence proper to the human process of coming to know."[155] Each is capable of breaking "often long-ingrained habits of thought and speech," of becoming "master in one's own house," an accomplishment attained "when one knows precisely what one is doing when one is knowing."[156]

As with all of the elements of conversion spoken of in the last section, reformation of the intellect often begins with a simple recognition in an unguarded moment that the domain of knowledge regarding a particular person, group, or set of phenomena is wrong, or at least incomplete. What sets it as a conversion as opposed to simply changing one's mind is the accompanying awareness, using Husserl's language, of the worlds beyond the enclosed world of the ego and an accompanying sense of both humility and a desire to further seek to explore the dimensions of those unknown but beckoning worlds. It is an embracing of the transcendent dimension at the heart of things. It is a recognition of the need for education—perhaps formal but always experiential—discipline, training, accountability, and the ever-greater expansion of one's cognitive framework. Such an accomplishment is what is meant by an intellectual conversion.

A moral conversion consists of the progressive movement from a-sociability or antagonism, or mere legal conformity (desistance) to recurrent other-centered motivation and action. Put into the words of Kant, the process of becoming "not merely *legally* good, but *morally* good . . . cannot be effected through gradual reform, but must rather be effected by a *revolution* in the disposition of the human being . . . And so a 'new man' can come about only through a kind of rebirth . . . a change of heart."[157]

Sociologists and psychologists have long reflected on the necessary political function of socializing the young to resist the selfishness of instinctual behavior or the "pleasure principle" and to learn, in effect, Freud's "reality principle."[158] One must sublimate narcissistic and destructive urges not only to enjoy the benefits of social conformity but also to avoid the painful consequences of delinquency. But this is a "low view" of the person, one devoid of a moral ontology predicated upon innate sociability and connectedness. Despite setting the moral bar at the most elementary level, the behaviorist and utilitarian view, consonant with Freud's moral perspective, is the coin of the social and legal realm. It is the currency with which the system of law and criminal punishment conducts its affairs and justifies its punitive arm.

In contrast, a moral conversion happens the same way all other conversions happen: through a sudden awakening to an integrated and interdependent world, normally with an experience of benevolence and acceptance. Substantive change in one's moral stance occurs not from being made to suffer for one's errors but in a gratuitous moment of illumination. Converts receive a message that they are decidedly not what they have done to others and to themselves; nor are they what has been done to them—however harsh and empty of concern the hurtful actions may have been. Converts are called to care for others in the same way the moment of radical acceptance has shown them to be fully worthy of care. In this there is an echo of the outward flow or ceaseless orientation of the life within. Yet, as has been discussed, it is an echo that must also register harmoniously in an interpersonal context, within a community committed to altruistic conduct. The community must be able to translate the "ineffable" experience of intrinsic goodness and worth into a language, a set of symbols, rituals, and relationships that nurture and assure the convert and enable him or her to retell their life story not as one of isolation, suffering, or vengeance but as the slow, painful, but redemptive journey to inner and outer wholeness: "[T]he group will bear witness to its founder . . . the witness it bears will be efficacious in the measure that the group is dedicated not to its own interests but to the welfare of [human]kind."[159]

Lonergan characterizes the moral conversion as the movement from satisfaction to value, from evaluating the worth of an encounter in terms of one's own perceived good (satisfaction) to one directed to the good of others (value).[160] It is reminiscent of the theological terminology of the transcendent and categorical self. Reinhold Niebuhr states the self that is absorbed in seeking accomplishment in the lifeworld is incapable of beholding its inner core of freedom and concern: "It can only recognize itself in loving relation to its fellows. Love is the law of its being. But in practice it is always betrayed by self-love."[161]

This is the universal journey from division, alienation, and binary opposites to participation and communion. Care is always summoned by care, never by neglect, objective distance, and certainly not by causing or administering pain. The existential crisis of confinement—or any of the tragedies that befall each of us in the span of our lives—conveys a quantum of anguish sufficient to break any hard or lonely heart and lay the necessary ground for the path of acceptance and healing. Like all conversions, an expansion of ethical responsibility does not happen unconsciously nor can it generate itself spontaneously—despite the grace of the peak experience—it can only respond to love and learn to love by being loved.

Spiritual conversion is the telos, the fullest expression, of the initial "religious" or ecstatic experience. In short, through a process of social realignment, affirmation, shifts in discourse and autobiography in light of a communal narrative, patient tutelage, and accountability, the novice becomes an adept and now embodies the openness, forgiveness, and unconditional regard that exactly mirror the moment when he or she, without reason for hope, was touched by an unexpected and undeserved gift of solicitude and acceptance. Lonergan calls this level of achievement "other-worldly falling in love. It is total and permanent self-surrender without conditions, qualifications, reservations . . . not as an act, but as a dynamic state."[162] For Conn, the convert has now become "a living principle of benevolence and beneficence."[163]

This way of being is analogous to Kohlberg's sixth level of moral development, wherein one has transcended the cultural and ethical barriers that separate one from all others. The person has become a universal thinker and cannot under any circumstances view even one who has committed murder as inferior to him or herself.[164]

This is the state in which the person has abandoned in great part the dualist, oppositional, judgmental framework that dominates the philosophical, social, and pragmatic assumptions of the judicial and penal systems. The vast "gulag" of correctional institutions and so many of the tens of millions of American citizens and countless others around the world who have been branded socially and psychologically by exclusionary and reductionist mechanisms of control bear witness to the alienation that these systems represent. The fully converted, in contrast, do not view one with a criminal record, or anyone for that matter, as "a milieu brushing against the skin . . . but as a face in which being faces me."[165]

At the spiritual level, in the words of Richard Rohr, "self-consciousness (in the negative sense) slowly falls away and is replaced by what the mystics call pure consciousness or unitive consciousness—which is love. Self-consciousness implies a dualistic split. There is *me* over here, judging, analyzing, labeling *that* or *me* over there. The mind is largely dualistic before spiritual conversion and even foolishly calls such argumentation 'thinking.' In true conversion the subject-object split is overcome at least for a moment. You can't maintain this non-dual state twenty-four hours a day . . . But now, maybe for the first time, you know there is something more and you will always long to return there."[166] Rambo and Farhadian state succinctly that conversion "invites us into the interconnectedness of all human phenomena."[167]

This state of wonder, presence, and compassion is the second naïveté in the thought of Paul Ricoeur. It is the movement beyond the judgmental "first outlook upon life" in favor of one that discovers "immediately, intuitively" a "world spread out in space endlessly, and in time . . . without end."[168]

The mature convert has become the most credible bearer of the metanarrative that provides the epistemological, moral, and relational contours for her life—for the narrative and the narrator have become to a large degree synonymous. In a semiotic sense, an ontological link has been forged between word and performance.[169] The utterances of the converted are more than indicators of preference or allegiance but constitute "a form of life, a way of being in the world, which itself corresponds to the . . . Ultimately Real."[170]

At this final stage, knowing has now become the process of seeking the unitive element in all dialectical formulations. As Walter Wink describes it: "Instead of the old dualism of matter and spirit, we can now regard matter and spirit as united in one indivisible reality, distinguishable in two discrete but interrelated manifestations."[171] At the moral level and spiritual levels, one is motivated more and more by acceptance, understanding, and care, and less and less by frustration and anger.[172] For Heidegger, one's "Being-in-the-world" has essentially become a "*Being towards*," a life of "care" that sums up "the totality of Dasein's structural whole," that "comports itself" with phenomena as "objects of . . . *solicitude*."[173]

Inasmuch as conversion redirects the will toward reconciliation and peaceful living, many of the compulsions that dominate the lives of those living in alienation from their relational center are overcome. The converted are far less interested in the acquisition and maintenance of material comforts and the simulacra of success. They are "no longer possessed by their possessions."[174] They have an overall sense of well-being and are grounded in a participative vision of life that better enables them to face crises with equanimity and hope.[175] Conversion thus affects all conscious and internal operations.[176] It is the end to which the inner life is directed.

As a systemic goal, conversion has been long interred in the forgotten crevices of history, yet, it provided the original meaning for the idea of the prison and remains the only hope for its rehabilitation.

Conversion and the State of Criminal Justice

I have tried to show in this chapter that "they" (those with criminal backgrounds) are not the problem. The universal problem is to think that others are the problem. The very act of thinking that I am superior to anyone and not an equal participant in the quest to live carefully with everyone and everything is the cause of the world's pain and it is the cause of each person's pain. That does not make me or you less than anyone else; it makes us *just* like everyone else. What is needed in confronting those who do evil to others is not someone, or some legitimate entity, to respond with acts of judgment, derision, and a deliberate dose of anguish. What those suffering under the burden of prejudice and rage need is a place of tranquility and solitude or, in the worst scenario, they need to have it created for them that they might come to realize that all feelings of antipathy are simply their own inner shadow turned outward.[177] They need to be accompanied and treated with patience and kindness in that sad inner pilgrimage that leads to a place of healing and peace—to conversion.

Fostering and sustaining conversion should be the governing logic of the criminal justice system. It would entail the adoption of a compassionate worldview: one that has been at the center of not only all of the wisdom traditions for the last two and a half millennia but has also been reproduced and re-emphasized in a wide array of secular academic disciplines. Its striking simplicity is that it enables us to eliminate virtually all of the binary, oppositional, and power-laden terms that dehumanize one wing of the human family—heavily defined by their race, ethnicity, and economic class—that is neither ontologically nor morally different from the rest of humanity. No one is above anyone in this schema and no one has to be hurt. They simply need to be provided with the environment in which they are enabled to face their isolation, the harm they have done to others, as well as the endless possibilities that are the fruit of entering into communion with the world around them.

The details of this refashioning of the penal system will be taken up in Chapter 5, but it is jarring in light of the presentation just concluded to reflect upon the prevailing philosophy of corrections that somehow seeks to affect a positive change in the future comportment of the offender by making the experience of confinement one that attacks his or her "very personhood" or, less dramatically but no less disturbingly, locates her in the precisely defined codes of criminogenic risk that require clinical intervention.[178]

The phenomenology of conversion attests to the vital importance of a supportive and peaceful community to affirm, sustain, and challenge the new convert on his or her path to wholeness. Lofland and Stark report that where the converted feel genuine acceptance, there is a desire to "melt into the collective."[179] It is, frankly, depressing to think of all the wasted lives and wasted opportunities for positive human transformation in a penal culture lost in the dualist and violent ideologies of pain delivery and in an ethos insensitive to the inner workings of grace in the human heart, particularly when it is suffering. Dorothy Soelle, describing the sensitivity to mystical experience that typifies native cultures, states that the questions raised by analytical research such as what kind of person is most susceptible to visions or what psychological state characterizes those likely to report such phenomena are those of detached academics who are "orphan-like in relation to nature." She suggests that the most important questions are the following: "Which culture works with such experiences? And which culture destroys them?"[180]

Reflecting on Adam in the Book of Genesis, giving names or labeling the various species of animals is tantamount to gaining power over them.[181] What takes place in the heart of the person who experiences the primal unity of all matter as well as its fundamental goodness is a gift that escapes the "fate" of any language that, remembering Foucault, "serves the exercise of power, control, and possession."[182] In the words of Wittgenstein, what takes place in the heart of the person overwhelmed by a sense of cosmic benevolence is "something that is inexpressible. Not as a result of a syllogism, but as that which shows itself. It shows itself as source, not in the sense of causality, but as transparency of the utterable toward a meaning that simply lies on the other side of the utterable, outside the world."[183]

For this reason, sociologists like Maruna and Kerley are correct in emphasizing the question of maintenance over the question of desistance. Instead of focusing exclusively on what interventions enable a former offender to adopt a legally cooperative lifestyle, the need is to focus on how to maximize the variables that both conversion literature and sociological analysis reveal to be the factors that help sustain the positive alteration of human lives.[184]

In this chapter, we have explored the concept of conversion and emphasized that experiences that invite a conversion are not only "a normal adolescent phenomenon" but also a normal result of the pains of imprisonment. It has been maintained that the seed of radical and positive character change always latent in these experiences will fall on hard and inhospitable ground in a social environment ill-attuned to the movements of the inner life; one that does not affirm and embrace an ontology of care and the endless hunger of the human heart for meaningful association with others; a heart that aches all the more when its bearer has violated the inner call to benevolence. Without such a culture—and such cultures are a rare find in our correctional institutions—a vast array of men and women who have uttered a cry for unity have seen it fall on deaf ears in institutions that run ceaselessly on rhythms of security, control, and suspicion. Small wonder so little good comes out of the penal experience and, given the conservative nature of its methodological starting points and the shallowness of its moral foundations, small wonder that most proponents of rehabilitation overlook the true source of sociability and fail to see that it is the institution of the prison, not its inhabitants, that needs to be rehabilitated.

4

What Is Wrong with Rehabilitation?

I BEGIN BY saying that, on one hand, I am not alone in wondering what precisely is meant when the term rehabilitation is invoked.[1] On the other hand, I think, in large part, I do know what is meant, and that leaves me even more dissatisfied. Scanning the copious literature on the subject, one continually reads that offenders can, cannot, or should be rehabilitated.[2] The conventional interpretation of the concept suggests several things. First, it means there is something wrong with people who are incarcerated or imprisoned. Second, what is wrong with them is that some blend of criminogenic or, more specifically, static (age, sex) and dynamic (antisocial cognitions) risk factors, or lack of self-discipline, or inappropriate peer associations, or the deleterious psychological effects of being labeled as delinquent have lead them into criminal activity.[3] Third, there is a group of professionals who are qualified to intervene in order to help them overcome said criminogenic factors. Fourth, the intervention is normally considered successful and rehabilitation accomplished if the offender refrains from criminal activity for at least three years. Fifth, there is a set of behavioral equivalents or benchmarks for one who has been rehabilitated that invariably appear in the literature. That is to say, the rehabilitated person, aside from now being "a law abiding citizen,"[4] has also learned to "settle down and become responsible,"[5] and/or has become "successful,"[6] or is now "a useful citizen,"[7] or, as still others claim, a "self-directed" citizen,[8] or now pursues a "productive and socially responsible" life.[9]

The argument to be made in this chapter is that the term and its widely held assumptions about personhood and society are laden with dualism, persistent social control inferences, the threat of coercion for noncooperation, and relatively easy accommodation to disproportionate class and racial penal demographics. For those reasons, it should be consigned to the long list of criminological innovations that failed both to anticipate and to address properly the complex internal and external factors that lead people to do harm.

Nor does changing the word to "desistance" relieve the problem. Let us assume, as Ward and Maruna suggest, that most prisoners desire to straighten out their lives yet "almost none will tell you that they need to be rehabilitated."[10] The term desistance (popular among criminologists) may avoid some of the terminological confusion of its conceptual sibling (found more often among psychologists) but still suffers from the same binary and conservative foundations. What is more, its proponents, like their colleagues committed to rehabilitation, either from conviction or due to the methodological constraints of their discipline, tend to cling stubbornly to a materialist raft in the midst of a spiritual ocean: a materialism inadequate to understand the deepest and most transformative levels of human experience. There is no formal, a priori commitment to human goodness, only the residue of evolutionary, biological, social, and cognitive influences that are common to all "animals" like "ourselves."[11]

We have already noted the well-worn path of current penal strategies. They share a prevailing binary perspective that inevitably features some form of deliberate coercion as a consequence of initial criminal misconduct and as a response to the failure to adjust to the conditions of confinement. The particular circular compromise endemic to the relation between retribution and rehabilitation (desistance) has been to seek to offset the pain of prosecution and punishment with the desire to help. In the words of Rotman, it is to view rehabilitation as a form of "compensation."[12] Hans Toch, reminiscent of David Rothman, has recognized that, in effect, the latter exists largely to seek to undo the problems caused by the former: "The combinatory political formula for arriving at a prison policy today requires legislators to be tough on crime and kinder and gentler to people with problems. But offenders are often people with problems which our toughness exacerbates . . . Instead of tempering justice with mercy, we temper retributive overkill with safety nets of remedial services that ameliorate the consequences of retributive policy."[13]

Another way to depict the general persona of rehabilitative proponents is that the carrot/stick, good cop/bad cop, healthy/sick, respectable/deviant, low-risk/high-risk dichotomies are ever present. Help is available and good intentions abound if the objects of the technologies of care are willing to oblige; if not, the state and its penal arm inevitably address the problem with their own uniquely persuasive, and sometimes terminal, measures. Gwen Robinson observes that this concession to power and methodological sleight of hand is the price that advocates of rehabilitation have had to pay to resurface the concept in the narrow, neoliberal moral register of protectionism, fear of the other, and hyper-retributivism. The cost of renewed relevance, in other words, has been to shrink the moral horizon of the old "welfarist" doctrine to programs answerable to "greatest good" utilitarian calculation, to actuarial/professional determinations of risk, and to the ephemeral moral expressions of public out-rage.[14] She concludes by saying that "it is arguably now the case that the 'pure' rehabilitative sanction is extinct."[15]

This chapter will first summarize the current state of the rehabilitation/ desistance conversation and offer a critique of the varying approaches in light of the issues of moral vocabulary, duality, and violence. It will then discuss the need to build cooperative bridges with advocates of rehabilitation as the problem is patently not with the many scholars, administrators, politicians, and private cit-izens in favor of doing *something* to amend the deleterious life conditions of the incarcerated. As we have noted, the problem with most criminological theory lies with the lack of a more comprehensive ethical starting point and with a general inattentiveness to the insights offered by theological, philosophical, and social scientific reflection on how conversion forms a time-tested link between human failure and human redemption.

The Proponents of Rehabilitation

We have thus far spoken of the parallel between rehabilitation and desistance in their current manifestations: each targets an "at risk" population and seeks programs and interventions to induce conformity with the regulatory norms of society. There are, however, significant shades of difference, particularly if one looks at two currently well-regarded approaches to the issue. The first, known as the Risk-Need-Responsivity (RNR) model, is concerned with identifying and addressing the set of criminogenic factors that lead a given person to engage in illegal activity whereas the Good Lives Model (GLM) primarily seeks to uncover and cultivate the internal and external, prosocial resources that can be utilized to induce desistance from future legal violations.[16]

Without sounding too euphemistic, the first tends to see the offender in terms of what is wrong with her or him (risk) and how those asocial tendencies can be ameliorated, while the latter tends to see the offender as possessing a set of "strengths" that can be summoned with the proper interventions.

Risk-Need-Responsivity

To illustrate the moral distinction between the two approaches, a critical one in my view, the authors who developed the RNR model ("the premier rehabilitative theory in existence in the world today"),[17] Andrews and Bonta, write: "Criminal acts, no matter which . . . definitions are employed, are part of a more or less gen-eral class of behavior that social psychologists have been calling 'problem behav-ior' or 'deviant behavior' since the 1970s."[18] The relevance of this starting point as a moral affirmation as well as a meta-analytical product of criminological data is revealed in the two ethical positions that provide the basis for the authors' analysis of illegal conduct and the substance of their design for its curtailment.

The first is a commitment to the utilitarian, pleasure/pain calculus as both an explanation and forecast of human action: "The chances of a criminal act (a) increase with the density of rewards signaled for that behavior and (b) decrease with the density of signaled costs of criminal behavior."[19] What we have here is an affirmation of the need to address "problem behavior" by negotiating the proper balance between the precise amount of negative pressure or "cost" to take the luster off a potentially deviant act and the application of rewards for socially approved comportment. While the authors affirm, in fidelity to Bentham, that punishing too much or too little is ineffective, their focus is clearly to foreground rewards for cooperative conduct and diminish the emphasis on punishment: "Reinforcement, compared to punishment, has two important advantages. First, only reinforcement can shape new behaviors; punishment only suppresses existing behavior . . . Second, reinforcement procedures avoid the obvious ethical and professional dilemmas associated with purposefully inflicting pain. We have learned that there are better ways to change behavior than to use punishment."[20] Thus, they conclude: "Increasing the rewards associated with prosocial behavior would make the rewards associated with crime less attractive."[21]

Theirs is a rehabilitative approach that in all respects is intended as an alternative to retribution and, for that matter, deterrence or incapacitation: "There is little evidence that 'get tough' interventions . . . deter crime."[22] The same is true of intermediate punishments such as electronic monitoring (EM) or intensive supervision (ISP).[23] Regarding incapacitation, they point out that "states that showed the highest increase in the rate of incarceration showed smaller decreases in crime than the states with below-average imprisonment rates."[24]

The RNR model may not be retributive in intent, but like all the rehabilitative approaches in the theoretical playing field, cannot function without the implicit threat or explicit use of violence. While it acknowledges that the benefits of criminal activity for "high-risk offenders" are considerable in terms of "intensity, immediacy, consistency, and variety," it wisely notes that those "behaviors are highly resistant to punishment."[25] The RNR approach seeks, therefore, to target clinically those factors in the personality that persistently cling to proscribed actions with an emphasis on positive incentives. However, the only alternative to noncooperation or for the failure to meet the minimum standards of social conduct is to inflict pain "dense" enough to pierce the layers of willful resistance.

In support of this latter option, the authors are convinced that punishment is effective if understood correctly within the utilitarian moral framework. Reflecting both Beccaria's and, later, Bentham's insistence on "certainty" and "celerity," they write that effectiveness is predicated upon "no escape or reinforced alternatives," only the "*immediate* delivery" of "*very intensive* levels of punishment" to counteract the illegal impulse: "Studies suggest that we have to turn the dial to full in order to stop the targeted behavior completely."[26]

Thus, despite the fact that "punishment creates more problems than it solves," the limited moral range of their theory of human nature means that the best that can be hoped for in the face of a lack of "responsivity" is that punishment be neither too lenient nor too excessive.[27]

The second moral commitment that the authors espouse is the "radical behaviorism" of B. F. Skinner whose work denies an inherent human nature and, *a fortiori*, the belief in a natural orientation to seek to live in peace with one's fellows.[28] In discussing the analysis of the personal, interpersonal, and communal reinforcement perspective (PIC-R) that they utilize, Andrews and Bonta write: "PIC-R draws upon radical behaviorism for its most fundamental principles in that the factors responsible for variation in human conduct are found in the immediate situation of action. Specifically, these include rewards and costs and those antecedents to behavior that signal the delivery of either rewarding or costly consequences for particular acts."[29]

With these starting points (constraints) firmly in place, the diagnostic analysis of the individual and the type of intervention based upon it are then methodically outlined. Offenders pose specific risks to themselves and the communities wherein they reside. The most significant of those risks are antisocial cognitions, antisocial attitudes, a history of antisocial behavior, and an antisocial personality pattern.[30] Those who are qualified and empowered to work with this population must identify the specific needs that each problematic individual possesses, the fulfillment/alleviation of which will lessen or eliminate the problem behavior. It is then the task of the therapist and/or trained professional to assess what specific interventions, given the cognitive/psychological state of the delinquent, will be most effective in diverting or disincentivizing criminal conduct.[31]

The results show that the model has indeed been successful. Ward and Maruna write: "In short, the RNR model of offender rehabilitation represents a significant achievement. Its application by correctional services throughout the world has resulted in reduced recidivism rates and safer communities."[32] Devon Polashek states that "the RNR model remains the only empirically validated guide for criminal justice interventions that aim to help offenders to depart from that system."[33] Francis Cullen adds that the methodology is inadequately characterized as a model, and he insists that it represents the new paradigm for rehabilitative efforts.[34]

Presuming these empirical claims to be correct, RNR represents the highest achievement of the positivist, scientific penology inaugurated in the Progressive

Era that replaced what remained of the ancient culture of promoting conversion with one based upon risk management and therapy.[35] It is the quintessential expression of the difference that De Beaumont and De Tocqueville in the early 1830s saw between the monastic configuration of the Eastern State Penitentiary and the strict administration of the Auburn prison factory: the first produced better human beings, the other "more obedient citizens."[36]

To return to the earlier reflection on the causal relationship of harming and then trying to help, twelve million people are sent to the more than three thousand jails in America each year with approximately two million people behind bars on any given day.[37] Many of these, teetering at the edge of the meritocracy due to racial and economic factors, have been destined for a life of depleted resources and opportunities that constitute a sort of "civil death."[38] Programmers thus have virtually limitless opportunities to target risk-laden candidates for intervention in remedial programs, particularly if "rewards" are attached to refraining from the proscribed activity.[39] They also can effectively target those who have been so traumatized by the degrading rituals of the courtroom and the frequent brutality of penal institutions that their "desistance" can be assured by the shock of "traumatic stress" as much as by the forensic interventions shown to effect a compliant lifestyle. Craig Haney notes that adjustment or conformity are frequently induced among those who have been exposed to the physical and psychological damage so often caused by an extended period of confinement. That said, this character adjustment often signals "counter-productive, dysfunctional long-term consequences," in that "they may lose the capacity to initiate activity, to use their own judgment to make effective decisions, or to engage in playful behavior of any kind."[40]

Undaunted by such criticisms, the strategy of most evidence-based meta-analyses and the programs that devolve from them is driven by the compelling mantra of "reducing recidivism" and proving that "something works." In so doing, they fall prey to the shifting constraints of the political climate and perpetuate the duality between the keepers and the kept and between the clinicians and their deviant subjects.[41]

Even a scholar such as Mark Brown who criticizes Bonta's "evolutionary catalogue of risk" and, as a result, seeks to humanize the subject/object relation by counteracting the reduction of rehabilitative language to the mechanics of inducing controlled behavior, still communicates in the same dualist language that inevitably summons images of power and manipulation: "Fluid risk carries with it a conception of the offender as an at least potentially knowable and manipulative entity."[42]

The authors of RNR and those who speak of its positive outcomes insist that care for the offender is a paramount concern. They subscribe to the clinical approach of Carl Rogers who emphasized "empathy, warmth, being open, and being genuine" in his work with clients.[43] They further stress that the services provided are enacted "in an ethical, just, moral, humane, and decent manner."[44]

I am confident that the interventions, at least in as much as the tactical style of the psychoanalyst can be made to reflect such laudable guidelines, are informed by these principles. Yet, while a warm bedside manner is, I am sure, welcome to the offender under the therapeutic microscope, this model takes its energy from an assessment of the person as a risk (writ deviant) whose attention can only be secured by the promise of rewards and the threat of punishments. As Ward and Maruna note, the "client, after all, is not the real focus of the intervention, only his or her outward behavior. In fact, offender rehabilitation may be one of the only forms of treatment in existence that is explicitly intended for the benefit of others . . . rather than for the person undergoing the counseling itself."[45]

Like its companion rehabilitation models, RNR surrenders to the ethically insupportable compromises that befall a worldview in which the security and harmony of the social body dominate its moral vocabulary. Clear states that "the evidence-based policy paradigm is, at its core, extraordinarily conservative."[46] It is an exemplar of the epistemological paradigm that Marie Gottschalk depicts as "slavery to the present" that cannot countenance and thus denigrates other sources of coming to know.[47] It is technological sociology, "simple operant conditioning," that assumes that correctional rehabilitation is usually resourced by, and accountable to government.[48] It is dominated by "technical values" by what is "expedient or effective rather than morally correct . . . conceived, talked about, and practiced, in these rational, passionless terms."[49]

Good Lives Model

The Good Lives Model (GLM) is an innovation in the field that, for Cullen, is on the brink of mirroring the paradigmatic status of RNR.[50] As stated above, it takes its primary energy not by an assessment of the risks posed by given offenders but, rather, by seeking to maximize the "strengths" that they possess both within themselves and as a result of their various social interactions. It is the cultivation of these character and communal strengths that leads persons with a troubled past to seek to amend asocial conduct. Desistance is not, as the authors of RNR claim, a calculation based on the attractiveness of conformity in light of the fear of punishment in which "[c]onsideration of offenders' welfare" is "secondary."[51] GLM's leading proponents, Ward and Maruna, state that their method treats offenders as subjects rather than objects.[52] In this way, as McNeill claims, it reflects the position commonly found in desistance literature that each person possesses the necessary wherewithal to live a peaceful and fulfilling life; the task of the intervention is to aid in accelerating and guiding that process.[53]

GLM insists that change cannot be imposed. It must come from within the given offender.[54] It shares much with Edgardo Rotman's position that rehabilitation evaluated strictly in terms of law abidance may well reveal outward conformity, but it will be based upon "cunning, calculation" or "sheer deterrence," and is, therefore, "fragile and transient."[55]

Ward and Maruna work from the hypotheses that all people seek to attain basic human goods (life, knowledge, excellence, agency, inner peace, friendship, community, spirituality, happiness, and creativity) but for varying reasons choose to attain these goods in ways that are harmful to others. Desistance will naturally flow from the redirection of a given client's goal orientation in a respectful and cooperative direction. The abiding concern is to demonstrate to the offender that his or her goals are not the issue in question, only the strategies chosen to achieve them.[56]

The treatment specialist is directed to work with persons with demonstrated criminogenic risk to aid them in reconstructing their prior history in such a manner that it becomes a "redemption script," one that allows the person "to rewrite a shameful past into a necessary prelude to a productive and worthy life."[57] As Maruna writes: "The life stories of desisting narrators ... maintain ... equilibrium by connecting negative past experiences to the present in such a way that the present good seems an almost inevitable outcome."[58]

In tacit rebuttal of RNR, the effort to see discrete events in the wider arc of one's autobiography reveals the goal of a "holistic reconstruction of the self," not simply an instrumental intervention in which the given offender is viewed as a means to an end.[59] For this to be the case, and not simply a less forceful version of a Procrustean bed seeking to amputate what does not fit into the social compact, the promoters of the model energetically defend the autonomy of the given client by magnifying what Ward refers to as "the first person perspective."[60] The task of the therapist is to work with clients to construct a life plan, reflecting the narrative focus; wherein the primary goods of existence are identified and prioritized; and practical, cooperative, and responsible formulae for their attainment clarified.[61]

Much of the literature on GLM suggests an affinity with the concept of conversion: it cannot be imposed; it seeks to mobilize resources internal to the individual; it involves narrative reconstruction; its proof is expressed in prosocial action; and it requires communal support. Despite these praiseworthy commitments, it shares more with RNR and other rehabilitative models, whose primary aim is social control, than might first meet the eye. After all, a good life, rather than criminogenic needs, may be on the marquis, but, inevitably, the feature will address how to overcome the very criminogenic needs that more deliberately prophylactic models aim to suppress: "criminogenic needs are *internal* or *external obstacles* that frustrate and block the acquisition of primary human goods."[62] Thus, proponents must, perhaps reluctantly, accede to the reduction of the offender to being a risk. Ward and Maruna admit that "there is a direct relation between goods promotion and risk management in rehabilitative work,"[63] while Ward (second author) and his colleagues claim: "The major aim of intervening with offenders is a reduction in recidivism."[64]

More to the point of this book's argument, and despite commitments that echo the methodology of the conversion paradigm, the most troubling aspect of the Good Lives approach is precisely its understanding of what constitutes a good life. Ward and Maruna state that their approach is Aristotelian in that it seeks to affirm Aristotle's claim that the purpose of life is happiness. Their nomenclature may be right, but if the reference is meant to refer to Aristotle's ethical project (the goal of achieving *eudaimonia* or happiness), then it is either a beguiling dissimulation (which I doubt) or a significant misreading. For Aristotle, happiness was the highest good. The desire for its achievement was the goal or telos of human existence inscribed in the very nature of human beings. The desire is, however, anything but the ego's relentless search for favorable circumstances. It is an ontological reality "because we always choose it for itself, and never for any other reason. It is different with honour, pleasure, intelligence and good qualities generally."[65] Happiness is "an activity of the soul" in accordance with virtue "of the best and most perfect kind."[66] It is divine, but it is not given by the gods, only acquired by "virtuous activity."[67]

Aristotle then proceeds in the remainder of the *Ethics* to expand on the connection between ontology, virtue, and happiness and, in so doing, approximates in significant ways the three kinds of conversion we spoke of in the last chapter. The virtues are not "self-determined" goals that take pride of place in so much of the rehabilitation/desistance literature: goals for which the only limiting qualifier is that they do not threaten the self-determined goals of others. Conversely, for Aristotle there are intellectual virtues (wisdom, understanding, and prudence) and moral virtues (liberality and temperance) that "we are constituted by nature to receive" but only by way of slow development in the human person subject to tutelage, training, and accountability.[68]

Finally, resembling once again our discussion in the last chapter, there is the highest virtue of all, and the one most pivotal for a stable sense of happiness, contemplation: "We conclude then, that the happy man will have the required quality, and in fact will be happy throughout his life; because he will spend all his time, or the most time of any man, in virtuous conduct and contemplation."[69] If one were to follow Aristotle's formula for happiness, one would see no need to speak of risk, desistance, or autonomy.

In contrast to Aristotle and what might be termed the perennial tradition—the compiled wisdom of religious traditions over the last two and one half millennia—virtually all proponents of rehabilitation and its pseudonyms adamantly maintain a materialist perspective. Despite their contention, Ward and Maruna are hardly "old-fashioned" in a statement such as this: "There is no assumption in the GLM that individuals are inherently or naturally good in an ethical sense. Rather, the presumption is that, because of their nature [natural selection is invoked], human beings are more likely to function well if they have access to the various types of good outlined above."[70] Fortune et al. maintain that "in order to be able to pursue a meaningful life, individuals must be able to identify what *they* find truly valuable and construct ways of living which will help them achieve outcomes . . . which reflect their identified values" [italics my own].[71]

The RNR and GLM models have garnered much enthusiasm (much of it deserved) for their impeccable research, particularly the detailed meta-analyses utilized by RNR; and for their clinical methodologies that, all things considered, not only seek to create better lives for offenders (the work of GLM with those convicted of sex crimes is especially commendable), but have also proven successful in steering antisocial individuals into cooperative paths. Still, the thinness of their moral imagination allows them few options but to affirm the only behavioral horizons permissible given their stated ethical commitments: the individual human ego and the state. For the autonomous individual in contemporary political economy, "what now matters . . . is not the proper object of desire but rather the promotion of desire itself and the manipulation and control of the process."[72] It is, of course, the state that regulates the expression of those desires, endlessly fabricated by the vast production and marketing sectors. And those desires are indeed inviolable, as long as the ego trims its expansive wish list to fit within the legal constraints established by the state, or, remembering Richard Quinney, has the power and privilege that give one the capacity to make laws to protect those privileges and turn them into constraints for everyone else.[73]

Other Rehabilitative Approaches

Among the noteworthy contributions to the effort to reorient the penal system to reflect rehabilitative concerns is the notion of the virtuous prison. In an article reprinted in an edited volume on rethinking the culture of criminal detention, Cullen, Sundt, and Wozniak write that prisons "should be considered moral institutions and corrections as a moral enterprise."[74] To that end, they perform a noteworthy service to the intent of this book in remembering, first, that an important part of the reason for confinement was instilling the virtues, spoken above in the discussion of Aristotle. They add further weight to their substantial contribution in seeking to bridge the lamentable and costly (human cost) barrier between the sciences and the humanities: "Because advocates often borrowed the language and logic of the medical model, offender treatment has at times been portrayed strictly as a scientific, technical task . . . But rehabilitation is, at its core, a moral enterprise."[75]

In a sense, they build on the idea of Goffman, spoken of in the last chapter, that in order to resist the dehumanizing atmosphere of the prison, "islands of civility" are required wherein, mirroring the conversion process, an experience that some sociologists call "encapsulation" can not only offer a humane locale for communication, education, and spiritual nourishment but also provide like-minded associates to aid in the mentoring and accompaniment essential to expand the frontiers of consciousness.[76]

Hans Toch also adopts this view of recapturing the original life-enhancing function of the penitentiary by establishing places or "niches" that mirror the sort of nurturing environment spoken of by Cullen and his colleagues: "Inmate-centered settings solve problems. They include 'niches.' These range from places of refuge to settings where inmates can grow, develop, and change."[77]

Of course, the idea of incarceration as a school for instilling virtues is not a new one. Although the earliest monastic rules reveal that imprisonment was solitary (save for the regular visit of a respected member of the community), we have evidence of a common gathering space in a prison adjacent to the monastery of St. Catherine in sixth-century Egypt. St. John Climacus visited the prison for thirty days and describes in vivid detail the common life of the repentant monks: "They did not even know that a thing as anger existed among men, because in themselves grief had finally eradicated anger. Where were disputes among them, or frivolity, or audacious speech, or concern for the body, or a trace of vanity . . .? For even the hope of all such things had been extinguished in them in this present world. Where amongst them is there any care for earthly things, or condemnation of anyone? Nowhere at all."[78]

Nor was the instilling of virtue foreign to the iconic symbol of nineteenth-century Progressive penology, the reformatory. Brockway, the warden of the first reformatory at Elmira, stated that "the religious instrumentality in prisons had not so generally effected a change of moral character and behavior with prisoners as to commend evangelism for the central guiding principle . . . Already hopefully loomed the formative value of good habits duly confirmed and the ennobling influence of established individual industrial efficiency."[79] Brockway implemented "a purely scientific process, the modification of character by the wise use of rational means and methods . . . socialization of the anti-social by scientific training under completest government control."[80]

The two descriptions are born of two radically different worldviews. In the first, a conversion model, we find St. John's affirmation: "Repentance is reconciliation with the Lord by the practice of good deeds contrary to the sins . . . A penitent is the inflicter of his own punishments."[81] Because people are inherently good and ontologically oriented to be in relationship with the social and natural environment, the "sin" of severing this fundamental orientation is the cause of suffering and, at the same time, in the proper "virtuous" environment, an invitation to face the alienating behavior, its effect on self and others, and seek reconciliation. How different is the carrot/stick mentality of the reformatory: "Most of the prisoners were unable of themselves, unassisted by some exterior compelling force, to effectually resist, even if they were so disposed . . . their inner tendencies . . . they were creatures of instincts."[82] Brockway adds in another report: "Friction occurred as was natural, and in our estimation desirable, for friction in the reformatory procedure is proof of effectiveness."[83]

As I have been saying repeatedly, this is to be expected in virtually all criminological literature—then and now—for lack of any other moral resources than enlightened self-interest, behavioral modification, sociobiological inheritance, and "completest government control." And this, sadly, is the very problem with the virtuous prison concept. The authors are using moral terms that are begging for further substance, but either ideological or methodological constraints prohibit any moral notions other than those grounded in utility and behaviorism.[84] So, after repeatedly affirming the commitment that criminal justice must be a moral rather than a strictly scientific enterprise, the authors lack a vision of what sort of virtuous person they want to create other than one compliant to the law: "[P]eople, including inmates, have an *obligation* to obey the law, not to harm others, and that societal institutions, including the prison, should be organized to facilitate this goal."[85]

This is substantially the same argument that Cullen and Karen Gilbert made in a volume some years ago in which they invoke a social contractarian vision of rehabilitation, a theory that (again) posits a dualist agreement between competing interest groups wherein the state upholds a rehabilitative focus that enables prisoners to pursue their needs for security, employment, and other human goods (e.g., a "virtuous" penal environment) in exchange for the obligation to refrain from illegal activity.[86] Sam Lewis follows a similar logic: "[R]ehabilitation is what the state owes to the disadvantaged offender in return for the offender's future compliance."[87] If the reader recalls David Rothman's thesis in *Conscience and Convenience*, each time there was an attempt in Progressive penology to modify a fundamentally coercive atmosphere with programs designed to offer treatment, the modification came at the expense of the program, not the power dynamics of the institution. Nowhere in the "new" rehabilitation literature can I find an antidote to the black hole of coercion, not only in the culture of the prison but in the very language of the reformers. There is nothing, in short, to counteract an epigram by an eighteenth-century penal reformer: "There are cords of love and fetters of iron."[88]

Another well-known alternative to the prevailing culture of punishment that is not only promising but also making significant strides throughout the world is restorative justice. I trust that most readers are familiar enough with this attempt to replace the adversarial environment of the courtroom, wherein victim and offender are generally nonparticipants, with a focus on seeking voluntary compliance from both parties to a mediated dialogue. In the ensuing interchange, the harm caused to the victim can be expressed; each is enabled to offer explanations and background; and, if amenable to both parties, a legally binding settlement is drawn up to assuage the anger and loss of the victim with concrete reparations; and, at the same time, enable the offender to avoid confinement and the demonstrated onus of a criminal record.[89]

It is important, as Stanley Cohen claims, to initiate and enthusiastically support such informal programs that emphasize "that the state has no monopoly on justice."[90] It is not my intention in any way to disparage the diversion of cases into honest conversations with opportunities for the demonstration of remorse and for concrete acts of restitution. The restorative justice movement can and should weaken the hold of the confrontational arm of justice and lead it in the direction of one aiming at restoration of relationship.

Having said that, the movement still suffers from many of the dilemmas that plague other models of criminal justice, dilemmas that, I believe, only the adoption of a conversion paradigm can satisfactorily address. For instance, we emphasized in the last chapter the distinction between the initial transcendent experience that so often invites a new intellectual, moral, or spiritual horizon and the long and challenging process of character transformation that characterizes a conversion. Since the primary emphasis of restorative justice is satisfying the needs of the victim for self-expression, compensation, and closure, the welfare of the offender beyond the willingness to listen, to express remorse, and to meet the obligations of the mediated agreement is normally forgotten. This lacuna is often glossed over beneath the rhetoric that a more humane form of justice has been accomplished and that the experience has been, to some significant degree, transformative for the offender. Cullen and his colleagues are among those who are skeptical: "The idea that the kind of hi-risk offenders who frequently populate prisons will, with any regularity, be morally regenerated by a two-hour victim-offender reconciliation meeting or merely by furnishing restitution strains credulity."[91] Maruna suggests something similar: "Although the metaphor of the 'moment of clarity' conversion experience is embedded in Western discourse, research on how people change entrenched patterns of behavior contradicts the image of self-change as a moment or event."[92]

Another area of concern regarding restorative justice, one that haunts all rehabilitative efforts, is what to do with the recalcitrant offender who refuses to offer apology or seek reconciliation, or to the half-hearted offender (divided soul) who submits to mediation solely to avoid criminal prosecution and confinement but lacks sincerity in apology or fails to honor the terms of the contract with the victim. For such persons, there is little else to offer save the traditional imposition of misery.

Braithwaite suggests that restorative justice, in itself, is incapable of providing a true alternative to the dominant rubrics of the court and the jail. It can only work in conjunction with deterrence and retribution/incapacitation, in what he calls a regulatory pyramid, if it has any chance at widespread success: "The design responds to the fact that restorative justice, deterrence, and incapacitation are all limited and flawed theories of compliance. What the pyramid does is cover the weaknesses of one theory with the strength of another. The ordering of strategies in the pyramid is not just putting the less costly, less coercive, more respectful options lower down . . . It is also that by resorting to more dominating, less respectful forms of social control only when more dialogic forms have been tried first, coercive control comes to be seen as more legitimate."[93]

The approaches to rehabilitation discussed in this section by no means exhaust all of the creative strategies that have been and are being designed and implemented to improve the conditions under which offenders endure their imprisonment and the conditions they must face during the reentry process. It is not my intention either to tire the reader with facts about programs that he or she understands better than me or to describe initiatives that may be unknown to the reader only to subject them to the same analytical scrutiny with the same critical brush. Best to say that if, in my research, I discovered programs that proceeded from a position that did *not* have to rely on coercion and violence to fill in the cracks in the treatment model, then I would not have needed to write this book.

Areas of Agreement and Possible Cooperation

The critique of rehabilitation, as I have hoped to show, reprises the same metaethical concerns that have been raised vis-à-vis other theories in the criminal justice field. It is one that has to do with moral language, human nature, and a view of consciousness that divides the objects of perception by means of value judgments rather than proceeding from a cultivated predisposition of inclusion and compassion. While I am indeed suggesting the need for a new moral paradigm in the study and practice of criminal justice based upon the conversion motif, I also want to emphasize that within the literature on rehabilitation/desistance, a parallel discourse is visible that only requires further elaboration and elongation to extend into the domain from which my own analysis proceeds.

Fergus McNeill states that desistance literature tends to focus upon three factors: age, life transitions, and re-narration with the understanding that the three often interact in a dynamic, integrative fashion.[94] This is pertinent as life transitions and amending one's autobiography are essential notions in the increasing self-transcendence that characterizes a conversion. I am struck by the frequency with which stunning and/or life-altering moments appear in the findings and discussion within criminological texts. I have already noted that Sampson and Laub resist the more static depictions of the criminal personality by authors such as Gottfredson and Hirschi and focus on the transitional experiences or "turning points' in an otherwise disenchanted individual such as gainful employment or falling in love: "The interlocking nature of trajectories and transitions may generate *turning points* or a change in the life course . . . the long-term view embodied by the focus on trajectories implies a strong connection between childhood events and experiences in childhood [Gottfredson and Hirschi's focus]. However, the simultaneous shorter-term view also implied that transitions or turning points can modify life trajectories—they can 'redirect paths.' "[95]

Similarly, Giordano and her colleagues performed a follow-up study on a cohort of female adolescent offenders by studying narratives and noting the factors leading to "transformation" in terms of "cognitive development."[96] Among the determining factors in biographical reconstruction we find, once again, an uncanny resemblance to the conversion literature. Like all converts, there is always a sense of dissatisfaction with the state of one's life and an "openness to change" that recalls Miller and Rollnick's use of the terms ambivalence and discrepancy.[97] Next, the authors replicate the transformative moment with their moniker, a "hook for change": "The second type of cognitive shift relates more directly to one's exposure to a particular hook or set of hooks for change . . . This type of cognitive transformation is central to our conceptual emphasis because it focuses direct attention on the reciprocal relationship between actor and environment. That is, while a general openness to change seems necessary, by itself it is often insufficient. A fundamental premise is that both exposure to a hook and one's attitude toward it are important elements of successful change."[98] Third, as with converts in general, the subjects in the Giordano study fabricated a "replacement self" to "supplant the marginal one that must be left behind."[99] Finally, the cognitive transformation is complete when the given person no longer recognizes her former self in light of the person she has now become.[100]

Yet another, perhaps less dramatic, instance in which a criminologist seeks to explain the movement to desistance can be found in Ward's notion of surprise. In one study, he attempts to marshal the most compelling set of "protective factors" that insulate the former offender from asocial influences and, thereby, promote a "first person perspective"—aided by a treatment regimen capable of fomenting the sort of cognitive transition about which Giordano and her co-authors write.[101] Despite the mechanistic language in which the offender benefits from psychological tools "that enable the mind to function as a predictive engine," he notes that the mind has a tendency to recalibrate in light of "error" or "surprise."[102] Such language is reminiscent of narrative accounts of human development that employ terms like "expectations gone awry" or twists in plot, or, perhaps, "hooks for change" or "turning points": "Surprise motivates a search for more data via active engagement with the environment or the alteration of causal models in some ways. In an important sense, error signals fuel learning and provide individuals with the chance to boost the predictive power of their models, to increase their level of skill in managing data, and to utilize this information to achieve goals."[103]

Granted, all of the authors follow the predictable binary path of interpreting the possible religious experience or conversion simply in terms of "informal social control" and reduced "crime and deviance." Sampson and Laub state: "[S]trong attachment to a spouse (or cohabitant) combined with close emotional ties creates a social bond or interdependence between two individuals that, all else being equal, should lead to a reduction in deviant behavior."[104] Giordano et al. place less emphasis than Sampson and Laub on the centrality of social control in stimulating desistance, but, like them, take a more "agentic" view of desistance," in which "intimate networks" play a vital role in opening the person in question to a new horizon.[105] Ward states: "I will begin with the problematic aspects of agency (causes of crime—dynamic risk factors) and then focus on how protective factors can be employed by practitioners to address these challenges."[106] But even such conservative language does not diminish the transitional and participative nature of a given incident of ethical clarity. Events like falling in love, or being overwhelmed by a sudden turn of events, or experiencing affirmation at a deep internal level are common and profoundly moving human experiences that cannot be accounted for (and can even be tarnished) by the restricted moral language available to and often utilized by researchers.

In a recent volume, Rodney Stark supports this conclusion by noting that the positive impact of religious or mystical experiences is not diminished by the inability of respondents or, for that matter, academicians to classify them in terms other than coincidence or behavioral modification or, perhaps, pathology.[107] Still, he notes that despite the general suspicion among scholars to give credence to a religious interpretation of transformative events, a large number of people claim to have had such numinous encounters. He cites a random sample that he did of churchgoers in Northern California in the late 1960s and found that 69 percent had felt the presence of God; more recently, in a 2009 Pew report, 49 percent of Americans claimed to have had a religious experience.[108]

There is a growing interest in exploring the dichotomy just alluded to between what "empirical" data seems to suggest regarding mystical encounters and the limited hermeneutical options open to many researchers. One finds evidence of an openness to broaden moral and even metaphysical categories to allow a more phenomenological approach to the study of religious experience and conversion. McNeill states that "the concept and project of rehabilitation compel and require the development of a more fully interdisciplinary perspective."[109] Ward writes of the "metaphysics of protective factors," that is, "the embodied nature of human functioning," and then concludes: "While criminological research has much to offer in terms of understanding and managing crime, on its own it lacks the theoretical resources to fully explain it. As embodied, evolved social animals, human beings are complex creatures and a single level of analysis is not rich enough to account for normative fullness."[110] Reminiscent of Rene Girard, Rotman decries the ease with which the offender in correctional discourse can so easily be relegated to a "stereotyped scapegoat at the service of the emotional needs of the public."[111]

All of the rudiments for a paradigmatic shift, perhaps germinating since the Progressives erected the reformatory on such sandy moral foundations, are beginning to emerge from incubation. There is a growing awareness of the need for a deeper vocabulary to view the human person in her cognitive, moral, and integrative development. More and more of the intellectually converted are seeing the removal of boundaries as necessary not only between scholars of different disciplines but also between the "us and them" structure of the ego that engenders a rubric of separation that is tribal and exclusionary unless named and replaced by what David Berreby calls "kind-mindedness."[112]

I have argued in this chapter that this default function of the ego that ceaselessly divides the world has given birth to terms like rehabilitation, desistance, recidivism, and going straight. Such terms and their resultant modes of analysis have led to objectifying millions of people from the start and remain, despite the signs of the renaissance of a more comprehensive discourse, the common parlance shared by even the most sympathetic and "progressive" criminologists. Such terminology reproduces the discourse of the courtroom where power relations determine outcomes and where "juridic subjects" (deviants, recidivists) are engulfed in an acrimonious and judgmental atmosphere tolerated by the buffers of objective distance and, if convicted, relegated to suffer in the penitentiary where an army of well-meaning professionals will be there to help them rehabilitate.[113]

5

How Conversion Can Rehabilitate the Penal System

THE CONFINEMENT OF persons against their will is more than a social practice; it is a tradition. It is an extended "socially embodied argument" about human nature; about what constitutes behavior so destructive that its perpetrator must be segregated from the community; about what, specifically, is the end to be sought in detaining him or her; and about the means by which that end can in some demonstrable way be achieved.[1]

Put another way, "incarceration signifies criminal justice: It is its symbol, its referent, its beating heart."[2] What I have been contending is that the argument about penal policy, if it is in any way to be true to the concept of a tradition, must be extended back to its religious roots and to the understanding of human nature that provided the impetus for its development.

The contemporary prison is a remarkably consistent sociological phenomenon and *does* represent a tradition, writ small, if we restrict our view to the birth of "scientific criminology" in the Progressive movement of the late nineteenth century. Within that framework, as Sykes contends, virtually any observer would, despite minor variations, "be struck by the basic similarities which exist among custodial institutions, for there seems to be a remarkable tendency to override variations of time, place, and purpose."[3] Those similarities remain despite substantive differences among theorists, penal professionals, and legislators over the functional significance of criminal detention. Arguably, the normative principle affirmed most consistently is an operational imperative of order and security, supported by the immanent or direct use of violence, that spreads like a canopy over scheduled activities, be they obdurate or benign. The prison official in the post-Weberian world may well be a bureaucrat, "but he is a bureaucrat with a gun."[4]

It is within this overarching ambiance of precaution that initiatives designed to serve both the temporal and spiritual needs of the confined population must function. Lin remarks: "Programs in particular and reforms in general can threaten the sense of order in prisons, not so much because they breed disorder, but because they often represent a challenge to established ways of keeping order."[5] Beckford and Gilliat write that prison chaplains are sometimes inhibited by their own ideological shortcomings from serving the religious needs of a diverse population, but "the organizational structures and physical surroundings ... [exercise] even more powerful influences over their capacity to give members of other faith communities access to the resources and facilities that they require for their religious practices."[6]

Such observations remind us that while prisons are a sociological phenomenon, they are also a spiritual or ideological one. Social theorists may use a specialized grammar in noting that the ethos of institutions sends the "mutual corroboration" of their interlocking functions "cascading through all levels of the information system."[7] This is, however, analogous to the observation that institutions possess a "spirit" that "enfolds" both employees and residents within a dominant discourse whose "privileged position entitles it to the designation of paramount reality."[8] The work of Walter Wink underscores the fact that "spirits," whether gracious or malevolent, are omnipresent in sacred texts and such entities, referred to in the Bible as "principalities and powers," are never "free floating" forces but always express and reproduce the ethos of a given institution or social configuration: "[T]o understand the New Testament we must move from the naïve assurance that the principalities and powers mentioned ... can be 'demythologized,' that is, rendered without remainder into the categories of modern sociology, depth psychology, and general systems theory."[9]

Thus, the remarkable consistency of today's penal culture is one that evidences, despite shades of difference in practical implementation or in discrete moments of manifest cruelty or tender grace, a distinct spirit expressed in a generally unified symbolic and moral framework. It is precisely at this spiritual level that it can be distinguished from that of its progenitor whose ethos, despite a weary historical catalogue filled with misanthropic decisions and gross instrumental errors, was fashioned upon the contention that a quantum of time in a carefully constructed environment is not only preferable to sanguinary punishments and the other justifications for confinement (pre-trial detention or the collection of ransom or debt), but morally and spiritually mandatory.[10] I have been arguing that any attempt to rethink or think constructively about the meaning of incarceration will simply rearrange the correctional décor using the same furniture until those initial moral and "spiritual" assumptions are introduced into the planning, design, and operation of the penal milieu.

From the perspective of that earlier design, we have been asking the wrong questions for well over a century: not how to mold productive and law-abiding citizens through penal practice; not how to discipline the potential lawbreaker by the swift and certain administration of the most efficacious and least invasive amount of pain; not to express communal dissatisfaction and, often, outrage through the infliction of suffering upon those who willfully disregard the law; and not the selective segregation of the most troublesome for no other reason than rendering them harmless through incapacitation. The question should be: How can the conditions be fostered for those who have brought harm upon others to discover or be reacquainted with their natural sociability and capacity for creativity and compassion at ever-widening levels without having to punish or correct them?

This chapter will begin with an overview of a theory of confinement based upon the centrality of conversion and, continuing to some degree the argument of the last chapter, it will discuss how even the most promising reformative templates remain in significant ways oblivious to the moral and methodological practices upon which that theory was configured. Next, an approach utilizing those historic ideas as a response to careless and violent behavior in lieu of confinement will be outlined. Finally, I will present what I believe to be the essential rudiments of a rehabilitated penal system.

Outline of a Penitential Model of Confinement

In his classic study of life in a maximum security prison, Sykes claims that the modern-day prisoner is "an unwilling monk" and, later in the volume, speaks of "the monastic life of the imprisoned criminal."[11] He is describing the daily regime of a group of persons who have been "literally buried from the world," deprived of freedom of movement, and forced to bear a degree of asceticism and self-denial to which they, presumably, are not accustomed and to which they do not provide their consent.[12]

There is a degree of truth to the comparison. The monk (or cloistered nun), especially during the first millennium of Christian monasticism, is a prisoner.[13] A statute of the Council of Chalcedon (451 CE) declares that monks shall "embrace a quiet course of life . . . remaining permanently in the places in which they were set apart."[14] The sixteenth-century mystic Teresa of Avila spoke in one of her letters of "the convent and its inmates" while Therese of Lisieux, a cloistered nun in nineteenth-century France, speaks of making herself "a prisoner at the age of fifteen."[15]

Granted, the monk or nun enters the monastery or convent voluntarily, but, just as the novice in a religious community seeks a goal of spiritual enlightenment, there is a latent or manifest desire even in the case of forcible detention that something demonstrable be attained in the life of the detainee—whatever the vision of human nature being utilized—that will, upon release, make him or her more prone to bear the hardships of life with equanimity.

What makes the monastic model so appealing as an institutional metaphor is that regardless of the free decision that may have led an aspiring ascetic to abandon the secular world, the same failures of character that induce men and women today to bring harm upon their fellows, for example, commit murder, assault, or thievery, appeared in the cloister. However, since the monk or nun was, in correctional argot, a "lifer," expulsion was, normally, not an option. They belonged to the brother or sisterhood; and if their destructive behavior was not amended, they were segregated from the common life in a cell; a designated room; or, as we saw in the last chapter with St. John Climacus, a monastic prison.[16]

Numerous authors corroborate that the prison as we know it was born in this framework, one that drew its inspiration from the New Testament and from the development of the practice of penance in the early Church.[17] Penance in the first centuries of Christianity localized "criminal justice" within the community since Christians were admonished not only in Scripture to abjure settling differences in civil, that is, Roman courts (Lk 12: 57–59; Mt 5: 25–26; I Cor 6: 1–8), but also had witnessed the violence to their own that was so often unleashed by the Roman judicial system during periods of persecution.[18]

The gospel (Mt 18: 15–18) had provided the outline for the adjudication of faults, later replicated in the first monastic rules. Repeated interventions with the defendant were called for, first, by the injured party and, afterward, by a delegation of concerned members of the community, prior to taking the matter, if still unresolved, before the entire assembly. The apostles, and their episcopal successors, were then empowered and delegated to perform the rituals of binding and loosing—imposing penance and reinstating the penitent to communal life upon its completion (Mt 16: 19; Jn. 20: 22–23).

Given the power to forgive sins, the early Church next had to determine what sins were in need of absolution by the bishop or priest and the extent to which that absolution could be offered. Actions requiring penitential expiation were found in various catalogues of negligent behavior in the New Testament.[19] For instance, Jesus tells his disciples: "Do you not see that whatever goes into a person from outside cannot defile, since it enters, not the heart but the stomach, and goes out into the sewer? . . . It is what comes out of a person that defiles. For it is from within, from the human heart, that evil intentions come: fornication, theft, murder, adultery, avarice, wickedness, deceit, licentiousness, envy, slander, pride, folly. All these evil things come from within, and they defile a person" (Mk 7: 18–23). Most behavioral flaws such as those just mentioned could be effaced by private acts of prayer and penance or through a communal sharing of faults.[20] However, certain breaches of conduct were considered too serious to be amended by personal asceticism or humble recognition alone. Their remission required absolution from a cleric before the assembled congregation.[21] The three offenses most commonly requiring the penitential ritual were idolatry, fornication, and the shedding of blood.[22]

Despite some early contentions that those who underwent the transformative power of baptism were morally a new creation and, as such, had overcome their sinful tendencies and need for penance, the overwhelming consensus among church authorities held that just as the moral frailty of the human condition was inescapable so also no limits were to be placed upon the clemency offered those seeking reconciliation.[23] In the Constitutions of the Holy Apostles, known as the *Didascalia*, a third-century document widely disseminated and emulated, bishops are counseled to resist any animosity or fear of disorder that would restrict forgiveness regardless of the nature of the offense: "Receive, therefore, without any doubting, him that repents."[24]

Given the authority to absolve all sin, the next issue concerned the method or, more properly, the rituals by which sin was to be confessed and pardon extended. In the early centuries of the common era, the guilty party seeking forgiveness appeared before the congregation and its presiding bishop. He or she was given a "binding" penance, received the laying on of hands (an ancient right of adoption and membership), and entered the order of penitents. The latter was a designation that mandated suppliants to undertake a series of self-disciplinary practices for a given time during which they were forbidden to participate fully in the mass or receive the Holy Eucharist.[25]

Persons undergoing penitential discipline were often required to wear a special garment, known as the cilicium, and, in the Eastern Church, were often assigned a designated place during the Sunday liturgy for a specific period of time, depending upon the nature of the offense.[26] There were normally four locales or, as they were called, stations: weepers, those guilty of the most serious infractions, gathered outside the worship space for a specified period of time; hearers remained in the vestibule or at the entrance of the sanctuary; kneelers assembled around the lectern where the Scriptures were read; and co-standers were allowed to attend the mass with the faithful, although restricted from reception of the consecrated bread and wine.[27]

The members of the congregation were also actively involved in the lives of those undergoing penance. They were charged to monitor the repentant and encourage them in the practice of the exculpatory acts.[28] When the time prescribed for the various ascetic practices was concluded, the suppliant came once again before the bishop, the cilicium was removed, there was a "loosing" of the penance through absolution, and (ideally) full communion was restored.[29]

Church historians confirm that the central issue in this extended ritual was not punishment but the procedures necessary to reestablish communion: "[E]xclusion, either voluntarily undertaken or indirectly or directly imposed upon the sinner was in no way a punitive action. It merely recognized externally what had occurred already due to sin; alteration of relationship . . . In the image of the early writers, it was a 'hard medicine'; nonetheless, it remained a medicine rather than a punishment."[30] In the same way, the idea of "excommunication" was not an act of severing the offender from the community but an attempt to create the conditions for the unruly to recognize the sorrow they had caused to others and to themselves by their self-preoccupation and alienation. It was the "supreme attempt to bring back certain recalcitrant sinners to repentance."[31] In speaking of the goal of dismissing the errant Christian, Tertullian, who in the second century wrote the first penitential handbook, states that the discipline casts him (or her) down but "it raises him up all the more; when it makes him sordid, it cleanses him all the more; when it accuses, it excuses; when it condemns, it absolves."[32]

Thus, by the end of the third century, a set of normative practices had been established in various parts of the Christian world that required the party guilty of serious misconduct to appear before the leader of the community, followed by a public imposition of penance, accorded in units of time, to be served in a specific series of locales. The penance featured a set of exercises that were believed to be essential to allow the penitent to overcome the internal disorder that had provoked the offense. There was a communal delegation charged with the task of encouragement and supervision of the errant member, and a ritual of reincorporation into the community at the conclusion of the sentence.

Here we have virtually all of the rudiments of the Western system of criminal justice. The only missing element was the practice of forcible detention. It was in the monasteries that this final step in the first penal regimen was to be systematically undertaken.

In Chapter 2, we spoke of the differentiation in Christianity between the unconditional love and mercy Jesus portrayed when confronted by human weakness and the numerous passages in Scripture that suggest a deity whose perfect compassion is limited by perfect justice—retributive justice at that. The point in putting primary emphasis upon what I see to be the "kerygma" (central message) of the Gospels is not to dismiss the ongoing and equivocal conversation within the tradition, it is to take a position on a matter that is foundational for how we are to live as social beings in the face of human weakness and, more to the point, malevolence.

One can read the history of monasticism and the origins of confinement as we know it within its walls with the same bifurcated vision we saw in relation to punishment. There is normally heartfelt solicitude when Scripture is invoked, as in Benedict's exhortation to treat the offending monk as Jesus did the lost sheep: carrying it upon his shoulders back to the flock (Lk 15: 3–6). However, one also finds violent frustration when those sources are overlooked in the desire to reinforce the regulatory norms. Benedict requires the abbot to meet twice with the disobedient brother, followed by communal admonition. If the given monk still persisted in his errant behavior, he was to be "excommunicated." For minor offenses, the excommunication meant exclusion from the common table. Failing to respond to that measure, the offender could also be subjected to corporal punishment.[33]

The ambiguous tone of the Benedictine Rule regarding coercion, however, changes dramatically in the approach to "graver faults" that merited incarceration. There, again remembering Scripture, Benedict writes: "Let the Abbot be most solicitous in his concern for delinquent brethren, for 'it is not the healthy but the sick who need a physician' (Matt 9:12). And therefore he ought to use every means that a wise physician would use. Let him send *senpectae*, that is, brethren of mature years and wisdom, who may as it were secretly console the wavering brother and induce him to make humble satisfaction; comforting him that he may not 'be overwhelmed by excessive grief' (2 Cor 2: 7), but that, as the Apostle says, charity may be strengthened in him (2 Cor 2: 8). And let everyone pray for him. For the Abbot must have the utmost solicitude and exercise all prudence and diligence lest he lose any of the sheep entrusted to him. Let him know that what he has undertaken is the care of weak souls and not a tyranny over strong ones."[34]

While there is legitimate dispute as to which "Benedict" was followed in the disciplinary regimen of the many hundreds of Benedictine monasteries that flourished in Europe for a millennium prior to the Reformation, the penitential practices and penal structure that were drawn upon and utilized in each had been in place since the early centuries of the common era.[35]

Although many of the rudiments of current correctional practice are a reflection of the various stages of penitential discipline just enumerated, the glaring lacuna in comparing the two systems is the belief of the latter that the person whose behavior has been found wanting does not need to be punished or made into an example for the censure to be effective because our early ancestors were steeped in an ethical framework that held that the fractious and undisciplined were already suffering—their destructive comportment in itself an acknowledgment of their own estrangement. The fact that many individuals failed to honor this ontological position does not diminish the centrality of the belief in each of the early monastic rules that the very practices that led inevitably to spiritual perfection and that formed the basis of monastic existence were the rituals that must, of necessity, be built into the carceral experience: solitude, prayer, work, self-denial, and spiritual direction from respected members of the community. Those environmental conditions are sufficient in themselves to lead those experiencing internal discord and social alienation to come into harmony with the transcendent core of the self and, at the same time, experience conversion.

In contrast, current proponents of penal reform may not be as sarcastic as David Hume in ridiculing "monkish virtues" such as "[sexual abstinence], fasting, penance . . . humility, silence [and] solitude," but most of what one reads in the literature reveals that "men of sense" still reject such eccentricities in favor of "normal" human pursuits—and more invasive forms of discipline.[36]

Edwin Sutherland highlights this crucial difference in noting that the fault line that separates the prototypical approach to criminal justice and current ones has to do with the question of the willingness to make the penal experience one in which the offender is made to suffer. He notes that reaction to offenses in premodern times was usually not characterized by such authoritarian measures: "It was not until the modern period that the clearly punitive reaction to crime—the purposive infliction of pain on the offender because of some assumed value of the pain—became popular."[37]

This is by no means to suggest that scholars today dismiss the importance of self-punishment. Rather, having abandoned, or perhaps never having considered, the idea that a nonviolent penology is possible, they are left with no other option than to leave violence looming in the background should more gentle means of persuasion fail to take root. This is true whether one weighs the phenomenon of punishment on either a utilitarian or Kantian scale. Braithwaite provides a case in point of the first approach: "The [regulatory] pyramid says that unless you punish yourself for lawbreaking through an agreed action plan near the base of the pyramid, we will punish you much more severely higher up the pyramid (and we stand ready to go as high as we have to)."[38] Duff might eschew Kant's *lex talionis* in his plea for self-punishment but cannot escape his patron's desire to make pain part and parcel of the correctional exchange. Writing of various forms of "hard treatment," he notes that these expressions of infliction "are communicative: they aim to communicate not merely censure, but a better understanding of what the offender has done. They also, therefore, aim to elicit an appropriate moral response from him; for an adequate understanding of what he has done must be a *repentant* understanding, involving his recognition of its wrongfulness."[39]

As we have been repeatedly pointing out, there is often this dualist tendency to do the right thing for the wrong reason in criminological thought. It is not that Braithwaite and Duff are unaware that the movement to empathic sociability must, finally, be one that expresses the will of the offender. It is that the ethical paradigm that sets "the poles of their moral understanding" simply does not allow for the trust in human beings to discover these compassionate instincts in their moral DNA without applying external pressure.[40] Thus there is no provision if, say, penal subjects are prone to violence, to find a way out of such reactive behavior by trusting that once placed in a humane environment organized upon a neo-monastic model, latent nonviolent and participative instincts could begin to flow outward. That is why Alasdair MacIntyre insists throughout his trilogy investigating the various streams that carry our notions of the good, that the main line of moral and epistemological tension is drawn between liberal individualism and the Aristotelian/Thomist notion of a tradition wherein virtues can be learned because the core of the person is ontologically oriented to live in accord with them.[41]

The same disjointed relationship between right intentions and insufficient ethical presuppositions, or, between communitarian vs. individualist worldviews, surfaces in the psychological literature. Treatises predicated upon psychological techniques often contend that the therapeutic initiatives they support are life affirming rather than punitive and are built upon working with a given offender to sort out the priorities necessary to escape the cycle of improper socialization and imprisonment.[42] The aim of such an approach could not be more appropriate. Yet, the subject/object dualism embodied in the moral theories they espouse reroutes the good intentions through the matrix of judgment; power; and, if necessary, violence.

Rotman, for example, proposes a "humanist anthropocentric model" based upon dialogue between the psychologist and client. Its aim is "to understand the psychological determinants leading to anti-social acts, so as to provide the key that will unlock the offender's conscience."[43] This is murky language, to say the least, since he also makes a point of dismissing "metaphysical fixations," among them, presumably, the *very* "metaphysical" concept of conscience. Perhaps, murky is not the proper adjective since the intervention is based upon the same kind of determinism that we saw underlying Andrews and Bonta's *Psychology of Criminal Conduct*. We are thus left with a neo-Freudian reading of conscience as the imprint of authoritarian rule upon the superego: one that now needs to be recalibrated through "constructive action" to make the offender "a useful citizen" who "[stays] out of prison."[44]

This is another way of saying that even as "inner freedom" and "self-discovery" are fostered—a "strength based" strategy, according to Lewis, since the offender is an active participant—there is no moral core or higher authority to which one can appeal save attention to the sages of self-interest and, presumably, the state with its threat to "correct" those who fail to be "useful."[45]

Most treatment strategies combine radical behavioral approaches based on classical and operant conditioning with those predicated upon cognitive skills development and social learning.[46] As shown above, and commensurate with their commitment to behaviorism and the hedonic calculus, these modes of intervention are accompanied by "appropriate and immediate reinforcement and punishment."[47] Such tactics echo the sort of "managerial criminology" that we spoke of in the critique of rehabilitation; "a framework of risk rather than a framework of welfare"; one that focuses on the "capacity of the law and social control system to structure the conduct and choices of individuals."[48] Despite Kohlberg's claim that "arbitrary cultural beliefs" like these are as erroneous as the ethical relativism upon which they are based, they are reproduced again and again in criminological literature and institutional practice.[49]

In most accounts, there is no substantial self beyond the roles we play. The symbolic interactionism of Erving Goffman is often invoked as an accurate portrayal of humans who are identical mirrors of the Sophists of old from whom ingenuousness would be considered "an optimistic ideal and in any case not necessary for the smooth working of society."[50] Rather, Goffman argues, since each individual seeks to control the definition of a social encounter, there is a certain "symmetry" to the communication process, "a kind of information game—a potentially infinite cycle of concealment, discovery, false revelation, and rediscovery."[51] What he means is there is an implied morality in the games we play since we ought to be honored for the person we claim to be even as we must demonstrate the skills and comportment appropriate to substantiate that claim.[52] MacIntyre notes that the self in this construction is considered to have no necessary social identity; it is "criterionless because the kind of *telos* in terms of which it once judged and acted is no longer thought to be credible."[53] Thus, once again, one detects in numerous studies a deep conflict between an honest desire to improve the lives of those suffering the pains of conviction, confinement, and social reprobation (the desire that the client "change for the better") and insubstantial moral resources to enable scholars to translate that concern into anything other than "language games" and the subtle give and take—the reality principle, if you prefer—that one learns in constantly seeking the upper hand in each social encounter.[54]

There are other authors whose commitments resonate to some degree with the model of criminal justice based upon conversion. Braithwaite and Petit's "republican" theory of criminal justice, like the ancient approach, eschews punishment and seeks to maximize humane official practices. For example, in a critique of other theories (incapacitation, rehabilitation, deterrence), the authors decry the common mantra of crime prevention whose objectives "look uncontroversial" but "are outrageously destabilizing and insatiable."[55]

Their argument is that internal regulations should be weighed not only on the scale of security but also on "a stable allocation of rights" within "uncontroversial limits" consistent with the ideals of capitalist democracies.[56] They maintain, for instance, that each confined person has the right "not to be victimized" and, while they respect that within the penal framework one should not have the right of movement, they lament that such a person is deprived of the right to vote.[57]

They are correct: humans should not be free to do harm but neither should their freedoms be constrained for the purpose of punishing them. They are also correct in their critique of retributivist theories which, when all is said and done, are focused upon "constraints" rather than liberties.[58] But the argument stalls for this reader because it has nowhere else to go than the maximization of rights within necessary, "uncontroversial" limits. We have already noted that all liberal theories, even those not consciously operating under an "us and them" duality, lack any substantive conception of the good strong enough to ward off violence or the petty tyranny of the penal culture's existent rationalizations that limit dominion in the name of safety and protection.[59] Any thought to consult a wider range of ethical guidelines than the ones provided by the current political economy is dismissed out of hand. As with most of their peers, Braithwaite and Petit only mention religion to reaffirm the refrain of its irrelevance: "Thus we would not take seriously any [theoretical] candidate which appeals to a conception of the good—say, a religious view of the point of life—that is radically incapable of commanding consensus in a pluralist society."[60]

To be fair, I am certain that the authors are working from a definition of the "religious view" that is predicated upon affirming certain metaphysical propositions regarding the divinity and allowing those dogmatic assertions to exert influence upon outward conduct. But it is precisely this narrow and hence dismissive reading of the collective practical insights of the Eastern and Western lineages of wisdom that makes all such arguments hollow and ineffectual. No one needs to profess a religious dogma to be believe that human beings have a moral center that is relational, participative, and oriented to self-transcendence; in other words, one need not be religious to be a humanist. Tarrou, the pacifist tourist caught in plague-stricken Oran in Camus's novel *The Plague* makes the ontological claim that violence is the "plague" that ravages humanity ("we all have plague") and that the "social order" is "based on the death sentence." He proclaims that the only thing he now wishes to do with each breath he emits is to avoid breathing the plague on anyone.[61]

Tarrou is an atheist and yet, he tells his colleague, Dr. Rieux, that he wants to be a saint: "But you don't believe in God. Exactly! [Tarrou replies] Can one he a saint without God?—that's the problem, in fact the only problem, I'm up against."[62]

Everything we have spoken of concerning conversion affirms Tarrou's desire—and his sainthood. All are meant by their nature to be "saints"; put negatively, to manifest in an ever-widening circle the profound hope never to breathe the stench of violence upon another human being; expressed in positive terms, to adopt a continuing attitude of intellectual humility, moral concern, and a pre-reflexive affirmation of unity with all.

These are fully human aspirations, not simply theological ones, within the reach of every man and woman. And, as I have pointed out continually, many secular philosophers and scientists proclaim their a priori status as energetically as religious adherents.

That does not mean that religion, precisely as a system of beliefs in a divine being who creates, sustains, and ultimately guides history into compassionate union, is to be excluded from the conversation over social policy. A healthy dose of what may be termed eschatological hope is a perfect balance—whether consciously tied to a doctrinal position or not—to materialist worldviews that have no transcendent barometer to aid in the measurement and interpretation of current events.[63] Charles Taylor takes a similar view in claiming that the kind of "self" that emerges from a staunch liberal individualism is "living beyond its moral means" in seeking to construct standards of justice. He claims that "adopting a stripped-down secular outlook, without any religious dimension or radical hope in history, is not a way of avoiding the dilemma . . . It involves stifling the response in us to some of the deepest and most powerful aspirations that humans have conceived. This . . . is a heavy price to pay."[64]

Furthermore, as I maintained in the opening pages of the book, if a revolution or paradigmatic shift is needed in criminal justice, it can neither be conceived nor communicated without an apocalyptic or some trans-historical metaphor. Positivism and its "progressive" offspring were constructed on such a cosmic scale—the upward and unstoppable movement of "progress" in which religion cedes its authoritative place to reason which, in turn, cedes explanatory priority to science.[65] When employed in such a schema, science as ideology can, as it did with Comte and his successors, be employed to strike religion from the index of intelligible subjects just as religion can be and often is employed to seek to impede the credibility of science. Ideological whitewashing, however, is the antithesis of conversion and fails in the task of seeking a metaphor that is spacious enough to embrace all creative efforts in the evolutionary process toward full harmony. Both science and religion must be freed from the stagnant and reactionary claims of zealots who fail to see that most of the scientific developments over the last century echo the theological belief in the relational propensity of all matter.[66] Alan Watts, in one of his early works, writes that in the wake of scientific developments in "field theory, ecological dynamics, and the transactional nature of perception" scientists "can no longer see man as the independent observer of an alien and rigidly mechanical world of separate objects . . . The sensation of man as an island-ego in a hostile, stupid or indifferent universe seems more of a dangerous hallucination."[67]

There are noteworthy efforts to bridge this unnecessary divide in the criminological community. Clear and his colleagues, for example, point out what every researcher into penal culture knows to be true: regardless of the personal agnosticism of many researchers, religion *is* important to the men and women in our jails and prisons. They also note that the social sciences often fail in their analysis of correctional dynamics due to this clash of worldviews: "Science deals with things that are observed, measured, and inferred by logic. Religion so often deals with mystery not to be captured by observation, namely, the experiences of the spirit that happen within individuals."[68]

Another area of promise in linking the prototypical model of justice and current formulations is found in the assertion that the ancient practice of welcoming the released captive back into the common life is not only necessary but must be ritualized, much like the ceremony in which the absolved penitent was shorn of the garment signifying his or her isolation from full social participation. Maruna writes that rituals are important in all meaningful social inter-reactions; none more important than "restoration of reputation and full citizenship."[69] In this, he recalls Braithwaite's important insight concerning the need of shaming rituals whose intent is "reintegration" as opposed to the shame and stigma that are so often exhibited in the rituals of arrest, prosecution, sentencing, and confinement; ceremonies whose result is "disintegration" and the attending alienation that, as we have seen, so often lead to antisocial conduct.[70] Mathiesen, too, laments the extravagant expenditure of resources allotted to dishonoring the convicted with no complementary rite of reincorporation that proclaims as loudly to the prisoner as the anterior sentencing "that now the time in prison is up, the disparagement is cancelled, dignity and honor are restored."[71]

The advocacy for a liturgy of reintegration, of course, does not dismiss the magnitude and critical importance of the reentry question; but it also recognizes that leaving prison is not simply a transactional incident in an otherwise coherent life narrative.[72] It honors the fact that significant damage has often been done to the person as a result of incarceration and not simply to her social or economic circumstances. If conversion teaches anything, it is that the process of healing and meaningful social interaction is always initiated when human beings are treated gently and with care.

The discussion need not end here, but I believe we have covered enough ground to meet the aim of this section: to provide an outline of the prototypical correctional paradigm and to point out that not a few of the historic assumptions have been suggested in the thought of contemporary scholars, albeit incompletely. Let us now turn to an outline of how conversion might be employed as the dominant metaphor for criminal justice.

Social Rudiments of a Conversion Paradigm

In speaking of a conversion paradigm, I am speaking to a substantial degree of a heuristic device that would emerge from an ongoing conversation among all disciplines committed to framing human conflict—whether involving actual crimes and torts or simply the host of real and narcissistic injuries that persons routinely encounter—within a nonjudgmental, compassionate, and dialogical perspective that eschews, in as much as possible, prior judgment and the willful infliction of suffering in any form, be it physical, emotional, or psychological.[73]

The qualifier on the heuristic nature of the dialogue would be an a priori affirmation of the inviolable dignity of life. The entire argument to this point has sought to lay the intellectual and instrumental value of this necessary commitment. The penal/legal system, indeed, the social system itself, cannot be rehabilitated without the assertion of an innate capacity and longing for participation and self-transcendence that is, at once, common in its unitive orientation yet exquisitely unique in each personal manifestation. I have repeatedly orchestrated the voices of secular scholars in a host of disciplines to show that such an ontological claim does not require subscription to theological propositions, but neither does it exclude them.

Furthermore, a conversion paradigm would take a patient view of asocial comportment, justice, community sanction, and reintegration by honoring the methodology of repeated intervention and self-disciplinary practices spoken of in the beginning of this chapter. It was only after a series of purposeful encounters that the phenomenon of "excommunication" as a means of reconnecting the penitent to life-affirming internal instincts was undertaken; an excommunication that, in the world outside the monastery, was neither punitive nor carceral but provided for active engagement between the penitent and his or her peers in the congregation.

These historical and ethical assumptions do not provide a fail-safe resolution to the endless expressions of human fallibility; rather, they set the conditions for seeking solutions to this primordial condition. They make solutions possible in a new and creative way—at least as far as the archetypal pattern is concerned. That is another way of saying that the conversion paradigm is not reactionary. True to the definition we have been speaking of, it seeks to broaden the frontiers of knowledge, empathy for others, and consciousness itself. As a result, multiple viewpoints should be welcomed in the conversation over the social response to destructive comportment since attentiveness to the distinctive insights of discrete persons, communities, and traditions are necessary to the methodological framework. Stanley Cohen points to the vibrancy of creative communal alternatives to uncivil conduct, any and all of which blend with the hope to create a dialogical and sensitive approach to human error: "[E]ven to its harshest critics, the informal justice movement has generated some interesting experiments: restitution programs, mediation projects, advisory sentencing panels made of local residents . . . these projects might clarify rather than obscure moral values; they might expose ordinary people to the nature of the formal machine, and remind them that the state has no monopoly on justice."[74]

Addressing everything from simple misconduct and conflictual situations to misdemeanors and low-level felonies in terms of conversion suggests a policy that might fruitfully employ the base of Braithwaite's restorative pyramid and the guidelines for addressing conflictual situations in Matthew's Gospel (18: 15–18). In such a framework, litigation would not be the normal means of resolving disruptive behavior. If the plaintiff and defendant are amenable, a negotiated settlement structured along the principles of restorative justice might be instituted. The encounter would "involve, to the extent possible, those who have a stake in a specific offense" who would then "collectively identify and address harms, needs, and obligations, in order to heal and put things as right as possible."[75] Carolyn Hoyle affirms that there is some empirical validity to such structured interactions: "Restorative justice has been shown to have enormous potential in dealing with conflicts in schools and neighborhoods, particularly for anti-social behaviours that do not warrant a criminal justice response."[76] She also affirms that studies show that relational rubrics along the lines described have shown positive outcomes in educational settings with regard to bullying, destruction of property, and disruptive conduct.[77]

Since persons are social beings and the steps in the conversion process reveal that the barometers of growth are expanded levels of communication, participation, and reconciliation, restorative justice in its basic format aligns properly with a conversion model. However, as I have mentioned in several places, it is, at the same time, another laudable attempt to refocus the legal system in a life-affirming direction that relies on the specter of "harsh justice" to coax the reluctant into dialogue or to punish them for their recalcitrance. Thus Zehr claims, restorative justice is "not about forgiveness or reconciliation" nor is it "the opposite of retribution."[78] It also falls prey to the criticism that, regardless of how favorable the outcome (e.g., the offender takes responsibility; the victim expresses the extent of personal hurt; the offender offers concrete reparation accepted by the victim; and the case is resolved without confinement or the stigma of conviction), the conditions that led to the offensive behavior have still not been substantially addressed. Additionally, as mentioned in the last chapter, its methodological guidelines indirectly verify neoliberal assumptions (and those of most proponents of rehabilitation) that the recalcitrant or poorly socialized individual, not the current alignment of power, wealth, and privilege, bears direct responsibility for the failure to submit to the sometimes brutal realities of his or her existence.[79]

Recognizing these limitations, a "decriminalized" method of seeking conflict resolution and some degree of reconciliation would honor the fact that individual manifestations of anger and destructiveness are signals of internal conflict and, as not a few studies have suggested, often the outcome of feeling deliberately targeted for social and economic failure by the depressed socioeconomic conditions in which so many are forced to live.[80]

In similar fashion, anger and feelings of revenge on the part of victims are equally understandable, even necessary, as they uncover the wounds that have been inflicted upon them. Yet, at the same time, in a conversion model, both are ultimately barriers to understanding the offender and to the recognition that the legally culpable are not the only ones called to conversion. If *either* party is incapable of seeing the "face" of the other, the satisfaction of the victim at an offender's show of remorse and promise of restitution is a hollow victory. Levinas writes: "Does not what we call the word of God come to me in the demand that challenges me and claims me, and before any invitation to dialogue, does it not break through the form of generality under which the individual who resembles me appears to me and only shows himself, and become the face of the other person? Does God not come to mind in that challenge?"[81]

If, as we have been claiming, persons are ontologically poised to transcend the limited, sheltered, defensive world built by the ego; if they are likewise capable of a shift in horizon that is more and more inclusive in its breadth, then the inner voice of each person is a summons to develop the contemplative stance that enables the compassionate center to envelop the fearful public persona. This, I believe, is what Levinas, who is not a professed believer, is getting at in the above quote. "God," in his language, as in agnostic thinkers such as Lacan and Heidegger, might be understood in the same imaginative way with which Camus develops the concept of the secular saint. It is a metaphor for the expansive love buried under the fabrications of what Thomas Merton calls the "false self," or Heidegger the "they-self."[82]

Not surprisingly, the development of a meditative or contemplative practice is at the heart of the monastic search for spiritual perfection, as well as the remedy for misanthropic alienation. It is also a growing worldwide phenomenon with millions and millions of adherents in a welter of traditional Eastern and Western formats, in New Age, native American, Aboriginal, or First Nation practices, and in a host of syncretic expressions. There are no theological or doctrinal prerequisites to learn and engage the achingly simple formulae unless one desires to develop a physical discipline, such as Yoga, to accompany one's attempt to enact a nonjudgmental, compassionate attentiveness to the moment. Presence to the real, to "what you have to deal with," is a discipline that takes a lifetime to master but is available with each breath one takes.[83] All traditions recommend that one take at least one period each day to "sit" or assume a meditative position of one's liking, follow one's breath accompanied often with the use of a mantra that expresses one's deepest inner longing, and gently acknowledge but not indulge thoughts and feelings. In the words of Alan Watts: "This is really all there is to contemplative mysticism—to be aware without judgment or comment of what is actually happening at this moment, both outside ourselves and within, listening to events even to our involuntary thoughts as if they were no more than the sound of rain."[84]

The transformative power of this practice enables one not only to view and acknowledge antisocial impulses but also diminishes their power each time they are beheld with equanimity and, with repeated practice, sympathetic understanding.[85] The veracity of these claims has been demonstrated through neuroscientific research. Meditative practice reconfigures brain synapses so that prior patterned responses to unpleasant stimuli that produced anger and violence are overcome by feelings of serenity and even benevolence. James Austin writes that "the human brain can be shaped, etched, and transformed . . . To what end? To yield striking, ongoing constellations of perception, insight, attitudes, and behavior. These flow spontaneously, blending conduct fully in harmony with whatever social setting prevails."[86]

That said, we know by simple acknowledgment of the anger and violence embedded in the world and in all who live within it that, however nourishing the well, contemplation is a source from which one cannot be forced to drink. I am convinced, however, by the historical imprint of the great spiritual traditions and the widespread contemporary appeal of mindfulness among those lacking religious affiliation that it is a discipline that ought to be at the forefront of the conversation over "justice." Among the many things that Gandhi correctly saw was the need to teach such practices to the young: "[A] child, before it begins to write its alphabet and to gain worldly knowledge, should know what the soul is, what truth is, what love is, what powers are latent in the soul. It should be an essential of real education that a child should learn, that in the struggle of life, it can easily conquer hate by love, untruth by truth, violence by self-suffering."[87]

While only a small percentage of children may derive the benefits of Gandhi's advice and the meditative lessons necessary to provide its ethical commitments room to be expressed, there is no situation in which young men or women find themselves that the introduction of such techniques would not be appropriate. That is to say, just as no "criminal" should ever be punished, so also no child or student should ever be punished. All should be taught that our outward misbehavior is not indicative of our true nature. In fact, we hurt others when we are not in harmony with our relational essence. It is for this reason that many mystics claim that what is termed "sin" in certain theological systems is a willful fracture of relationship. It is not expressive of the inner life but only its negative image. It can only urge the angry to turn away or hide in fear from their internal sense of intimacy with everything and everyone.[88]

According to some criminal justice scholars, there is evidence revealing that informal means of confronting disruptive behavior often result in lower rates of incarceration; just as there is equally disquieting evidence that excessive surveillance of the "dangerous" results in "net widening" and, ineluctably, an expanded carceral population.[89] Ruth Wilson Gilmore, following Todd Clear, reinforces this point and then notes that "increased use of policing and state intervention in everyday problems hastens the demise of the informal customary relationships that social calm depends on."[90] Robert Sampson and Charles Loeffler state that the reason that mass incarceration is not a concern for many is due to "spatial inequality" in which there is direct correlation between "concentrated disadvantage" and incarceration.[91]

The reader may remember that I began this book stating that its intention was to engage criminal justice at the metaethical rather than at the practical level. I suggested that a revolution is needed that will introduce a new model to replace one whose foundational commitments are laden with unsubstantial ethical presuppositions and their resultant systemic contradictions. All of us know it is easier to tear down than to construct, and so I make these "front-end" recommendations because they are, from my theological and criminological perspective, truthful. They are practices that have outlived all of their undertakers, but they cannot be reduced to a fabricated solution that ignores the complexity of the human psyche or the persistence of social inequality. Each life, like each case of antisocial comportment, is unique; and each solution, if it is to honor the unfolding plot of a human life, is also unique. What is being suggested are methodological starting points. The invitation to dialogue, introduction to the practice of meditation or contemplation, creating the conditions for peaceful exchange, all done with neither the threat nor the demonstration of force, are vital resources in the collective effort to address the very real tensions that disfigure human relationships, human hearts, and human bodies.[92]

More to the point, teaching persons whose physiological and psychological constitution seems incapable of sitting in silence, focusing on the moment, and suspending judgment in favor of kind-mindedness is a difficult and frustrating process. This is due, however, at least in part, to the fact that many have lost touch with the resources of what Aldous Huxley calls the "perennial philosophy."[93] At their deepest level, these wisdom sources unite in teaching that with the proper guidance and practice any person, no matter how suffused with rage and self-hatred, can discover inner peace and live without resorting to violence in the face of life's misfortunes. While this strategic starting point is eminently possible in all cases of mild discord, there is a far more serious question from both the social and criminological perspectives: How are we to address those who are unwilling to respect the life and goods of others and brusquely disdainful of the practices that lead to inner and outer harmony?

Confinement and Conversion

As noted at the beginning of this chapter, the prison is a symbolic universe. Berger and Luckmann use this term effectively to describe institutions as "bodies of theoretical traditions that integrate different provinces of meaning and encompass the institutional order in a symbolic totality."[94]

Penal reformers have been far from blind to this reality since the inception of the prison. We have already noted that institutions have an identity, a spirit or ethos, that, remembering Marx's famous aphorism, is not altered by human consciousness but invades and fashions human consciousness.[95] This functional requirement of symbolic coherence was evident in the monastic prison whose cells were often built into the walls of the chapel so that the inhabitant's only window was into the sanctuary of the church.[96] The establishment of such a unified symbolic vision was the clarion call of the first architects of the American penitentiary movement, one heard literally around the world. Governmental representatives came from as far away as Japan to learn of this "new" "total institution," whether Auburn or the Eastern State Penitentiary, that sought to imprint on residents a regime that integrated every aspect of daily life around either a monastic framework or one patterned on silence and a congregate work ethic.[97] Progressive penal institutions, too, were to be integrated in all respects. Enoch Wines writes: "As a principle that crowns all, and is essential to all . . . We ardently hope yet to see all the departments of our preventive, reformatory and penal institutions in each state moulded into one harmonious and effective system; its parts mutually answering to and supporting each other; and the whole animated by the same spirit."[98] Such coherence is what lies at the heart of the "faith-based prison" that seeks to reinforce a (normally) Christian ethos and worldview in every aspect of the daily life of those under its care.[99] Not surprisingly, some present-day scholars are now convinced that if the prison is to remain the prototypical expression of societal disapproval for serious misconduct, its internal culture must reflect a system-wide, integrated program of reform.[100]

The unifying element in each prison, as with the guidelines for addressing disruptive behavior discussed in the last section, should be built around the commitment to honor life as sacred, possessing inherent and unimpeachable dignity; a dignity that precedes temperament, socialization, will, and the errant paths that each to a different degree treads upon. All theories and all social experiments proceed from first principles that are not in themselves rational. Rather, they proceed from beliefs that to varying degrees suggest trans-historical metaphors. A well-known case in point are the words in the American Declaration of Independence: "We hold these truths to be self-evident that all . . . are created equal."

A penal framework fails from the start if it is conceived in binary and oppositional terms; the religious-secular distinction being a good case in point. The latter, in a democratic context such as the United States, is an issue of concern only if church and state are understood in the parochial terminology with which the First Amendment is written. There is no violation of the integrity of either when they meet on the common ground assumed in documents such as the Declaration of Independence that hallow the inherent worth of each human being. To affirm the sacredness of life, according to Ronald Dworkin, is the most natural of all human affirmations (perhaps the "Founding Fathers" would call such an affirmation, "self-evident"). Dworkin scolds "pro-choice" advocates in the abortion controversy for ceding to their opponents the moniker of "pro-life." He wisely states that no one seriously contends that life is *not* sacred. The discussion of abortion, in his mind, can only proceed in a fashion that transcends tribal affiliation and acrimony when both parties in the debate hallow this mutual commitment to honor life at every stage of development, even if, always regrettably, some choose to terminate a pregnancy.[101]

As we noted in the last chapter, the withering of an ethics of care was intensified in the correctional arena with the demotion of rehabilitation in the latter decades of the twentieth century. Despite the latter's withered legacy of trying to offset coercion with treatment, its welfarist orientation was its ideological selling point. All current approaches, as noted in the last chapter, have been forced since the decline of the rehabilitative ideal to "reinvent themselves" by catering to political/populist pressure aimed at relinquishing the welfare of the prisoner as a primary goal in favor of utilitarian "greatest good" concerns, or attention to criminogenic needs and risk, or to instrumental interventions based upon behavioral modification.[102] In other words, as Ward and Maruna suggest, rehabilitation is no longer undertaken solely for the benefit of the offender but, primarily, for that of the community.[103] Gwen Robinson attests not only that "the 'pure' rehabilitative sanction is extinct," but also that ethical commitments are no longer ends in themselves but tools "to regulate individual conduct and . . . help maintain order and obedience to law."[104]

While the affirmation of the primacy of each life as an end in itself has been lost even among some of the most ardent supporters of salutary aid to the captive, one does find that transcendent commitment in the most enduring ethical theory, one that traces itself back to the Greeks: natural law. Aristotle distinguishes that which is "legal and conventional" with that which "never changes at all."[105] Aquinas's formulation is the best known. It proceeds from the universal dictum that all are ontologically motivated "to do good and avoid evil" and that the most primal and universal application of this guideline—one that "all substances" share in common—is the affirmation of the irreducible integrity of life and resistance to those things that seek to disfigure or destroy it.[106]

Places of detention should have as their overarching principle the belief that conversion, an ever-expanding affirmation of the sovereignty of life, is a state of being toward which all are "naturally" pointed in a teleological sense. The reader may recall the assertion of William James that ineffable moments of *ecstasis*, wherein recipients are carried beyond the shell of their self-understanding, are common occurrences among the young.[107] The issue to be addressed in correctional policy, therefore, is not whether the young are lacking extraordinary interventions that open doorways to a "pro-social" existence, but whether they have the aid of sensitive and knowledgeable mentors (St. Benedict called them "senpectae") to enable them to interpret the noetic and moral message they have received. A reformed prison would recognize not only that instinctual affirmations of life arise often among those under its custodial care, but also that they arise with greater ease and frequency when the conditions spoken of regarding conversion are respected and set in place.[108]

The notion of accompaniment as a necessary element in the process of character transformation is a direct response to the failure of many of the reform movements in Britain in the late eighteenth and early nineteenth centuries, as well as some of the early incarnations of the penitentiary in the United States, that sought to create a religious renewal among the confined by the imposition of solitary confinement.[109] The same policy has been instituted with far more draconian intentions and the same depressing results with the phenomenon of supermax prisons in which the prisoner is isolated in a cell twenty-three hours each day.[110] In the words of De Beaumont and De Tocqueville, "this absolute solitude, if nothing interrupt it, is beyond the strength of man; it destroys the criminal without intermission and without pity; it does not reform, it kills."[111]

A reformed prison would be familiar with the harmony among spiritual traditions in providing the methodological pathways by which ego barriers can be lowered to give way to feelings of unity.[112] While some traditions, such as Buddhism, feature specific postures and techniques to center the person in a meditative state, all unite in seeking the cultivation of an attitude of openness to the moment and the transformation that it inevitably brings to those who make it a daily practice. As those who respect and engage this discipline relate repeatedly, the divided self of which James speaks must recede before the true participative self can be born. The theme of death leading to new life is commonly invoked. William Miller writes: "To be an inquirer . . . means that one takes the unknown so seriously that, instead of setting out to master it, one gives up all one thinks and becomes its servant. To make that turn, to undergo that conversion, seems to those who look at it from the perspective of what it leaves behind, like a kind of death . . . To the one who understands it, who awakens in wonder to the other in its otherness, it seems like the birth of genuine thinking."[113] Levinas conceives the inner world of the self and its material manifestation in terms of instinct and exteriority: "The relationship of instinct and exteriority is not a knowing but a death. Through death, the living being enters the totality."[114]

An acknowledgment of the sacred within and the attempt to create the conditions for its deeper unveiling would mean the expurgation of virtually all the language used to speak of the process of confinement. Nomenclature, often degrading, must be excised from the penal domain: not only terms like criminal and inmate but also procedural terminology such as referring to a person as "a body" or meals as a "feeding." It would also put an end to the reduction of religion to an instrument of social control—the latter being the one consistent value that religion is seen to possess in the penal environment according to many studies.[115]

The conversion model reverses this negative ideology. Conversion creates the conditions for self-punishment and, inevitably, empathic behavior by affirming the innate capacity of each person to mature in the ways of relational harmony. With such an affirmative starting point, the phenomenological emphasis on encountering the other "in a spirit of meekness and voluntary poverty" can be honored and its transformative effects on the knower and known put into motion.[116] An approach that honors interiority and the inherent longing for community is echoed by some psychologists: "Those who work in the helping professions often are inclined to believe that what causes change is the service provided, be it counseling, treating, advising, or teaching . . . It is now widely accepted that in many problem areas, positive change often occurs without formal treatment . . . Change occurs naturally."[117] Increasingly, correctional scholars are beginning to acknowledge the power of respecting the inner movement of the human spirit: "Telling someone to stop being a criminal may work for a period of time, but that person needs a replacement identity, and this identity may be chosen only by the individual who is in the process of change . . . No matter how coercive or punitive, corrections can't do it, nor can treatment. The most these organizations can do is create the environments and conditions in which change is most likely to occur."[118]

This spirit of acceptance and affirmation was the initial inspiration for the faith-based prison movement. It began when the abandoned Humaita Prison in Brazil was converted into a facility run entirely on Christian principles at the behest of two Catholic laypersons in the mid-1970s. The organizers asked only that the state provide the residents with food. Charles Colson visited the facility after his own release from custody and provided this description: "Instead of seeing the usual grey, dingy walls, I was met by a clean, inviting atmosphere. The prison had a well-tended garden with signs prominent everywhere, most them taken from the Psalms or Proverbs . . . I was met at the gate . . . by a guard who was actually an inmate . . . a convicted murderer, swinging a huge chain of keys from this belt. When inmates arrived at Humaita, their chains were removed, and they were told that in this prison they are not constrained by steel but by the love of Christ."[119]

What the founders of the prison knew from their religious training was that every person has done shameful things, and every person longs for reconciliation and loving relationships. They understood that the best way to summon the repentance necessary for humble admission of fault, re-narration, and living peacefully with self and others is to treat each person, regardless of who they are or what they have done, with kindness. A warden at the New Jersey State Prison reminds us of some of this practical wisdom in his remark that it is the relationships between the incarcerated themselves, not with professional caregivers, that determine whether incarceration would render any substantive change in their affective lives: "The welfare of the individual inmate, to say nothing of his welfare and dignity, does not importantly depend on how much recreation and consultation he receives but rather depends on how he manages to live and relate to other inmates who constitute his crucial and only meaningful world. It is what he experiences in this world, how he attains from it, how he avoids its pernicious effects—how, in a word, he survives in it that determines . . . whether he will emerge from prison with an intact or shattered identity."[120]

This focus on care and the centrality of communal interchange is the only deficient element in the theories of mid-level retributivists like Duff, Jean Hampton, and Graeme Newman and abolitionists like Laura Magnani and Harmon Wray. Each affirms that repentance is the goal of detention but they cannot conceive of a non-punitive way to enable its expression to emerge. Duff states repeatedly throughout his work that punishment is a "penance" initially "imposed by others on the criminal" that "he should ideally come to accept and will for himself."[121] Hampton's moral education theory of punishment is, in her words, "nonretributivist" since its aim, similar to Duff's schema, is to induce contrition.[122] Thus, she states that "if there were clear evidence that a criminal was very remorseful for his action and had already experienced great pain . . . this theory would endorse a suspension of his sentence or else a pardon."[123] Newman gives explicit reference to the sagacity of the monastic ethos in viewing human malevolence in a fully moral way, "which is to say that the offender has a guilty mind, and that only by a series of ritually purgative functions can this this guilt be assuaged."[124] He then offers this critique: "Unfortunately, penologists have lost sight of this important function of retribution, so that they allowed punishments to destroy souls rather than save them."[125] Magnani, a regional director for the American Friends Service Committee, has written position papers for this social service arm of the pacifist Quakers.[126] She and her co-author, remembering the example set by the Truth and Reconciliation Commission in South Africa, contend that forgiveness must be preceded by truth telling and reparations.[127]

What is missing in these writers is not their appreciation of the need for contrition among those who have done harm to others but their general inability to see that no one needs to be harmed or be forced to make a confession in order to bring it about. Sykes (once again) perceptively saw that what makes prison "exceptionally negative" is not imprisonment itself; "what makes this pain of imprisonment bite most deeply is the fact that the confinement of criminals represents a deliberate moral rejection by the free community. Indeed . . . it is the moral condemnation of the criminal—however it may be symbolized—that converts hurt into punishment."[128]

In an environment of care and accompaniment, whose life-affirming ethos refuses to judge the person even if the action that brought him or her to prison is deeply appalling, the conditions for the initial impetus of conversion are enacted. Recall that the event that breaks open the shackles that bind the heart is always experienced by the convert as one of unconditional regard, never "righteous" anger or condemnation.

Theological and philosophical scholarship on the notion of forgiveness is helpful in amplifying the deep significance of this unexpected graciousness. Linda Ross Meyer conflates mercy and punishment to such a degree that punishment morphs into "a shared remembering of one's self-alienation . . . and responsibility for others."[129] She contends that the true understanding of punishment is an "undeserved leniency" that mirrors the trust involved in any committed relationship; it is the risk of "being-with" that looks with confidence to the future "rather than settling accounts with the past."[130]

Derrida also emphasizes the sense of trust involved in a correct understanding of forgiveness but emphasizes the impact of the Abrahamic faiths and of Christianity in particular in underscoring its "exceptional and extraordinary" nature.[131] Forgiveness, in his view, is decidedly not a transaction meant to satisfy the complaint of the victim but a prodigal expression of benevolence: "forgiveness forgives only the unforgiveable."[132] He then claims (also invoking Abrahamic language) that the frequent "hypocrisy, calculation, and mimicry" that coalesce in the ritual of accusing others of unspeakable crimes is borne by "parasites" who are blind to the fact that "if we were to begin to accuse ourselves . . . of all the crimes of the past against humanity, there would no longer be an innocent person on earth."[133]

Forgiveness, for Derrida, is a "madness" that must plunge "into the night of the unintelligible"; a faith in the power of human and humane contact between victim and offender that gives birth to something creative and new: a bond of care and intimacy which is always the "the end of pure forgiveness."[134] It comes as no surprise, at least to me, that Derrida emphasizes that to achieve such a demonstration of kindness would require "an immense scene of confession in progress . . . a virtually Christian convulsion-conversion-confession" that can be effected without "need for the Christian church"[135]

Theological reflection upon forgiveness adds a further dimension to this relational aspect in addressing the psychological conditions that make possible the sort of internal revolution that conversion symbolizes. In this view, what one must comprehend on the question of supererogatory actions such as mercy is the proper, indeed temporal, relationship between grace and judgment on one hand and between forgiveness and repentance on the other.

If people are simply pleasure seekers and pain avoiders, then the relationship must move from back to front: judgment first and then, possibly, mercy or grace; repentance first and then, possibly, forgiveness. However, if people are meaning seekers; if they long for love, community, acceptance, and participation as fundamental to their humanity, then the equation must proceed exactly as written: mercy followed by judgment; forgiveness followed by repentance.

A key biblical text demonstrating this counterintuitive relation is the story of the repentant woman in the Gospel of Luke (7: 36–47). A woman who is a "sinner" (a euphemism for a prostitute) enters uninvited into a dinner given by a master of the law (Pharisee) because she wants to show reverence to Jesus in a way that manifests her sorrow over the life she has lived. She weeps at his feet as she anoints them. The legal scholar is repulsed since the class and purity codes common in first-century Palestine would find such comportment anathema.[136] Jesus, intuiting his embarrassment and disdain, then says to his host: "I tell you, her sins, which are many, are forgiven, for she loved much; but he who is forgiven little, loves little." The point of the story, in other words, is she is not weeping because she is seeking forgiveness; she is weeping because she has been forgiven. The outpouring of love is the result of the grace and mercy bestowed upon her.

The renowned theologian Paul Tillich adds a parallel interpretation of the story: "Jesus does not forgive the woman, but He declares that she is forgiven. Her state of mind, her ecstasy of love, show that something has happened to her. And nothing greater can happen to a human being than that he is forgiven. For forgiveness means reconciliation in spite of estrangement; it means reunion in spite of hostility; it means acceptance of those who are unacceptable; and it means reception of those who are rejected."[137] In like manner, Gregory Jones writes that the forgiveness one receives from God "is a judgment of grace that requires and enables our repentance."[138] On this view, one predicated upon a relational and participative ontology, the person living in fear, anger, and isolation is already suffering. Further pain, witnessed in the pejorative and venal behavior of the legalist in the story, reinforces her isolation and self-recrimination.

What Tillich and Jones are saying is that the act of kindness, the invitation to communion in spite of what one has done, is the decisive act that, at once, judges the conduct of the offender but in a way that invites her to measure the conduct she has shown to others against the unqualified acceptance with which she has been received. The lesson for us is plain: "We are to give up that judgmental*ism* by which we sit in self-righteous condemnation of others. We need to learn . . . how to receive and offer a discerning judgment that occasions new life."[139] Simply put, forgiveness is the path to reconciliation which occasions regret for past errors. That would be a primary task of a rehabilitated penal system. Like the guard at the gate of the Humaita Prison, its task is to remove the chains that bind the offender in shackles of denunciation and self-hatred and invite him or her into a communion without judgment that will, in turn, plant or nourish the seed of conversion. In such an atmosphere, to borrow a phrase from Charles Taylor, "we flourish even though we fail."[140]

This leads us back to the central issue we have raised throughout the book: the poverty of the moral language used in writing about and conceiving the dimensions of criminal justice. The prevailing discourse is incapable of offering such a life-giving and life-transforming message. The inevitable result of this truncated vision of the moral life is the "exceptionally negative," "degrading" atmosphere of the prison.[141]

Concluding Thoughts

I would like to conclude with some concrete pathways that might be adopted in a conversion model of confinement. I offer them somewhat reluctantly as I am convinced that no single discipline and, certainly, no single person is capable of charting the exact course that society should adopt in dealing with the very real and very troubling threats to the peace and safety of the body politic by individuals bent upon violence against others. The best one can do is make informed suggestions and invite observations to craft a system of justice and criminal detention that seeks to do no harm.

One area of both promise and concern is the relation between faith-based penal initiatives and the ideas being raised here.

There are numerous reasons to applaud this attempt to offer religious programs in a prison environment virtually "around the clock."[142] The movement traces its initiative to Charles Colson and the life-changing visit he made to the prison in Brazil we spoke of earlier. Like his associates who undertook the task of re-conceptualizing the role of the correctional facility, Colson wisely intuited the need to view the functional areas of institutional life as spheres of meaning whose discrete modes of action must be made into a unified whole. Describing the "Inner Change Freedom Initiative," the first of its kind in the United States, implemented at a Texas prison in 1997, Byron Johnson states that it "promotes adult basic education, vocational training, life skills, mentoring, and aftercare, while linking each of these components in a setting permeated by faith."[143] Furthermore, the anthropological assumption of the program is based on the belief "that men and women in prison are not incorrigible criminals. Instead . . . have the potential to be reformed."[144] Additionally, the curriculum is augmented by the important commitment to assure that the individual participant is aided, encouraged, and challenged by mentors who embody the level of spiritual development to which she or he is challenged to attain.[145]

In this scenario, there are certainly hints of and lines of connection with the virtuous prison or the "islands of civility" metaphor. In such a setting a buffer is established "against the assaults of the total institution."[146] To the degree that a penal system were to be organized to foster conversion, it would incorporate these positive guidelines. Unlike the faith-based model, however, selection would be universal rather than restricted to those drawn by a specific religious orientation. The entire facility would be organized to foster the progressive expansion of intellectual, moral, and spiritual vision but, due to its commitment to unity over dualism, would favor no specific secular or religious point of view.

Furthermore, the patient accompaniment of the confined person and the positive relational outcomes that flow naturally from the conversion experience would provide an ongoing barometer of the growth of what Giordano et al. call the "replacement self" or what the perennial tradition would term the "true self." In contrast to the "symbolic interactionism" of Goffman or the canons of behaviorism, there *is* a core self that is expressed in relations of equanimity and care, especially in moments of frustration that had previously summoned anger and asocial behavior. While it is possible to "manage" a given situation through a disingenuous demonstration of sociability, the moment to moment attentiveness, humility, and tolerance of the converted would be evident and impossible to feign over an extended period of time, thus verifying that a given person is ready to rejoin the wider community.[147]

All aspects of the schema we have presented avoid the obvious constitutional breach of fostering a religious denomination or metaphysical system of belief.[148] This latter trait is the criticism that can be brought against some of the faith-based ventures that are not only specifically Christian but also often take a disparaging if not hostile attitude toward those outside their theological purview. Colson himself, after diminishing the importance of all of the major religions, save his own, states: "So deeply ingrained in the human soul is the need for salvation, an answer to the dilemmas of life, that advertisers, philosophers, teachers, and others across the board attempt to address this deepest of all human needs. But the truth is that only Christianity deals directly with what individuals most long for: true redemption, true forgiveness of sin."[149] In a study of the various Christian prison experiments, Winnifred Fallers Sullivan observed evidence of a hyper-evangelicalism that centered around individual salvation for the born-again Christian and a smug dismissiveness of the validity of other expressions of belief. In one course regularly featured, entitled "Freedom From Addiction," participants were required to renounce sixty-five different non-Christian denominations, including New Age, Christian Science, Mormonism, Unitarianism, Buddhism, Hinduism, and Islam.[150]

The enclosed nature of the catechesis described above exemplifies Nock's employment of the term adhesion as a misguided synonym of conversion. No such provincialism can be countenanced in the portrait of a rehabilitated penal system that has been presented in this volume. As Becci accurately states, religious practice should lead one to overcome "feelings of revenge, sadness, and anger," not to mention mockery of other systems of belief or unbelief.[151]

The prison based on conversion has no need for self-selection. The only selection criteria would be a negative one: the vast majority of the men and women currently under lock and key in America have no need to be confined. As mentioned earlier in the chapter, patient mentoring, social support, and some introduction to unitive spiritual practices could and should empty out a large portion of the jail and prison population. Bail reform would release even more.[152]

The population that the prison should serve is precisely the people that no other program wants: the unrepentant; the cruel; the violent; and those who prey upon the weak, either physically, emotionally, or financially—in old school theology, "the damned." It is they who need to recover their natural belonging to the human community; it is they who are in need of the methodological discipline and gentle accompaniment that inevitably summon conversion; it is they whom the facility ought to welcome, and welcomed they should be. The chains should be removed and love should be shown to them. The rest is an act of faith in the goodness of human nature, the irresistible nature of grace and mercy, of kindness and attentiveness, and of a forgiveness that inevitably summons repentance.

Conclusion

WE BEGAN THIS theological rereading of criminal justice with the claim that a revolution is needed: one that demands far greater changes than attention to systemic details, be they mass incarceration, or decarceration, or even abolition; whether they be the lopsided demographic portrait of the imprisoned, or institutional violence, or which of the contending penal organizational theories is the most advantageous. What could be bigger or more important than any or all of these vital matters? The language we use to speak about them.

Without a commitment to life as sacred in each and all of its forms, without a commitment to the belief that there are ethical truths that precede the imprint of socialization, and without a commitment to the belief that all are ontologically directed to participation in ever-widening circles of inclusion and care, we are left to forage off the meager moral pickings of dualist social categories that can do no other than further divide an already fractured world.

The list of categories and "variables" is endless but all of the ones currently in the criminological vocabulary can do no other than label, compare, analyze, threaten, discipline, deter, rehabilitate, and punish to varying degrees those who are, to put it simply, different; and yet, in all things that matter, no different than ourselves.

In this, I share the "sentimental bias" of John Lofland that the only proper perspective is one that includes and embraces all social categories under the one "category of humanity." Therefore, to further his thought equation, to reduce anyone to a label other than that of one to whom I am intrinsically bound is to commit a "crime against humanity."[1]

I have attempted to show from a theological perspective (my own) that of all the static and oppositional systems and concepts, perhaps the most pressing one to address on the topic of criminal justice is that between science and religion.

That issue is important not only because the preceding chapters have emphasized the indelible trace of penitential and monastic influences on the inauguration and conceptual lexicon of criminal justice, but also because the way the world works and how people are affected by it matters as much to those of us who profess faith in a divine being as it does to those of us who do not. For Whitehead, such basic coherence is at least an implicit recognition that no element of the universe, no fact, can be isolated from its association with all others.[2] It is also a recognition that we can only be liberated from the dominance of a system for which coercive power is its stock in trade by something that in all conceivable ways eschews the use of such power.[3]

This need for a broader interpretive schema is very much in order in the discussion of criminal justice since, as Sutherland claims, criminology is not strictly scientific. He notes that science is directed to discover "general propositions of universal validity" by the analysis of "stable and homogeneous units."[4] Not only is human nature "endemically diversified, erratic and unpredictable," but also, beyond a coherent research design with the proper methodological framework for determining how offenders (and victims) are treated, there is more often than not a concern among criminologists (and other analysts of the justice system) with the ethical validity of those interventions.[5]

This concern with the ethical over the simply technical or pragmatic highlights a necessary tension—one that this book has been keen to explore: the tension that exists between the social and cultural structures that condition intersubjectivity on the one hand and "the self-transcendence of the intentional consciousness" on the other.[6] I have argued that this tension need not be hardened into competing frameworks. Rather, I have emphasized the non-duality of a significant portion of philosophical and social scientific literature that honors the dynamic relation between the transcendent dimension and the experiential with an overarching commitment to the primacy of the "we-relation."[7]

I have also repeatedly "demythologized" the church-state dichotomy by underscoring the possibility and unifying power of a joint, inclusive moral language that is shared among the humanities and the sciences, between believers and nonbelievers. This, in turn, creates the dialogical space for all disciplines to contribute to the conversation over social policy generally and correctional policy in particular. If Whitehead is correct, this union of perspectives is the basis of all creativity in its endless reach to move from disjointed existence or, as we have termed it, alienation, to what he terms "concrescence": " 'Creativity' is the universal of universals characterizing ultimate matter of fact. It is that ultimate experience by which the many, which are the universe disjunctively, become the one actual occasion, which is the universe conjunctively. It lies in the nature of things that the many enter into complex unity."[8]

Such agreements would enable social ethics to move beyond H. L. A. Hart's attenuated natural law theory of the state in which the minimum level of common agreement on moral rules is the only possible and necessary requirement to enable a society to remain viable.[9] In the manner of a retort, Robert Cover seeks a new context of "legal meaning" to supplant the current model in which the cultural world (nomos) of a given group is circumscribed by "arbitrary power and violence" due to its incoherence with prevailing judicial precedent. Instead, he claims, "we ought to invite new worlds."[10] Ronald Preston, in similar fashion, asserts that we must not content ourselves with envisioning the state as concerned "with no more than the question of how we can make the necessary technical arrangements to survive together; it must be concerned with richer, more common, human values than this."[11] It is no threat to democracy to believe in the fundamental goodness of its citizenry: a contention which, despite the mythic national doctrines of natural equality, has been undermined as a matter of course in the day-to-day experience of the poor and, especially, that of the confined population.

As I have noted in consort with many scholars, however truncated the current state of our common moral language may be, it bears the marks of the theological systems from which it grew. Marcel Gauchet writes that it is not coincidental that a religious worldview "preoccupied our forefathers and dominated practically all of history." He claims it represents a fundamental human longing "that even today resonates in our innermost being and whose imprint can be found in the very dispositions that have separated us from it. We have broken away from religion only by finding substitutes for it at every level."[12]

There can be no true interpretation of reality without taking the spiritual and religious into account and, doctrine notwithstanding, each of the great religious traditions orchestrate the irreducible value of life and its careful cultivation as essential commitments. This is not a question of imposing an absolute concept of the good in some architectonic sense. It is an affirmation of the fact that some conception of the good frames all partial conceptions since, as Taylor writes, one cannot know where one is in any theoretical or institutional framework unless one has determined where one is going.[13] I have attempted to show that all conceptions of the good in the modern history of penal discourse have led into a moral wilderness incapable of demonstrating to the millions trapped in the grip of the correctional empire what I suppose to be the most elemental of human moral expressions: that their lives are precious and they should never be harmed. With apologies to Durkheim, a new sociological paradigm is necessary to enable scholars to move beyond a binary worldview emphasizing the chasm between the sacred and the profane and the lawful and the outlaw to a perspective wherein "*nothing* here below is *profane* for those who know how to see."[14] For Derrida, it is to uplift the "sacredness of the human."[15]

A richer moral framework is also necessary to understand the most significant model of human development, echoed endlessly in theological, philosophical, and, increasingly, in social scientific literature: the rupturing of parochial barriers of knowledge, moral commitment, and consciousness that characterizes conversion.

I have argued that since conversion is the normal means of nurturing the creative impulse of which Whitehead speaks, most of the current uses of incarceration are meaningless. The goal of developing unitive consciousness infinitely surpasses the callow fascination with venting personal and social frustration by justifying the infliction of pain on someone else; such a goal provides an opportunity to cultivate life at a level at which rivalry and anger recede naturally by developing the practice of transcending the egoic fascination with separation and judgment. This is a discipline that completely forgoes the need for a disciplinarian.

Conversion is the most life-affirming and life-changing model for an institution whose purpose is to receive those members of society incapable of resisting the impulse to bring harm upon others. As I have stressed, to be faithful to the roots of confinement as a social practice, it is immoral to will or to bring harm upon the prisoner. What she or he requires is a daily framework to confront loneliness, anger, and the inevitable sorrow they produce in an atmosphere of accompaniment. Linda Ross Meyer sounds a lot like St. Benedict in her appeal for witnesses whose task it is to listen and offer comfort to the guilty. Such solace is needed, she observes, because in "causing, even innocently, a trauma of suffering, I am implicated in that pain . . . The more pain I cause, the more pain I will feel."[16] From a psychological point of view, what is required of the witness is compassionate presence more than a mastery of counseling techniques. Once again recalling Miller and Rollnick, it is "clear that it is possible to speed or facilitate change . . . The fascinating point is that so much change occurs after so little counseling"[17]

Simmel provides a compelling and disturbing portrait of the manner in which urban life both exacerbates the alienation that is the cause of so much misery and deadens the heart to feelings of remorse or compassion for those who have been harmed. The *"intensification of nervous stimulation"* produces a "blasé attitude" that "agitates the nerves to their strongest receptivity for such a long time that they finally cease to react at all."[18]

People who suffer loneliness, anxiety, and hostility to this extent are not in need of repudiation and further isolation; they are in desperate need of an environment like the Humaita Prison or the penitentiary envisioned by Dom Jean Mabillon, a seventeenth-century Benedictine historian. In an influential essay, Mabillon decried some monastic prisons of his day where wanton cruelty and general mistreatment had led those in their icy grip to "become insane, hardened or desperate." Conversely, he pondered the immeasurable good that would result if the confined "saw that one had compassion [for] them, that one tried to spare them as much as possible, that one assisted them in carrying out their penances, that one sustained them in their shame and humiliation." They then "might be touched by such charitable behavior and disposed to receive the impressions of grace," and (paraphrasing him) be drawn to spend the rest of their lives in the company of those who demonstrate such kindness.[19]

Everything in the nature of the ones who have acted cruelly is seeking participation, integration, and an honest confrontation with the pain they feel and the pain they have caused. Though perhaps muted by a lifetime of brutal memories, there is a persistent internal cry to allow the compassion in which they are ontologically rooted to flow out of them and, at the same time, have it flow into them. All they require for a conversion to this level of sociability is a safe and affirming environment and a proper balance of solitude and companionship. The goodness that resides at the center of all things will do the rest.

Notes

INTRODUCTION

1. Most works seeking to reform the practice of criminal justice from a theological perspective focus (rightly) on the very shortcomings detailed with great effectiveness by criminologists and social theorists: the unprecedented number of people in penal detention, especially in the United States but in many other nations as well; the disproportionate racial demographics of the sentenced population; the over-reliance on retribution as an institutional philosophy with the accompanying despair of mercy, decarceration, and a commitment to assure that the released offender be given the opportunity to return to society with a support network, educational and vocational training, and help with problems related to substance abuse. What they do not do adequately is address the fragile moral and philosophical assumptions underlying current penal practice, nor do they, by and large, point to institutional failure in terms of the rupture with and professed disregard for the theological sources that provided the basis for the practice of confinement as a social strategy. For works that seek penal reform from a denominational perspective, see Catholic Bishops of the United States, *Responsibility, Rehabilitation, and Restoration* (Washington, DC: U.S. Catholic Conference, 2000); Evangelical Lutheran Church in America, *The Church and Criminal Justice: Hearing the Cries* (Evangelical Lutheran Church, 2013); Unitarian Universalist Association, *Criminal Justice and Policy Reform*, 2005. Among the works that provide a critique of the penal system in terms of the conditions mentioned above but find no positive role for confinement other than selective incapacitation of those unwilling to conform to the social contract or offer appropriate repentance, see James Samuel Logan, *Good Punishment* (Grand Rapids, MI: Eerdmans, 2008); Laura Magnani and Herman L. Wray, *Beyond Prisons: Biblical Perspectives on Prison Abolition* (Minneapolis: Fortress, 2006); Christopher Marshall, *Beyond Retribution* (Grand Rapids, MI: Eerdmans,

2001); Gerald McHugh, *Christian Faith and Criminal Justice* (New York: Paulist, 1978); T. Richard Snyder, *The Protestant Ethic and the Spirit of Punishment* (Grand Rapids, MI: Eerdmans 2001). For works that offer critique of the retributive nature of contemporary penality and the prison as such but provide no clear understanding of either the history of confinement or a substantive account for addressing the truly violent, see Timothy Gorringe, *God's Just Vengeance* (Cambridge: Cambridge University Press, 1996); Lee Griffith, *The Fall of the Prison: Biblical Perspectives on Prison Abolition* (Grand Rapids, MI: Eerdmans, 1993); Mark Lewis Taylor, *The Executed God: The Way of the Cross in Lockdown America* (Minneapolis: Augsburg Fortress, 2001) [reprinted 2015]. For works that provide a theological defense of a limited retributivism, see Peter Paul Koritansky, *Thomas Aquinas and the Philosophy of Punishment* (Washington, DC: Catholic University of America, 2012); Oliver O'Donovan, *The Ways of Judgment* (Grand Rapids, MI: Eerdmans, 2005); Jean Porter, *Ministers of the Law* (Grand Rapids: Eerdmans, 2010).

2. Harold Berman, *Law and Revolution* (Cambridge, MA: Harvard University Press, 1983), 18–23.

3. Berman argues that the revolution that most dramatically impacted history, certainly in the West, was the declaration of Gregory VII making the Catholic Church independent of all outside political influence. The results included the beginning of secularism and a legal revolution that established the world's first universal legal system, canon law, as well as the foundations of the legal and judicial professions. See Berman, *Law and Revolution*, 49–50.

4. David Garland, *Punishment and Modern Society* (Chicago: University of Chicago Press, 1990), 292.

5. David Rothman is one of many authors who, while in no way endorsing the prescriptive claims I am making, points to the inherent contradictions at the root of contemporary penal models, particularly that of the Progressives in the late eighteenth century. See *Conscience and Convenience* (Boston: Little Brown, 1980). Other noted authors have pointed to the inherent incongruities involved in both justifying and maintaining the prison. See, e.g., Michel Foucault, *Discipline and Punish*, trans. Alan Sheridan (New York: Vintage, 1979); Michael Ignatieff, *A Just Measure of Pain* (New York: Columbia University Press, 1978); Blake McKelvey, *American Prisons: A History of Good Intentions* (Montclair, NJ: Patterson Smith,1977); Gresham Sykes, *The Society of Captives* (Princeton, NJ: Princeton University Press, 2007).

6. Mary Douglas, *How Institutions Think* (Syracuse, NY: Syracuse University Press, 1986), 45, 112.

7. Robert Cover, "Nomos and Narrative," *Harvard Law Review* 97 (1983): 4–68 at 4–5.

8. The concept of civil religion provides an example of this claim, whether in the writings of Rousseau, Comte, or Robert Bellah. The latter details the religious imagery in all American presidential inaugurals and its necessary, though neglected, role in providing a transcendent dimension that relativizes and contextualizes

discrete historical events. See Robert Bellah, "Civil Religion in America" in *Beyond Belief* (Berkeley: University of California Press, 1970), 168–190; Auguste Comte, *A General View of Positivism*, trans. J. H. Bridges (New York: Robert Speller, 1975), Ch. VI; Jean Jacques Rousseau, *The Social Contract*, trans. Wilmoore Kendall (Chicago: Henry Regnery, 1954), IV, 5–9. On the concept of epistemological crisis, see Alasdair MacIntyre, *Whose Justice? Which Rationality?* (South Bend, IN: Notre Dame University Press, 1988), 361–369.

9. Tal Asad argues that the "conceptual geography" of Christian and post-Christian history "has profound implications for the ways in which non-Western traditions are now able to grow and change." To study any religion, he argues, one must be familiar with "how 'religion' has come to be formed as concept and practice in the modern West." I think his remarks apply to the way law, justice, and forms of punishment have evolved in Christian history and have provided a significant portion of the judicial and moral templates that other traditions draw upon. See Tal Asad, *Genealogies of Religion* (Baltimore: Johns Hopkins University Press, 1993), 1.

10. Precisely because Purgatory functioned as a divine prison in which one served a penitential sentence, certain Catholic clergy made "indulgences" available that lessened the time of one's sentence if one contributed one's wealth to the support of the Church. See Henry Charles Lea, *A History of Auricular Confession and Indulgences in the Latin Church* (New York: Greenwood Press, 1968). On the development of the concept of Purgatory see, Jacque LeGoff, *The Birth of Purgatory*, trans. Arthur Goldhammer (Chicago: University of Chicago Press, 1981).

11. Andrew Skotnicki, "God's Prisoners: Penal Confinement and the Creation of Purgatory," *Modern Theology* 22 (2006): 85–110.

12. On the creation and continued relevance of Purgatory see, Richard Fenn, *The Persistence of Purgatory* (Cambridge: Cambridge University Press, 1995). On the normalization of the prison, see Edward Peters, "Prison Before The Prison" in *The Oxford History of the Prison*, eds. Norval Morris and David J. Rothman (New York: Oxford University Press, 1995), 3–47.

13. Wines was the secretary of the New York Prison Association, and Brockway was the warden of the Detroit House of Correction, soon-to-be warden of the Elmira Reformatory. Carl Schmidt writes: "All significant concepts of the modern theory of the state are secularized theological concepts." See Carl Schmidt, *Political Theology*, trans. George Schwab (Chicago: University of Chicago Press, 1985), 36. On the secularization of Christian millennial beliefs, see Christopher Lasch, *The True and Only Heaven* (New York: W. W. Norton, 1991).

14. Those of a more skeptical nature, like Brockway, maintained the wisdom of silence, but in his biography, he wrote: "[A]t the time of assuming management of the Elmira Reformatory I had emerged from the traditional theological or fictional stage of mental attitude into the evolutionary stage." See *Fifty Years of Prison Service* (New York: Charities Publication Committee, 1912), 174.

15. Michael Buckley, *At the Origins of Modern Atheism* (New Haven, CT: Yale University Press, 1987); Charles Taylor, *A Secular Age* (Cambridge, MA: Harvard University Press, 2007), Chs. 6–7.

16. "The treatment of criminals by society is for the protection of society. But since such treatment is directed to the criminal rather than to the crime, its great object should be his moral regeneration." *Transactions of the National Penal Congress on Penitentiary and Reformatory Discipline*, ed. E. C. Wines (Albany, NY: Argus, 1871), 541.

17. Perhaps the most influential of the American contributions at the Cincinnati Penal Congress were from Zebulon Brockway's groundbreaking innovations at the Detroit House of Correction. Also lauded were earlier experiments by Alexander Maconochie in Australia and especially the ticket of leave (later parole) and graded prisons utilized by William Crofton in Ireland. Brockway and others saw the reformatory as the institution capable of forming productive citizens in service to America and its thinly disguised mission to save the world. Zebulon Brockway, "The Ideal of a True Prison System for a State" and Sir Walter Crofton, "The Irish System of Prison Discipline" in Wines, *Transactions of the National Penal Congress*, 38–65, 66–74. On the reforms initiated by Maconochie, see Robert Hughes, *The Fatal Shore* (New York: Knopf, 1987).

18. David J. Rothman, *Conscience and Convenience*, 10.

19. Charles C. Cole, *The Social Ideas of the Northern Evangelicals 1826–1860* (New York: Octagon Books, 1977); Timothy L. Smith, *Revivalism and Social Reform* (New York: Abingdon, 1957).

20. Edward Shils writes that technological sociology is a "conception of society and of those within it which stresses the ordering of society in light of the progressive growth of rational-empirical knowledge. It serves power. Government is the independent variable; the subjects are dependent variables." It is "an aid in the execution of policy." Edward Shils, *The Calling of Sociology and Other Essays on the Pursuit of Learning* (Chicago: University of Chicago Press, 1980), 35–36. One example will serve to portray the conservative grammar of this ubiquitous methodology: the goal of "desistance" (or rehabilitation, if you will) is "a successful life course," "to settle down and become responsible," an "airtight" story of change; all of which are "corroborated by low self-reported deviance and the absence of recent arrests." See Peggy C. Giordano, Stephen A. Cernkovich, and Jennifer L. Randolph, "Gender, Crime, and Desistance: Toward a Theory of Cognitive Transformation," *American Journal of Sociology* 107 (2002): 990–1064 at 1001, 1028, 1031.

21. Garland, *Punishment and Modern Society*, 185. See also, McKelvey, *American Prisons*, 146.

22. Todd Clear, Patricia L. Hardyman, Bruce Stout, Karol Lucken, and Harry R. Dammer, "The Value of Religion in Prison," *Journal of Contemporary Criminal Justice* 16 (2000): 53–74 at 54.

23. Alasdair MacIntyre writes that in the current moral consensus in which individuals make up their own minds concerning their values and life course (within legal parameters), "[t]here are only two alternative modes of social life open to us, one in which the free and arbitrary choices are sovereign and one in which the bureaucracy is sovereign so that it may limit the free and arbitrary choices of individuals . . . Thus the society in which we live is one in which bureaucracy and individualism are partners and antagonists." See *After Virtue* (South Bend, IN: University of Notre Dame Press, 1981), 33.

24. Husserl writes that "in the transcendental sphere we have an infinitude of knowledge previous to all deduction, knowledge whose mediated connections . . . have nothing to do with deduction, and being entirely intuitive prove refractory to every methodically devised scheme of constructive symbolism." See Edmund Husserl, *Ideas: General Introduction to Pure Phenomenology*, trans. W. R. Boyce Gibson (London: George Allen & Unwin Ltd, 1931), 12. Maurice Merlau Ponty writes: "Consciousness is, therefore, coexistence with all being of which we can gain any knowledge." *The Primacy of Perception* (Chicago: Northwestern University Press, 1964), 55.

25. Jerome A. Miller, *In the Throe of Wonder* (Albany: State University of New York Press, 1992), 6.

26. Zygmunt Bauman, "Social Issues of Law and Order," *British Journal of Criminology* 40 (2000): 205–221 at 206.

27. Patrick McNamara, *The Neuroscience of Religious Experience* (Cambridge: Cambridge University Press, 2009), 231; T. Richard Snyder, *The Protestant Ethic and the Spirit of Punishment*, 11–15.

28. Owen Barfield, *Saving the Appearances* (New York: Harcourt Brace, 1965).

29. Lynne Anderson makes this point in an essay criticizing the conjoining of "legality" with emotional detachment—particularly regarding the feeling of empathy. See "Legality and Empathy," *Michigan Law Review* 85 (1987): 1574–1653.

30. Karl Jaspers, *The Origin and Goal of History* (New Haven, CT: Yale University Press, 1953), 1.

31. Ibid., 1, 6.

32. Richard Rohr, *Immortal Diamond, The Search for Our True Self* (San Francisco: Josey-Bass, 2013), 108, 112–114.

33. Alfred Schutz, *The Phenomenology of the Social World*, trans. George Walsh and Frederick Lehrer (Chicago: Northwestern University Press, 1967), 103; Shils. "The Calling of Sociology," 13–14.

34. Martin Heidegger, *Being and Time*, trans. John Macquarrie and Edward Robinson (New York: Harper & Row, 1962), 52.

35. Husserl, *Ideas*, 150.

36. Charles Taylor, *Sources of the Self* (Cambridge, MA: Harvard University Press, 1989), 137–142.

37. William James, *The Varieties of Religious Experience* (New York: Collier, 1961), Lectures 9–10.
38. James Q. Wilson, *Thinking About Crime*, Revised ed. (New York: Vintage, 1985).
39. Ibid., 145.
40. Jurgen Habermas, *Legitimation Crisis*, trans. Thomas McCarthy (Boston: Beacon Press, 1975), 4.
41. Ernst Troeltsch writes perceptively of the need to suspend judgment regarding the compromises made in Christian history with biblical and especially New Testament teaching. Such judgmental interpretations, so much a part of the polemics in the post-Reformation era and nineteenth-century historicism, miss the necessary "mutual inward penetration" of the church with the social system. The same can be said of penal history. See *The Social History of the Christian Churches*, Vol. I, trans. Olive Wyon (Chicago: University of Chicago Press, 1931), 204–207.
42. "What has been done in the past and is done today to those humans classified as deviant . . . is in many respects a crime against humanity." John Lofland, *Deviance and Identity* (Englewood Cliffs, NJ: Prentice Hall, 1969), 12. Laura Magnani and Harmon L. Wray state: "The penal system all too easily becomes the repressive arm of the state that reinforces the oppression of the exploited . . . the justice system . . . has become a monstrous crime against humanity." *Beyond Prisons*, 9. Jeffrie Murphy states that what is important in the legal curriculum is not just what is taught but what is omitted: "What is omitted is what makes our overall system of what we presume to call 'criminal justice' a disgrace to the ideals of the United States." See "'In the Penal Colony' and Why I Am Now Reluctant to Teach Criminal Law," *Criminal Justice Ethics* 33 (2014): 72–82 at 75.
43. Clifford Geertz, *The Interpretation of Cultures* (New York: Basic Books, 1973), 28–29.

CHAPTER 1

1. In speaking of the Pueblo Indians and their system of religious symbols, Carl Jung writes that such a transcendent worldview provides them "with a perspective (and a goal) that goes far beyond their limited existence. It gives them ample space for the unfolding of personality and permits them a full life as complete persons. Their plight is infinitely more satisfactory than that of a man in our own civilization who knows that he is (and will remain) nothing more than an underdog with no inner meaning to his life." See "The Importance of Dreams" in *Man and His Symbols*, ed. Carl Jung (New York: Dell, 1964), 3–94 at 76. On the influence of populist conceptions of criminal justice upon political rhetoric and institutional practice, see David Garland, *The Culture of Control* (Chicago: University of Chicago Press, 2002), 145–146; Julian V. Roberts, Loretta J. Stalans, and David Indemauer, *Penal Populism and Public Opinion: Lessons From Five Countries* (New York: Oxford University Press, 2002); Michael Tonry, "Rebalancing the Criminal Justice System

in Favour of the Victim: The Costly Consequence of Populist Rhetoric" in *Hearing the Victim: Adversarial Justice, Crime Victims and the State*, eds. Anthony Bottoms and Julian V. Roberts (Uffcolme, UK: Willan Publishing, 2010), 72–103.

2. "It is not possible to offer theological responses without making suggestions about a way of life, just as it is not possible to analyse the context and implications of criminological confusion without falling into questions about ways of life presupposed, promoted or hindered by the society whose responses to crime we are considering." David Jenkins, "Possible theological responses to apparent criminological confusion" in *The Coming Penal Crisis*, ed. A. E. Bottoms and R. H. Preston (Edinburgh: Scottish Academic Press, 1980), 173–213 at 194–195. On theology as a meta-discourse, see also John Milbank, *Theology and Social Theory* (Oxford: Blackwell, 1990), 1–2; Taylor, *Sources of the Self*, 41–52.

3. Tony Ward and Shadd Maruna shed further light upon the relation between destructive behavior and alienation. In their words, "the failure to meet the basic needs of autonomy, relatedness, and competence will inevitably cause psychological distress and will likely result in the adoption of maladaptive defenses." *Rehabilitation: Beyond the Risk Paradigm* (London: Routledge, 2007), 48.

4. "Precisely because punishment involves moral condemnation, but cannot by itself produce moral attachment, it serves to alienate further offenders rather than to improve their conduct." Garland, *Punishment and Modern Society*, 74–75. Malcolm Feeley and Jonathan Simon contend that punishment is a side effect in a system-wide policy to isolate the socially and economically marginal from the common life: "The new penology is neither about punishing nor about rehabilitating individuals. It is about identifying and managing unruly groups." See Malcolm Feeley and Jonathan Simon, "The New Penology," *Criminology* 30 (1992): 449–474.

5. Walter Wink phrases nicely what I perceive to be at the root of the metaethical crisis in the penal milieu: one that I hope to address by suggesting the frequent commensurability of religion and the social sciences. For that to take place, however, the materialist reluctance to countenance the insights offered by theological ethics must be overcome: "Christianity's lack of credibility is not a consequence of the inadequacy of its message, but the fact that its intrinsic message cannot . . . be communicated within a materialist cosmology." See *Unmasking the Powers* (Philadelphia: Fortress, 1986), 6.

6. Michael Sandel, *Liberalism and the Limits of Justice*, 2nd ed. (Cambridge: Cambridge University Press, 1998), x. As many readers know, John Rawls developed a highly influential procedural theory of justice based upon Utilitarian and Kantian moral commitments. He argued that if persons had no foreknowledge prior to birth of the conditions of their existence, they would adopt two principles: an expansive set of human rights (equal liberty) and a level of economic security that would provide a floor beneath which no one could descend (difference principle). See *A Theory of Justice* (Cambridge, MA: Harvard University Press, 1971).

7. Marie Gottschalk, *Caught: The Prison State and the Lockdown of American Politics* (Princeton, NJ: Princeton University Press, 2015), 17.

8. Ibid. Even the early American penal experiments were constantly evaluated in terms of economic pragmatism. See Andrew Skotnicki, *Religion and the Development of the American Penal System* (Lanham, MD: University Press of America, 2000), 68–83.

9. Garland, *The Culture of Control*, 18.

10. Wolf Heydebrand and Carroll Seron, *Rationalizing Justice: The Political Economy of Federal District Courts* (Albany: State University of New York Press, 1990), 13. On the influence of neoliberal economic policy on legal and penal systems, see Loïc Wacquant, *Punishing the Poor* (Durham, NC: Duke University Press, 2009).

11. The literature on this topic is vast. See, e.g., Michelle Alexander, *The New Jim Crow* (New York: New Press, 2010); Garland, *Culture of Control*; Gottschalk, *Caught*; Jeffrie Murphy, " 'In the Penal Colony' and Why I Am Now Reluctant to Teach Criminal Law"; Craig Haney, *Reforming Punishment* (Washington, DC: American Psychological Association, 2006); Wacquant, *Punishing the Poor*; James Whitman, *Harsh Justice* (Oxford: Oxford University Press, 2005).

12. Whitman, *Harsh Justice*, 23.

13. David Garland, *Punishment and Modern Society*, 6. The classic work detailing the demotion of rehabilitation is Francis Allen's, *The Decline of the Rehabilitative Ideal* (New Haven, CT: Yale University Press, 1981). There were also numerous studies that led to the crisis in rehabilitative confidence and a turn toward other, more punitive strategies. See American Friends Service Committee, *Struggle for Justice* (New York: Hill & Wang, 1971); Andrew Von Hirsch, *Doing Justice* (New York: Hill & Wang, 1976); Wilson, *Thinking About Crime*.

14. Habermas, *Legitimation Crisis*, 1–8.

15. Tom R. Tyler, *Why People Obey the Law* (New Haven, CT: Yale University Press, 1990), 26.

16. Ibid., 161.

17. Jeremy Travis, *But They All Come Back* (Washington, DC: Urban Institute, 2005), xix.

18. MacIntyre, *After Virtue*, 236.

19. Martin Buber, *I and Thou* (New York: Scribner, 1958).

20. Sykes, *The Society of Captives*, 18.

21. Various scholars have chronicled the ideological foundations of the penitentiary and have varying degrees of commitment to the religious foundations of the pro- totypical experiments at Auburn, New York and at the Eastern State Penitentiary in Philadelphia. Gustave de Beaumont and Alexis de Tocqueville stated that "the prisoner in the United States breathes in the penitentiary a religious atmos- phere." *On the Penitentiary System in the United States and Its Application to France* (Philadelphia: Carey, Lea & Blanchard, 1833), 94. David Rothman underplays the religious influence in favor of a more Jacksonian inspired vision for the nation and its institutions. *The Discovery of the Asylum* (Boston: Little, Brown, 1971), Chs. 3–4.

Adam Hirsch disagrees with Rothman's focus on Jacksonian influence, focusing, instead, upon pragmatic, social control emphases but, like him, downplays the religious influence. *The Rise of the Penitentiary* (New Haven, CT: Yale University Press, 1992). Michael Hindus offers a more Marxist inspired reading of the period in *Prison and Plantation: Crime, Justice, and Authority in Massachusetts and South Carolina, 1767–1878* (Chapel Hill: University of North Carolina Press, 1980). My own study argues that the combination of orthodox Calvinism and, especially, evangelical millennialism provided the dominant cultural sources for the movement. Skotnicki, *Religion and the Development of the American Penal System*.

22. Shadd Maruna, Louise Wilson, and Kathryn Curran, "Why God Is Often Found Behind Bars: Prison Conversions and the Crisis of Self-Narrative," *Research in Human Development* 3 (2006): 161–184 at 173.

23. Brockway, *Fifty Years*, 165.

24. Edgardo Rotman, *Beyond Punishment* (New York: Greenwood Press, 1990), 8.

25. Frank K. Willets and Donald M. Crider, "Religion and Well-Being: Men and Women in the Middle Years," *Review of Religious Research* 29 (1988): 281–294 at 281.

26. Rodney Stark, Lori Kent, and Daniel P. Doyle, "Religion and Delinquency: The Ecology of a 'Lost' Relationship," *Journal of Research in Crime and Delinquency* 19 (1982): 4–24 at 22.

27. Rodney Stark, *Why God? Explaining Religious Phenomena* (Conshohocken, PA: Templeton Press, 2017), 81.

28. Byron Johnson, *More God, Less Crime* (Conshohocken, PA: Templeton Press, 2011), Ch.1.

29. Michael Buckley, *At the Origins of Modern Atheism*, 39.

30. Gibson Winter, *Elements for a Social Ethic* (New York: Macmillan, 1966), 256.

31. Emmanuel Levinas, *Entre Nous: On Thinking of the Other*, trans. Michael B. Smith and Barbara Harshav (New York: Columbia University Press, 1998), 23, 27–28.

32. Thomas Hobbes, *Leviathan*, ed. C. B. McPherson (London: Penguin, 1968), IV, xlvi. Hobbes consciously spars with Aquinas's belief that the natural law is the moral trace of the eternal law of God in the human mind. For the latter, human laws proceed from and must necessarily cohere with the principles of natural law. See St. Thomas Aquinas, *Summa Theologica*, trans. Fathers of the English Dominican Province (New York: Benziger, 1947), I–II, q. 95.

33. Rousseau, *Social Contract*, IV, 8.

34. Ibid. On Machiavelli's suspicion of the Catholic Church, see Niccolo Machiavelli, *The Discourses*, trans. Leslie J. Walker (Harmondsworth: Penguin, 1988), I, xii.

35. Hobbes, *Leviathan*, II, xxviii.

36. Rousseau, *Social Contract*, II, 12.

37. Ibid., II, 5.

38. "It is very strange and unreasonable to suppose innate practical principles that terminate only in contemplation." John Locke, *An Essay Concerning Human*

Understanding (Oxford: Clarendon, 1924), I, III, 3. Locke used the term but, for him, it was the process retaining or "keeping . . . in view" ideas conceived through sensory experience or reflection upon that experience. Ibid., II, X, 1.

39. Ibid., I, II, 1.

40. Ibid., I, II, 15; II, I, 2.

41. Ignatieff, *A Just Measure of Pain*, 67–68.

42. Taylor, *Sources of the Self*, 169.

43. Locke, "Essay," II, XXVIII, 8.

44. Ibid., I, I, 5.

45. Taylor, *Sources*, 248.

46. "Pleasure and pain are the only springs of action in beings endowed with sensibility." Cesare Beccaria, *On Crimes and Punishments*, trans. Henry Paolucci (Indianapolis, IN: Bobbs-Merrill, 1963), Ch. VI. "Nature has placed mankind under the governance of two sovereign masters, pain and pleasure. They alone point out what we ought to do and determine what we shall do." Jeremy Bentham, *An Introduction to the Principles of Morals and Legislation* (London: Forgotten Books, 2012), I, 1. On the inhumane punishments regularly inflicted at the time, see John Howard, *Prisons and Lazarettos* (Montclair, NJ: Patterson Smith, 1974) [orig. pub. 1789]; Louis Masur, *Rites of Execution* (New York: Oxford, 1989); Randall McGowen, "The Body and Punishment in Eighteenth Century England," *The Journal of Modern History* 59 (1987): 651–679.

47. Quoted in Janet Semple, *Bentham's Prison* (Oxford: Clarendon, 1993), 25. See also Bentham *Introduction to the Principles*, I, 13, 2.

48. Ibid., XIII, 2, fn. 1.

49. Beccaria, *On Crimes and Punishments*, Ch. VI.

50. Bentham states that each human being "from the very constitution of his nature, prefers his own happiness to that of all sensitive beings put together." Quoted in Semple, *Bentham's Prison*, 22.

51. Bentham, *An Introduction*, I, 14.

52. Winter, *Elements for a Social Ethic*, 178.

53. "The idea of the modern constitutional state triumphed together with deism, a theology and metaphysics that banished the miracle from the world. The rationalism of the Enlightenment rejected exception in every form." Schmidt, *Political Theology*, 36–37.

54. Buckley, *Origins of Atheism*, 40. On the moral sense theorists and their Deist notions, see Taylor, *Sources of the Self*, 248–265.

55. Adam Smith, *The Theory of Moral Sentiments* (New York: Augustus M. Kelley, 1966), II, II, 2 [orig. pub. 1759].

56. Ibid., II, II, 1.

57. Ibid., I, I, 5.

58. MacIntyre writes that emotivism fails because it conflates personal preference and moral evaluation and yet "to a large degree people now think, talk and act *as if*

emotivism were true . . . [It] has become embodied in our culture." MacIntyre, *After Virtue*, 12, 21.

59. Friedrich Nietzsche, *The Genealogy of Morals*, trans. Carol Diethe (Cambridge: Cambridge University Press, 2007), 11.

60. Kant makes clear how difficult it is to judge properly between one's feelings about a given object or state of affairs and the actual reality one perceives: "All satisfaction . . . is itself sensation . . . Consequently everything that pleases is pleasant because it pleases . . . But if this be admitted, then impressions of Sense which determine the inclination, fundamental propositions of Reason which determine the Will, mere reflective forms of intuition which determine the Judgment, are quite the same, as regards the effect upon the feeling of pleasure . . . men could indeed blame each other for stupidity and indiscretion, but never for baseness and wickedness. For thus they all, each according to his own say of seeing things, seek one goal, that is, gratification." *Critique of Judgment*, trans. J. H. Bernard (New York: Barnes and Noble, 2005), I, 3. Linda Ross Meyer calls the reduction of Kant's ideas on justice to the exaltation of reason as opposed to correct judgment, "kanticism." *The Justice of Mercy* (Ann Arbor: University of Michigan Press, 2010), 9–21.

61. Kant thus rejects the "eudaimonism" of philosophers like Beccaria and Bentham for whom the desire to achieve a "hypothetical" goal of deterrence was more important than the criminal infraction. "The Metaphysics of Morals" in *Immanuel Kant: Practical Philosophy*, trans. Mary J. Gregor (New York: Cambridge University Press, 1996), 6: 331.

62. Kant, "Metaphysics of Morals," 6: 332.

63. Ibid.

64. Ibid., 6: 333.

65. For Taylor, the view of the self that is disengaged and in rational control was spearheaded by Descartes. It developed in full with Locke and the Enlightenment. Taylor states that "the 'punctual self' . . . gains its control through disengagement. [It] is always correlative of an 'objectification' . . . Objectifying a given domain involves depriving it of its normative force for us." *Sources of the Self*, 160. Max Weber is the author most identified with the term "disenchantment." "Science as a Vocation" in *From Max Weber*, trans. H. H. Gerth and C. Wright Mills (New York: Oxford University Press, 1946), 129–156 at 155. Christian Wiman writes of this disenchantment as cause for apprehensiveness: "Consciousness among contemporary Western intellectuals is an 'apprehensive' quality: that is to say, we become conscious by taking a hold of, or apprehending, ourselves and reality, by standing apart from them—and, not at all coincidentally (for where, exactly, are we standing?), we grow apprehensive as we do so. There are other, fuller ways of being in the world, which Eastern religions, as well as Christian mysticism, strive to articulate." Christian Wiman, *My Bright Abyss* (New York: Farrar, Strauss, and Giroux, 2013), 95.

66. Bernard Lonergan, S.J., *Method in Theology* (New York: Herder and Herder, 1972), 130.

67. John Milbank, *Being Reconciled* (London: Routledge, 2003), 8–10; Taylor, *Sources*, 139–142.

68. Milbank, *Being Reconciled*, 10; Augustine, "On True Religion" in *Augustine: Earlier Writings*, trans. John H. S. Burleigh (Philadelphia: Westminster, 1953), 39, 72. Augustine also writes: "Free will can also be understood to be given for this reason: if anyone uses it in order to sin, the divinity redresses him [for it]. This would happen unjustly if free will had been given not only for living rightly but also for sinning. How would God justly redress someone who made use of his will for the purpose for which it was given? Now, however, when God punishes the sinner, what does he seem to be saying but: 'Why did you not make use of free will for the purpose for which I gave it to you?'—that is, for acting rightly." See "On the Free Choice of the Will" in *On the Free Choice of the Will, On Grace and Free Choice and Other Writings*, ed. and trans. Peter King (Cambridge: Cambridge University Press, 2010), 2. 1. 3. 6.

69. *City of God*, trans. Henry Bettenson (Harmondsworth: Penguin, 1972), XIV, 7.

70. I capitalize "Church" when referring to the Roman Catholic Church, not as a means of comparison with other denominations but in its historical role in the development of law and systems of criminal justice. I use the lower case "church" when referring to religious denominations in general.

71. Milbank, *Being Reconciled*, 11–12.

72. Jean Delumeau, *Sin and Fear*, trans. Eric Nicholson (New York: St. Martin's, 1983), 5. See also Rene Girard, "Mimesis and Violence" in *The Girard Reader*, ed. James G. Williams (New York: Crossroad, 1996), 9–19 at 16–17.

73. Marcel Gauchet, *The Disenchantment of the World*, trans. Oscar Burge (Princeton, NJ: Princeton University Press, 1997), 35–36.

74. Schmidt, *Political Theology*, 36.

75. Aquinas, *Summa*, I–II, q. 90–95.

76. Zygmunt Bauman, "Legislators and Interpreters" in *Intimations of Postmodernity* (London: Routledge, 1995), 1–25 at 4.

77. Valerie Toureille discusses what she understands to be the commonly held misnomer that "la justice du Moyen Age ne serait qu'une parodie de justice, usant a l'occasion de procedes aussi cruels." *Crime Et Chatiment Au Moyen Age* (Paris: Editions de Seuil, 2013), 7–10. Regarding institutions of confinement, Guy Geltner states that the popular conception of the medieval prison as a "hell hole . . . is simply untenable." Rather, he states, "incarceration meant more than simple sequestering. Prison walls, rather than severing the inmate community from the outside world, actually helped structure prisoners' interaction with various members of free society." See *The Medieval Prison* (Princeton, NJ: Princeton University Press, 2008), 101, 106.

78. Gauchet, *Disenchantment*, 38. Irene Becci writes: "During the Reformation, the state lost its natural legitimacy and was newly conceived as a human necessity one had to accept because some kind of power was preferable to anarchy." *Imprisoned Religion* (Farnham Surrey: Ashgate, 2012), 9.

79. Harold Berman, *Interaction of Law and Religion* (Nashville: Abingdon, 1974), 109.

80. Milbank, *Theology and Social Theory*, 4. "What is the key to the social content of emotivism? It is the fact that emotivism entails the obliteration of any genuine distinction between manipulative and non-manipulative social relations." MacIntyre, *After Virtue*, 22. For a contrasting view that argues for a more robust moral consensus in liberal democracies than MacIntyre recognizes, see Nicholas Wolterstorff, *Justice: Rights and Wrongs* (Princeton, NJ: Princeton University Press, 2010).

81. "Any order is, after all, a desperate attempt to impose uniformity, regularity, and predictability on the human world, the kind of world that is endemically diversified, erratic, and unpredictable." Bauman, "Social Issues of Law and Order," 206.

82. Robert Cover, "Violence and the Word," *Yale Law Journal* 95 (1986): 1601–1639 at 1606–1607.

83. Ibid., 1609.

84. Rothman, *Conscience and Convenience*, 420.

85. Garland, *Punishment*, 3, 47.

86. Walter Wink, *Naming the Powers* (Philadelphia: Fortress, 1984), 135. Peter Berger and Thomas Luckmann make a similar argument (minus the theological language) about the determinative character of the spirit of an institution. *The Social Construction of Reality* (New York: Anchor, 1966), 53–72, 92–104.

87. Roberts et al., *Penal Populism*, 76–86.

88. William G. Staples, *Everyday Surveillance*, 2nd ed. (Lanham, MD: Rowman and Littlefield, 2014), 39.

89. David Garland writes that "it is clear enough that criminal conduct does not determine the kind of penal action that a society adopts . . . penal systems adopt their practices . . . in ways which are heavily mediated by individual considerations such as cultural conventions, economic resources, institutional dynamics, and political arguments." *Punishment*, 20. Edward Sutherland and Donald Cressy state that crime begins with the values hallowed by the politically powerful. Those who endanger or disregard those values are criminally negligent and they must endure coercive treatment as a consequence. *Criminology*, 10th ed. (New York: J. P. Lippincott, 1978), 12. See also Richard Quinney, *The Social Reality of Crime* (Boston: Little, Brown, 1979), 15–25.

90. Alan Hunt writes: "Moral regulation comprises 'moralization' rather than 'morality,' and thus is relational, asserting some generalized sense of the wrongness of some conduct, habit or disposition. One important aspect of moralization involves what Foucault has called 'dividing practices.'" See *Governing Morals: A Social History of Moral Regulation* (Cambridge: Cambridge University Press, 1999), 8.

91. Loic Wacquant argues that "mass incarceration" disguises the fact that class and race largely determine who goes to jail and prison. "Class, Race & Hyperincarceration in Revanchist America," *Daedalus* 139 (2010): 74–90. The elevation of the value of harm has been widely explored; see, e.g., Nils Christie, *Limits to Pain: The Role of Punishment in Penal Policy* (Eugene, OR: Wipf and

Stock, 1981); Todd Clear, *Harm in American Penology* (Albany: State University of New York Press, 1994); Garland, *Culture of Control*; Thomas Mathiesen, *Prison on Trial* (London: SAGE, 1990); Whitman, *Harsh Justice*.

92. MacIntyre, *After Virtue*, 2.

93. Dorothee Soelle, *Political Theology*, trans. John Shelley (Philadelphia: Fortress, 1974), 105.

94. Ibid., 105.

95. Mathiesen, *Prison On Trial*, 137–138.

96. Richard Rohr, *Simplicity* (New York: Crossroad, 2003), 80–81.

97. Timothy Barnes, *Constantine: Dynasty, Religion, and Power in the Later Roman Empire* (Chichester, UK: Wiley-Blackwell, 2013); *Caroline* Humfress, "Law and Legal Practice in the Age of Justinian" in *The Cambridge Companion to the Age of Justinian*, ed. Michael Maas (Cambridge: Cambridge University Press, 2005), 161–184. Numerous theologians and Christian philosophers have decried the negative influence of Christianity's establishment after the conversion of Constantine. See, e.g., Stanley Hauerwas and William H. Willimon, *Resident Aliens* (Nashville: Abingdon, 1989), Ch. 1; Soelle, *Political Theology*, 55; Taylor, *A Secular Age*, Ch. 15; John Howard Yoder, *The Politics of Jesus* (Grand Rapids, MI: Eerdmans, 1972).

98. On dualism in Christian thought, see Delumeau, *Sin and Fear*. Walter Wink writes that "the universe is late in arriving at awareness of itself as a unity . . . We can actually date the moment of its dawning in the axiological period." *Naming the Powers*, 114.

99. Berman, *Law and Revolution*, Ch. 2; Andrew Skotnicki, *The Last Judgment: Christian Ethics in a Legal Culture* (Farnham Surrey: Ashgate, 2012), 63–85.

100. Anselm of Canterbury, *Why God Became Man (Cur Deus Homo)*, trans. Joseph Colleran (Albany, NY: Magi, 1969).

101. Numerous scholars have pointed the finger of guilt to Anselm in the systematic reliance on retribution in Western jurisprudence. See, e.g., Cynthia Crysdale, *Embracing Travail* (New York: Continuum, 1999); Gorringe, *God's Just Vengeance*; Darby Kathleen Ray, *Deceiving the Devil* (Cleveland, OH: Pilgrim, 1998).

102. "[M]y reason convinces me that I ought not the less carefully to withhold belief from what is not entirely certain and indubitable, than from what is manifestly false, it will be sufficient to justify the rejection of the whole if I should find in each some ground for doubt" Rene Descartes, *Meditations*, trans. John Veitch (Buffalo, NY: Prometheus, 1989), Meditation I. Descartes's spiritual director, Cardinal Beruelle, encouraged the former's approach as an answer to the "skeptics and atheists" whose materialist assumptions needed to be met on their own ground. See Buckley, *Origins of Modern Atheism*, 72.

103. Taylor, *Sources*, 157. See also, Buckley, *At the Origins*, 69–98; Taylor, *A Secular Age*, 125–127.

104. Taylor, *Sources*, 177.

105. Berman, *Interaction of Law and Religion*, 109–110. On the "hyper-Augustinianism" of the leaders of the Reformation and Descartes's "disengaged reason," see Taylor, *Sources*, 246, 143–158.

106. Husserl, *Ideas, General Introduction to Pure Phenomenology*, 81.

107. George Herbert Mead, *On Social Psychology* (Chicago: University of Chicago Press, 1956), 21, 23, 25.

108. Husserl, *Ideas*, 82.

109. Garland, *Punishment and Modern Society*, 9.

110. On situational and dispositional variables, see Lee Ross and Donna Shestowsky, "Contemporary Psychology's Challenges to Legal Theory and Practice," *Northwestern University Law Review* 97 (2003): 1081–1114.

111. Lofland, *Deviance and Identity*, 9.

112. "We must see to it with scrupulous minuteness that we do not put into the experience anything which is not really included in the essence, and that we 'lay it in' precisely in the way in which it already 'lies' in the essence itself." Husserl, *Ideas*, 265. On the concept of a second naivete, see Paul Ricoeur, *The Symbolism of Evil*, trans. Emerson Buchanan (Boston: Beacon, 1967), 351–353.

113. Wink, *Naming the Powers*, 141–142; G. G. Scholem, *Major Trends in Jewish Mysticism* (New York: Schoken, 1965), 46–47. Freud constructed his anthropological and moral insights into the psyche by the employment of the myths of Oedipus and the murder of the primal father. On Oedipus, see Sigmund Freud, *The Ego and the Id*, trans. Joan Riviere (New York: Norton, 1960), Ch. 3; on the primal father, see *Totem and Taboo* trans. A. A. Brill (London: George Routledge, 1919), IV, 5. Jung perceived primordial archetypes as the driving force in human social and psychological development. Carl Jung, *The Collective Unconscious and Its Archetypes* (Ghent: Satsang, 2010).

114. Immanuel Kant, "Groundwork of the Metaphysics of Morals" in *Kant: Practical Philosophy*, 4: 433–34, 437.

115. Mathiesen writes that "for prison to lose its irrational grip, the very concept of 'crime' has to be abandoned as a tool." See *Prisons on Trial*, 168.

116. Norval Morris, "Race and Crime: What Evidence Is There That Race Influences Results in the Criminal Justice System?," *Judicature* 72 (1988): 111–113 at 113. Among the works pointing to the historical linking of race and criminality, see W. E. B. Dubois, *The Souls of Black Folk* (New York: Signet, 1969):199–202; Elizabeth Hinton, *From the War on Poverty to the War on Crime* (Cambridge, MA: Harvard University Press, 2016); Hindus, *Prison and Plantation*; Khalil Gibran Muhammad, *The Condemnation of Blackness* (Cambridge, MA: Harvard University Press, 2010). On the new penology and its selective determinations of "risk," see Alexander, *The New Jim Crow*; Feeley and Simon, "The New Penology"; Garland, *Criminology* 30 (1992): 449–474; Garland, *Culture of Control*; Naomi Murakawa, *The First Civil Right* (Oxford: Oxford University Press, 2014); Wacquant, *Punishing the Poor*.

117. Troy Duster, "Crime, Youth, Unemployment, and the Black Urban Underclass," *Crime and Delinquency* 33 (1987): 300–316 at 303.

118. Michael Hardt and Antonio Negri, *Empire* (Cambridge, MA: Harvard University Press, 2000); Wacquant, *Punishing the Poor*. David Rothman's historical perspective reveals that immigrants, the poor, and the mentally ill have been long fated to pay the price of their alienated status behind bars: "Since inmates . . . were typically the immigrant and the poor, incarceration seemed a convenient policy, at least to a society that was acutely apprehensive about alien hordes and dangerous classes." *Conscience and Convenience*, 23.

119. Wacquant, *Punishing the Poor*, xviii.

120. Joan Petersilia, *When Prisoners Come Home* (Oxford: Oxford University Press, 2003); Travis, *But They All Come Home*; Bruce Western and Becky Pettit, "Incarceration and Social Inequality," *Daedalus* 139 (2010): 8–19.

121. Mathiesen, *Prison on Trial*, 70–71.

122. Foucault, *Discipline and Punish*, 207; Feeley and Simon, "The New Penology," 468.

123. Selective incapacitation as a correctional strategy emerged in the wake of the influential work of James Q. Wilson who argued that a significant percentage of "crime" was committed by a small percentage of the population. Crime rates would fall dramatically, he argued, if these repeat offenders were aggressively sequestered. *Thinking About Crime*, Ch. 8. On the link between repressive social structures and mental illness, see Haney, *Reforming Punishment*, 244–245; Wink, *Naming the Powers*, 108–111.

124. Ronald Goldfarb, *Jails: The Ultimate Ghetto* (Garden City, NY: Anchor, 1975), 4. John Irwin makes a similar argument, terming those minor deviants without social capital, "the rabble." *Jail* (Berkeley: University of California Press, 1985), 2. The derivation of the jail from the workhouse in England and Holland has been well-documented. See Randall McGowen, "The Well-Ordered Prison" in Norval Morris and David Rothman, eds. *The Oxford History of the Prison* (New York: Oxford University Press, 1995), 79–109; David Garland, *Punishment and Welfare* (Aldershot: Gower, 1985), 37–40; Thorsten Sellin, *Slavery and the Penal System* (New York: Elsevier, 1976), 23–24, 71–74. On the concept of "waste management," see Feeley and Simon, "The New Penology," 470. On penal institutions as the new asylums see, Garland, *Culture of Control*, 178–179. Gottschalk takes issue with the claim that the carceral state focuses unduly on racial minorities. Rather, she claims, not unlike Goldfarb and Irwin, that its target is a far broader range of "partial citizens." *Caught*, 242.

125. Diana Gordon, *The Justice Juggernaut* (New Brunswick, NJ: Rutgers University Press, 1990), 164. David Garland makes a similar point in his description of the operational concept he terms "criminologies of everyday life." *Culture of Control*, 127–131.

126. Milbank, *Theology and Social Theory*, 105–106.

127. Levinas, *Entre Nous*, 8.

128. Pope Francis, as quoted by Gerard O'Connell, "Pope Francis Opens Holy Door says: 'We Have to Put Mercy before Judgment,'" *America Magazine*, December 8, 2015. http://americamagazine.org/content/dispatches/pope-francis-opens-holy-door-says-we-have-put-mercy-judgment.

129. Bryan Stephenson, *Just Mercy* (New York: Spiegel & Grau, 2014), 294.

130. Levinas, *Entre Nous*, 66.

131. Schutz quoted in Winter, *Elements*, 96.

CHAPTER 2

1. Parts of this chapter derived from a paper, "Theological Perspectives on Wrongdoing, Punishment, and Forgiveness," presented at the "Interdisciplinary Roundtable on Punitiveness in America" at John Jay College in New York City in April 2015 and from, "Punishment and the Limits of Love," *Journal of Catholic Social Ethics* 13 (2016): 261–284.

2. Aquinas, *Summa*, I–II, q. 46, a. 6.

3. Sutherland and Cressey, *Criminology*, 24. Gresham Sykes states: "Imprisonment should be punishment, not only by depriving the individual of liberty but also by imposing painful conditions under which the prisoner must live within the walls." Sykes, *The Society of Captives*, 9.

4. Haney, *Reforming Punishment*, 70. See also Clear, *Harm in American Penology*; Whitman, *Harsh Justice*.

5. A significant percentage of people who are incarcerated are there for social and genetic conditions (poverty, race, and ethnicity) rather than for serious infractions. I use "asocial" to denote doing deliberate harm to others. I am not referring to what are called "nuisance crimes" that "exclude 'disorderly' individuals from public spaces wherever they are seen as interfering with commercial interests or the 'quality of life' demanded by more affluent residents." See Garland, *Culture of Control*, 178–179. John Irwin refers to most of those in America's jails as guilty of "crimes of restricted relevance." *Jail*, 16. See also, Goldfarb, *Jails*, 3–4. For a study detailing how the poor are more and more being restricted from public spaces for the reasons alluded to above and punished for violating the terms of expulsion, see Katherine Becket and Stephen Herbert, *Banished*. The racial overtones of such an approach are addressed in Alexander, *The New Jim Crow*; Jerome G. Miller, *Search and Destroy*, 2nd ed. (Cambridge: Cambridge University Press, 2010); Khalil Gibran Muhammad, *The Condemnation of Blackness*.

6. Aquinas, *Summa*, II–II, q. 108, a. 4. Aquinas has a much thicker understanding of punishment than these references reveal. In fact, there is a clear retributive component (e.g. *Summa*, I–II, q. 87, a. 1, 6) as well as a reformist one. I am using the definition due to its clarity and adopting the medicinal metaphor since it is the one that I think best conforms to the original understanding of confinement. For my own critique of St. Thomas and, in particular, the way that his ideas on

punishment have been underrepresented in Catholic doctrine, see Skotnicki, "Punishment and the Limits of Love," 271–276.

7. Walter Wink summarizes Andrew Bard Schmookler's thesis that human beings did not exhibit violent tendencies toward their fellows until the development of agriculture. The latter, in turn, spurred population growth, conflict with neighboring clans, and the rise of authoritarian figures to galvanize group fear. Schmookler, *The Parable of the Tribes: The Problem of Power in Social Evolution* (Berkeley: University of California Press, 1984); Walter Wink, *Engaging the Powers* (Minneapolis: Fortress, 1992), 39–43.

8. Quoted in Alex Tuckness and John M. Parrish, *The Decline of Mercy in Public Life* (New York: Cambridge University Press, 2014), 92.

9. Ibid., 93.

10. The movement to reframe the justice system in terms of repairing relationships is the hallmark of the Restorative Justice movement. As Howard Zehr writes, it is predicated upon "changing the lens," of criminal justice from one that is adversarial to one that is relational or restorative. Despite the different approaches of its advocates, and the critiques to which it is subject, the reconciliatory nature of its methodology is forwardly placed in the literature. See, e.g., John Braithwaite, *Restorative Justice and Responsive Regulation* (Oxford: Oxford University Press, 2002); Howard Zehr, *Changing Lenses* (Scottdale, PA: Herald Press, 1990).

11. Taylor, *A Secular Age*, 302. Karl Menninger phrases this invulnerability somewhat sarcastically but not without justification: "Perhaps our worse crime is ... our love of vindictive justice, our generally smug detachment, and our prevailing public apathy." *The Crime of Punishment* (New York: Viking, 1968), 3–4.

12. James Whitman, *The Origins of Reasonable Doubt* (New Haven, CT: Yale University Press, 2008), 211–212.

13. Pieter Spierenburg, *The Spectacle of Suffering* (Cambridge: Cambridge University Press, 1984). See also Ann Douglas, *The Feminization of American Culture* (New York: Knopf, 1977); McGowen, "The Body and Punishment in Eighteenth Century England"; Svend Ranulf, *Moral Indignation and Middle Class Psychology* (New York: Schocken, 1964).

14. Ignatieff, *A Just Measure of Pain*, 75–76.

15. The moral summons to abandon punishment was the subject of Karl Menninger's classic study: "All legal sanctions involve penalties for infraction. But the element of punishment is an adventitious and indefensible *additional* penalty; it corrupts the legal principle of *quid pro quo* with a 'moral' surcharge. Punishment is in part an attitude, a philosophy. It is the deliberate infliction of pain in addition to or in lieu of penalty. It is the prolonged and excessive infliction of penalty, or penalty out of all proportion to the offense." See Menninger, *The Crime of Punishment*, 203.

16. I am consciously using the terminology of John Braithwaite here. He emphasizes the importance of shaming as a necessary step in the process of reintegration. He distinguishes between shaming that integrates by recognizing the humanity of

the offender and shaming that labels and stigmatizes the offender. He calls the latter "disintegrative." *Crime, Shame, and Reintegration* (Cambridge: Cambridge University Press, 1989), 55.

17. Linda Ross Meyer has a similar understanding of punishment: "Wrong is no longer the irrational but the indifferent . . . to our nature as 'with others.' Punishment is no longer the universalizing of a maxim but the pain of a shared remembering of one's self-alienation from the connection and responsibility for others." *The Justice of Mercy*, 4. Haney, in like manner, contends that the suffering of prisoners is contained in their isolation from the world they knew; intending anything more would be the infliction of "gratuitous pain." See *Reforming Punishment*, 308.

18. Blaise Pascal, *Pensees*, trans. W. F. Trotter (New York: Modern Library, 1941), II, 131.

19. St. Benedict, *Benedict's Rule*, trans. Terrence Kardong (Collegeville, MN: Liturgical Press, 1996), Ch. 27.

20. Tanya Erzen, *God in Captivity* (Boston: Beacon, 2017), 22–25; Maruna et al, "Why God is Often Found Behind Bars: Prison Conversions and the Crisis of Self-Narrative," *Research in Human Development* 3 (2006): 161–184.

21. Arthur Shuster, *Punishment and the History of Political Philosophy* (Toronto: University of Toronto Press, 2016), 138–139.

22. Ronald Dworkin, *Taking Rights Seriously* (Cambridge, MA: Harvard University Press, 1977), 15.

23. Traditional Catholic theology uses restoring the balance of justice in its justification for punishment. See Anselm of Canterbury, *Why God Became Man* trans. Joseph M. Colleran (Albany, NY: Magi, 1969); St. Thomas Aquinas, *Summa Theologica*, I-II, 87, 6; II-II, 108, 4. Just deserts, or the punishment fitting the crime, is found in numerous works, for example, Ernest Van Den Haag, *Punishing Criminals* (New York: Basic Books, 1975); Andrew Von Hirsch, *Doing Justice* (New York: Hill & Wang, 1976). The "lex talionis," aside from its place in the Hebrew Bible (Ex. 21: 22–25; Lev. 24: 17–21), is invoked by Immanuel Kant: "[O]nly the *law of retribution (ius talionis)* . . . can specify definitely the quality and the quantity of punishment." "The Metaphysics of Morals," 6: 332. The idea of negating the negation is found in Hegel, *Philosophy of Right*, trans. T. M. Knox (London: Oxford University Press, 1952), 97. The unfair advantage theory is often associated with Herbert Morris. See "Persons and Punishment," *The Monist* 52 (1968): 475–501. On the educational theory and expressive theories of punishment, the latter sensitive to the needs of victims, see Jean Hampton, "The Moral Education Theory of Punishment, *Philosophy and Public Affairs* 13 (1984): 208–238; "An Expressive Theory of Retribution" in *Retributivism and Its Critics*, ed. Wesley Cragg (Stuttgart: F. Steiner, Verlag, 1992), 1–25. On the notion of communal solidarity, see Emile Durkheim, *The Division of Labor in Society*, trans. W. D. Halls (New York: Free Press, 1984), 60–64; Joel Feinberg, "The Expressive Function of Punishment" in *Doing and Deserving* (Princeton, NJ: Princeton University Press, 1970), 95–118.

24. Quoted in Bruce N. Waller, *Against Moral Responsibility* (Cambridge, MA: MIT Press, 2011), 16.

25. H. L. A. Hart, *Punishment and Responsibility* (Oxford: Clarendon, 1968), 28.

26. Garland, *Punishment and Welfare*, 17. Jonathan Simon writes: ". . . the neo-liberal techniques re-emphasize the individual as a critical manager of risk. . . . The new strategies aim to hold the individual more accountable." "Governing Through Crime" in *The Crime Conundrum*, ed. Lawrence M. Friedman and George Fisher (Boulder, CO: Westview, 1997), 171–189 at 177–178.

27. Meir Dan-Cohen quoted in Meyer, *The Justice of Mercy*, 14–15.

28. Von Hirsch, *Doing Justice*, 49.

29. Hegel, *Philosophy of Right*, 93, 97, 100.

30. Wollerstorff, *Justice: Rights and Wrongs*, 4, 106.

31. R. A. Duff, "Punishment and Penance—A Reply to Harrison," *The Aristotelian Society* 62 (1988): 153–167 at 155–157.

32. Feinberg, "The Expressive Function," 97–98.

33. Von Hirsch, *Doing Justice*, 6.

34. "The rekindling of the 'just deserts' approach has helped to restore the focus on the criminal act rather than the criminal actor." Malcolm Davies, *Punishing Criminals* (Westport, CT: Greenwood Press, 1993), 10.

35. Michael J. Sandel, *Liberalism and the Limits of Justice*, 2nd ed. (Cambridge: Cambridge University Press, 1998), 1.

36. Immanuel Kant, *Religion Within the Boundaries of Mere Reason*, trans. Alan Wood and George DiGiovanni (Cambridge: Cambridge University Press, 1998), 6: 41.

37. Van den Haag, *Punishing Criminals*, 11, 16–17, 57–58.

38. Von Hirsch, *Doing Justice*, 40.

39. Kant, "The Metaphysics of Morals," 6: 231, 256–257.

40. R. A. Duff, "Restorative Punishment and Punitive Restoration" in *Restorative Justice and the Law*, ed. Lode Walgrave (Cullompton, UK: Willan, 2002), 82–100 at 92. Durkheim, *The Division of Labor in Society*, 44–52.

41. Joseph Raz, *The Authority of Law*, 2nd ed. (Oxford: Oxford University Press, 2009), 104.

42. Carl Schmidt speaks of the noted legal scholar Hans Kelsen who "stressed since the 1920's the methodical relationship of theology and jurisprudence . . . At the foundation of his identification of state and legal order rests a metaphysics that identifies the lawfulness of nature and normative lawfulness." Schmidt, *Political Theology*, 40–41.

43. I am thinking here of Eastern as well as Western religions, not only with the concept of karma but also in sacred lore such as Krishna ordering Arjuna to slay the rebellious warriors, Bhishma and Drona. See *Bhagavad Gita*, Second Teaching.

44. Leibniz as quoted in Schmidt, *Political Theology*, 37. Schmitt goes on to comment on the similarities between jurisprudence and theology: "Both have a double principle, reason (hence there is a natural theology and a natural jurisprudence) and

scripture, which means a book with positive revelations and directives." *Political Theology*, 37–38.

45. Karl Rahner, *Foundations of Christian Faith*, trans. William V. Dych (New York: Seabury Press, 1978), 105.

46. Ibid., 52, 97–105. It is thus that Heidegger claims that those who confront their past with "resolution" hear the conscience cry, "guilty." *Being and Time*, 322.

47. Moses Maimonides, *The Guide of the Perplexed*, trans. Shlomo Pines (Chicago: University of Chicago Press, 1963), I, 31, 34.

48. Al-Ghazzali, *Al-Ghazzali on Repentance*, trans. M. S. Stern (New Delhi: Sterling, 1990), 42–43.

49. Alan Bernstein, *The Formation of Hell* (Ithaca, NY: Cornell University Press, 1993), 3, 154–161.

50. David Burrell, *Towards a Jewish-Christian-Muslim Theology* (Chichester: Wiley-Blackwell, 2011), 87, 96.

51. Martin Luther, "Secular Authority: To What Extend Should It Be Obeyed?" in *Martin Luther: Selections from His Writings*, ed. John Dillenberger (Garden City, NY: Anchor, 1961), II.

52. "[Christians] consider in humility the sins which have moved God's indignation so that he has filled the world with dire calamities. And although they are free from criminal and godless wickedness, still they do not regard themselves as so far removed from such wrongdoing as not to deserve to suffer the temporal ills which are the recompense of sin." St. Augustine, *City of God*, trans. Henry Bettenson (Harmondsworth: Penguin, 1984), I, 9. Herbert Fingarette writes that in the Hebrew Scriptures "a primary mode, perhaps *the* primary mode, of our relationship to God is that of responsibility to the law. According to this view, God's will is our law; the authority even of human law lies in its claim to express, or at least to implement, God's will." "The Meaning of Law in the Book of Job" in *Revisions*, eds. Stanley Hauerwas and Alasdair MacIntyre (South Bend, IN: University of Notre Dame Press, 1983), 249–286 at 250. See also Remi Brague, *The Law of God*, trans. Lydia G. Cochrane (Chicago: University of Chicago Press, 2008), 41–49.

53. John Calvin, *The Institutes of the Christian Religion*, trans. Henry Beveridge (Grand Rapids, MI: Eerdmans, 1953), IV, 10, 25.

54. John Neville Figgis, *The Divine Right of Kings* (New York: Harper, 1965), 5–6.

55. Erzen, *God in Captivity*, 18.

56. Paul Simpson Duke, *The Parables* (Nashville: Abingdon, 2005), 50–51.

57. Samuel Y. Edgerton, Jr, *Pictures and Punishment* (Ithaca, NY: Cornell University Press, 1985), 27.

58. Ibid., 23.

59. Ibid., 15–16, 132. Johan Huizinga writes: "During the Burgundian terror in Paris in 1411, one of the victims . . . being requested by the hangman, as was the custom, to forgive him, is not only ready to do so with all his heart, but begs the executioner to

embrace him. There was a great multitude of people, who nearly all wept hot tears." *The Waning of the Middle Ages* (Garden City, NY: Doubleday, 1954), 11–12.

60. Luther, "Secular Authority," I, V; Augustine, *City of God*, XIX, 17. Oliver O'Donovan writes: "For the proposition that the authority of the government resides *essentially* in the act of judgment, we must turn to the New Testament where St Paul described the function of civil authority as to reward the just and punish the evil" (Rom 13: 4). *The Ways of Judgment* (Grand Rapids, MI: Eerdmans, 2005), 4.

61. Luther, "Secular Authority," I, VI.

62. For contrasting views on Paul and his use of the law, see E. P. Sanders, *Paul, the Law, and the Jewish People* (Philadelphia: Fortress, 1983); Francis Watson, *Paul and the Hermeneutics of Faith* (London: T&T Clark, 2004).

63. Luke Timothy Johnson, *Reading Romans* (New York: Crossroad, 1997), 185, 189–190.

64. Ernst Kasemann, *Commentary on Romans*, trans. Geoffrey W. Bromily (Grand Rapids, MI: Eerdmans, 1980), 351, 354.

65. On legal ethics, see Eliezer Berkovits, *Essential Essays on Judaism*, trans. David Hazony (Jerusalem: Shalem Press, 2002); Mark Biddle, *Missing the Mark: Sin and Its Consequences in Biblical Theology* (Nashville: Abingdon, 2005); Roland DeVaux, *Ancient Israel: Its Life and Institutions*, trans. John McHugh (New York: McGraw Hill, 1961), 149–161. On the infrequency of the death penalty after the exile, see E. Christian Brugger, *Capital Punishment and Roman Catholic Tradition* (South Bend, IN: University of Notre Dame Press, 2003), Ch. 3.

66. J. A. T. Robinson is one of many scholars who do not see the passage in Romans as antithetical to Paul's overall theological schema: "[Paul] never purchases his high doctrine of the church at the expense of a low doctrine of the state." *Wrestling with Romans* (Philadelphia: Westminster, 1979), 137. On the Christian obligation to obey the government save in any attempt to force Christians to act or believe in defiance of their faith, see Luther, "Secular Authority," II.

67. For a summary of O'Donovan's position, see Stanley Hauerwas, "Punishing Christians" in *Performing the Faith* (Grand Rapids, MI: Brazos, 2004), 185–200 at 190–195. O'Donovan writes: "So although private vengeance has to be condemned, the desire for vengeance must be allowed its proper point of entry into the public realm, where it both commands and legitimates political authority." *The Ways of Judgment* (Grand Rapids, MI: Eerdmans, 2005), 25.

68. Saint Augustine "On the Predestination of the Saints" in *A Select Library of the Nicene and Post-Nicene Fathers of the Christian Church*, Vol. 5, trans. Peter Homes and Robert Ernest Wallis (Edinburgh, T&T Clark, 1887), Ch. 16.

69. Pelagius was a fifth-century theologian whose work denied the reality of original sin and asserted that humans were capable of achieving a virtually sinless life.

70. Calvin, *Institutes*, III, 21, 5.

71. On the influence of Puritan Calvinism on the American ethos, see Ann-Marie Cusac, *Cruel and Unusual: The Culture of Punishment in America* (New Haven,

CT: Yale University Press, 2009), Ch. 1; James A. Morone, *Hellfire Nation: The Politics of Sin in American History* (New Haven, CT: Yale University Press, 2003), Chs. 1–2; Kai Erikson, *Wayward Puritans* (New York: Wiley, 1966).

72. Perry Miller, *The New England Mind: The Seventeenth Century* (Cambridge, MA: Harvard University Press, 1939), 49.

73. Erikson, *Wayward Puritans*, 48.

74. Ibid., 190.

75. It is true that, unlike Luther for whom the value in law was to remind sinners of their incorrigible nature and justify their righteous punishment, Calvin affirmed a third pedagogical function of law that enabled persons to pattern their so-cial behavior in conformity to legislative demands. Proceeding from this, and aided immeasurably by the optimism and social reformist agenda of the Second Great Awakening, many of the evangelicals in nineteenth-century America who championed the penitentiary were Calvinists who would have subscribed to this use of the law to imbue virtuous habits upon those whose former lives may have lacked the necessary discipline and structure. But they were fiercely opposed by the "old lights" who strictly maintained that fallen humanity was doomed to repression in this life and eternal punishment in the next. See W. D. Lewis, *From Newgate to Dannemora* (Ithaca, NY: Cornell University Press, 1965), 57–63, 72–77; Andrew Skotnicki, *Religion and the Development of the American Penal System*, 24–26, 68–79; Smith, *Revivalism and Social Reform*, 143–149.

76. T. Richard Snyder, *The Protestant Ethic and the Spirit of Punishment*, 12.

77. Hunt, *Governing Morals*, 198.

78. St. Anselm, *Proslogion*, trans. M. J. Charlesworth (Oxford: Clarendon, 1965), Ch. X.

79. St. Anselm, *Why God Became Man*, I, 11, cf. I, 22.

80. Ibid., I, 19.

81. Ibid., II, 6.

82. Calvin, *Institutes*, III, 20, 45. Tuckness and Parrish claim that Luther and Calvin restated the basic ideas of Anselm, Abelard, and Aquinas on the justice/mercy rela-tion; ideas that, in large part, trace back to Augustine. *The Decline of Mercy*, 125–133.

83. Hans Boersma, *Violence, Hospitality, and the Cross* (Grand Rapids, MI: Baker Academic, 2004); Cynthia Crysdale, *Embracing Travail*; Timothy Gorringe, *God's Just Vengeance*; Darby Kathleen Ray, *Deceiving the Devil: Atonement, Abuse, and Ransom*.

84. Burrell, *Towards A Jewish-Christian-Muslim Theology*, 94.

85. Gorringe, *God's Just Vengeance*, 101, 103.

86. Boersma, Hans. "Eschatological Justice and the Cross," *Theology Today* 60 (2003): 186–199; D. Bentley Hart, "A Gift Exceeding Every Debt," *Pro Ecclesia* 7 (1998): 333–349.

87. Gorringe, *God's Just Vengeance*, 55; Rene Girard, *The Girard Reader*, ed. James G. Williams (New York: Crossroad, 1996), 178.

88. Girard, *Girard Reader*, 9–19.

89. Emile Durkheim, *Elementary Forms of the Religious Life*, trans. Karen Fields (New York: Free Press, 1997), II, 7.

90. Rene Girard, *Violence and the Sacred*, trans. Patrick Gregory (Baltimore: Johns Hopkins University Press, 1977), 1–13, 144–146.

91. Ibid., 12.

92. Girard, *Girard Reader*, 183.

93. Ibid., 16–17.

94. Aquinas, *Summa Theologica*, I–II, q. 87, a. 6.

95. United States Conference of Catholic Bishops, *Catechism of the Catholic Church* (New York: Doubleday, 1995), 2266.

96. The topic is voluminous and the reader can consult a storehouse of literature. Some works approaching this topic are Berman, *Law and Revolution*; Stanley Chodorow, *Christian Political Theory and Church Politics in the Mid-Twelfth Century* (Berkeley: University of California Press, 1972); Gabriel LeBras, "Canon Law" in *The Legacy of the Middle Ages*, eds. C. G. Crump and E. F. Jacobs (Oxford: Clarendon, 1926), 321–361; Andrew Skotnicki, *The Last Judgment: Christian Ethics in a Legal Culture* (Farnham Surrey, VT: Ashgate, 2012), Ch. 3; Walter Ullmann, *The Growth of Papal Government in the Middle Ages* (London: Methuen, 1955); *Law and Politics in the Middle Ages* (Ithaca, NY: Cornell University Press, 1975).

97. R. G. Helmholz, "The Early History of the Grand Jury and the Canon Law," *University of Chicago Law Review* 50 (1983): 613–627; Edward Peters, "Prison Before The Prison" in *The Oxford History of the Prison*, 29–30.

98. "If the law is not external to God, man's relationship with the law puts him in contact with God." Brague, *The Law of God*, 219.

99. St. Benedict, *Rule*, Chs. 23, 27.

100. John of Paris, *On Royal and Papal Power*, trans. J. A. Watt (Toronto: Pontifical Institute, 1971), Ch. 12.

101. Soelle, *Political Theology*, 24.

102. Ibid., 34.

103. Ibid., 37. George Lindbeck argues that being religious is more about an active engagement, a "how" one becomes a credible example of a given tradition rather than in learning "about" history or dogmas. He goes on to say, similar to Soelle, that there is a basic grammar to Christian faith, a set of "regulative principles" that consists of "affirmations about the inner being of God," whereas dogmas are "secondary guidelines." See *The Nature of Doctrine* (Philadelphia: Westminster, 1984), 35, 94.

104. Cover, "Nomos and Narrative," 8–9.

105. Aquinas, *Summa Theologica*, I–II, 91, 4.

106. Miroslav Volf writes that victims also have the responsibility to remember rightly. This implies knowing that the memory of abuse can make the victim into an abuser; that the social context plays a significant role in what the offender did; that there is a tendency to cluster more harm around the incident than was caused

by its perpetrator; that the evil act was not the entire life but a single incident in the life of the offender; and that the victim, like his or her attacker, is also a sinner. See *The End of Memory* (Grand Rapids, MI: Eerdmans, 2006), 11–16.

107. Waller, *Against Moral Responsibility*, 13.

108. "The special character of American criminal justice lies in the high degree of direct and indirect popular influence over its administration." Samuel Walker, *Popular Justice* (New York: Oxford University Press, 1980), 3.

109. "Some of the harshest policies . . . bear the clear imprint of populism." See Roberts et al., *Penal Populism*, 3. Laura Magnani and Harmon Wray state: "It is difficult to overstate the role of fear in driving public policy on crime and punishment." *Beyond Prisons*, 6.

110. Soelle, *Political Theology*, 105.

111. Garland, *Culture of Control*, 13–15, 180.

112. Haney, *Reforming Punishment*, 128.

113. Durkheim, *The Division of Labor in Society*, 45. Jonathan Simon notes, "the passion to punish remains a powerful political phenomenon." See "The Emergence of the Risk Society: Insurance, Law, and the State," *Socialist Review* 17 (1987): 61–89 at 81.

114. Feinberg, "Expressive Function," 100.

115. Elaine Scary, *The Body in Pain* (New York: Oxford University Press, 1985). 4.

116. Robert A. Ferguson, *Inferno* (Cambridge, MA: Harvard University Press, 2014), 3.

117. Garland, *Punishment and Modern Society*, 243. John Braithwaite and Philip Pettit are more imaginative in their portrayal of the horrors of imprisonment: "A society which feels morally comfortable about sending thousands of terrified young men and women to institutions in which they are bashed, raped, and brutalized, stripped of human dignity, denied freedom of speech and movement, has a doubtful commitment of freedom." See *Not Just Deserts* (Oxford: Clarendon, 1990), 6.

118. Levinas, *Entre Nous*, 3. Heidegger, *Being and Time*, 238.

119. Doris L. MacKenzie and David P. Farrington, "Preventing Future Offending of Delinquents and Offenders: What Have We Learned from Experiments and Meta-analyses?," *Journal of Experimental Criminology* 11 (2015): 565–595 at 574.

120. Sykes, *Society of Captives*, 67.

121. William R. Miller and Stephen Rollnick, *Motivational Interviewing*, 2nd ed. (New York: Guilford Press, 2002), 8.

122. Gottschalk, *Caught*, 242.

123. "Punishment, after all, is dictated as much by the character of the punisher as by that of the punished." Ferguson, *Inferno*, 7.

124. Lofland, *Deviance and Identity*, 302. Alan Hunt reinforces Lofland's claim with the support of social history: "[I]n the economic realm the ethically neutral 'unemployed,' who were the subject matter of economic and social policy for most

of the twentieth century, have been reconstructed as 'welfare scroungers' in a way that is reminiscent of the 'paupers' and 'undeserving poor' who inhabited earlier periods of the politics of poverty. New categories of the socially dangerous (youth gangs, drug dealers, sex offenders, persistent offenders) inhabit a space that in the nineteenth century was occupied by the 'dangerous classes.'" *Governing Morals*, 6.

125. "Punishment does involve treating people as inferiors, and the role of 'inferior' is largely defined by the structure and tradition of social status in a given society." Whitman, *Harsh Justice*, 26.

126. Pierre Teilhard de Chardin, *The Divine Milieu* (New York: Harper, 1960), 56.

127. Meyer, *Justice of Mercy*, 44.

128. Mathiesen, *Prisons on Trial*, 48–49. Michael Tonry and Andrew von Hirsch are among those who claim that utilitarian theories which feature deterrence have declined as correctional ideals. Michael Tonry, "Purposes and Functions of Sentencing," in *Crime and Justice: A Review of Research*, ed. Michael Tonry (Chicago: University of Chicago Press, 2006): 1–53 at 1–2; Von Hirsch, *Past or Future Crimes* (New Brunswick, NJ: Rutgers University Press, 1985), 7.

129. Stanley Cohen, *Visions of Social Control* (Cambridge: Polity Press, 1985), 262.

130. Magnani and Wray, *Beyond Prisons*, 151–152; John Pfaff, *Locked In: The True Causes of Mass Incarceration* (New York: Basic Books, 2017), 193–195.

131. Hegel argues that deterrence (and rehabilitation) fail to "honor" the offender as a rational human being who chose the unwarranted action and knows that punishment is required to set it aright. See *Philosophy of Right*, 99, 100. Kant says the offender must "never be treated merely as a means to the purposes of another . . . and woe to him who crawls through the windings of eudaimonism in order to discover something that releases the criminal from punishment." See "The Metaphysics of Morals," 6:331. Herbert Morris writes that teleological theories (like deterrence and rehabilitation) claim: "We have to change [the offender] and his judgments of value. In doing this we display a lack of respect for the moral status of individuals . . . thy are but animals who must be conditioned." See "Persons and Punishment," *The Monist* 52 (1968): 475–501 at 487. Duff states that in his theory the offender is "a person with whom communication is primarily or directly attempted, whereas if we talk only of expression, we may be accused of using the offender "as a means" to expressing something to others." See "Penal Communications: Recent Work in the Philosophy of Punishment" in *Criminal Justice: A Review of Research* 20 (1996): 1–97 at 33.

132. Sykes, *Society of Captives*, 11.

133. Mill's emendation of Bentham's calculus posits "higher" pleasures that require a longer view of personal and social policy than the satisfaction of the present. Still, he remains aligned with Bentham in the utilitarian need to punish: "The sentiment of justice, in that one of its elements which consists of the desire to punish, is thus, I conceive, the natural feeling of retaliation or vengeance, rendered by intellect and sympathy applicable to those injuries, that is, to those hurts, which wound

us through, or in common with, society at large." John Stuart Mill, *Utilitarianism* (Indianapolis, IN: Bobbs-Merrill, 1957), Ch. 5, p. 64.

134. Von Hirsch, *Past or Future Crimes*, 13. Although in his earlier work, he did feel that deterrence could be fruitfully combined with retributivism since deterrence suggests "that punishment 'may' prevent more misery than it inflicts." *Doing Justice*, 53–54.

135. Ferguson writes: "Legal systems are invariably comfortable with where they are. They depend on the status quo and profit from it." *Inferno*, 4. See also Winter, *Elements for a Social Ethic*, 178.

136. Shuster, *Punishment and the History of Political Philosophy*, 9.

137. Richard Fraher, "Preventing Crime in the High Middle Ages," in *Popes, Teachers, and Canon Law in the Middle Ages*, eds. James Ross Sweeney and Stanley Chodorow (Ithaca, NY: Cornell University Press, 1989), 212–233 at 219.

138. Ibid., 220–221.

139. "Bureaucratization of the conditions of life and limitations upon personal freedom are inevitable features of imprisonment . . . [thus the] inner contradiction which underlies every reform program to a greater or lesser degree. No reform program has been willing to abandon the principle that the living standard of the prisoner must be depressed in order to retain the deterrent effects of punishment." Georg Rusche and Otto Kirchheimer, *Punishment and Social Structure* (New York: Russell & Russell, 1968), 159.

140. Von Hirsch, *Past or Future Crimes*, 5.

141. Wilson, *Thinking About Crime*, Ch. 8. John Pfaff agrees that, whatever its moral and social pathologies, the mass imprisonment phenomenon, bolstered immeasurably by selective incapacitation, has been successful in reducing the crime rate. *Locked In*, 10–11.

142. Ruth Wilson Gilmore, *Golden Gulag* (Berkeley: University of California Press, 2007), 2.

143. Garland, *Punishment*, 288.

144. Gordon, *The Justice Juggernaut*.

145. Nietzsche, *Genealogy of Morals*, Second Essay, 14.

146. Winter writes: "[M]uch of the methodological discussion in the human sciences has been superficial; it has taken the possibility of a human science for granted and preoccupied itself with methods for improving precision in objective observation and increased power of mathematical manipulation of data. One begs the real question if one starts with a human science and proceeds to settle methodological questions by sharpening instruments of observation—simply refusing to ask what one is actually observing." *Elements for a Social Ethic*, 53–54.

CHAPTER 3

1. Aristotle states that "man is by nature a political animal." *The Politics*, trans. T. A. Sinclair (Harmondsworth: Penguin, 1962), 1253a1. Aquinas writes: "Yet it

is natural for man, more than for any other animal, to be a social and political animal, to live in a group." *On Kingship: To the King of Cyprus*, trans. Gerald B. Phelan (Toronto: Pontifical Institute of Medieval Studies, 1949), I, 1, 4.

2. Arnold Gehlen describes the "natural attitude" as an "a priori" conception of reality that views the world "as caught in a rhythmic, self-sustaining, circular process of motion." *Man in the Age of Technology*, trans. Patricia Lipscomb (New York: Columbia University Press, 1980), 13. See also Berger and Luckmann, *Social Construction of Reality*, 21.

3. Becci, *Imprisoned Religion*, 2.

4. Todd R. Clear, Patricia L. Hardyman, Bruce Stout, Karol Lucken, and Harry R. Dammer, "The Value of Religion in Prison: An Inmate Perspective," *Journal of Contemporary Criminal Justice* 16 (2000): 53–74 at 57–58.

5. Abraham Maslow, *Religious Values and Peak Experiences* (New York: Viking, 1970), 4.

6. Shadd Maruna, *Making Good* (Washington, DC: American Psychological Association, 2001), 95, 96.

7. Kent Kerley, *Religious Faith in Correctional Contexts* (Boulder, CO: First Forum Press, 2014), 64.

8. Braithwaite, *Crime, Shame, and Reintegration*, 64–65. Braithwaite does add an addendum that the nurturance is provided after the offender has been duly shamed for his or her bad conduct. In this and other matters to be addressed ahead, I am in disagreement with him. However, restorative justice is indeed predicated upon the sort of innate openness to transcendence about which I am speaking.

9. Katherine Becket, *Making Crime Pay* (New York: Oxford University Press, 1999), 10.

10. Lawrence Kohlberg, *The Philosophy of Moral Development* (San Francisco: Harper & Row, 1981), 15.

11. Ibid., 19.

12. Jean Piaget, *Six Psychological Studies*, trans. Anita Tenzer (New York: Vintage, 1968), 46, 79.

13. Josef Pieper, *Leisure: The Basis of Culture*, trans. Gerald Malsbury (South Bend, IN: St. Augustine's Press, 1998), 16–17.

14. Heidegger, *Being and Time*, 167.

15. Clear et al., "The Value of Religion in Prison," 58–59.

16. Joe Edward Barnhart and Mary Ann Barnhart, *The New Birth: A Naturalistic View of Religious Conversion* (Macon, GA: Mercer University Press, 1981), 22.

17. Levinas, *Entre Nous*, 28, 18.

18. Winter, *Elements for a Social Ethic*, 108.

19. Jacques Lacan, *Speech and Language in Psychoanalysis*, trans. Anthony Wilden (Baltimore: Johns Hopkins University Press, 1968), 44.

20. Karl Barth, *Church Dogmatics IV, Part 2*, trans. G. W. Bromiley (Edinburgh: T. & T. Clark, 1958), 560; Tanya Erzen, *God in Captivity*, 4; Peggy Giordano, Stephen

A. Cernkovich, and Jennifer L. Rudolph, "Gender, Crime, and Desistance: Toward a Theory of Cognitive Transformation," *American Journal of Sociology* 107 (2002): 990–1064; Maslow, *Religious Values and Peak Experiences*; William Miller, "The Phenomenon of Quantum Change, *JCLP/In Session* 60 (2004): 453–460.

21. "[W]e cannot apply the classical definition of form and matter to perception, nor can we conceive of the perceiving subject as a consciousness which 'interprets,' 'deciphers,' or 'orders' a sensible matter according to an ideal law which it possesses. Matter is 'pregnant' with its form, which is to say that in the final analysis every perception takes place within a certain horizon and ultimately in the 'world.'" Maurice Merleau-Ponty, *The Primacy of Perception* (Chicago: Northwestern University Press, 1964), 12.

22. Henri Bergson, *The Two Sources of Morality and Religion*, trans. R. Ashley Audra and Cloudesley Brereton (Garden City, NY: Doubleday, 1935), 32.

23. Ibid.

24. Ibid., 227.

25. Lonergan, *Method in Theology*, 237–238.

26. Miller, *Quantum Change*, 457.

27. Miller, *In the Throe of Wonder*, 1.

28. Heidegger, *Being and Time*, 387.

29. Maslow, *Religious Values and Peak Experiences*, 62, 63.

30. Merleau-Ponty, *The Primacy of Perception*, 50.

31. Lonergan, *Method*, 241.

32. Winter, *Elements*, 107.

33. Heidegger, *Being and Time*, 387.

34. Walter Conn, *Christian Conversion* (New York: Paulist, 1986), 69.

35. Kerley, *Religious Faith*, 58.

36. Rotman, *Beyond Punishment*, 31.

37. Maslow, *Religious Values*, xiii–iv.

38. Husserl, *General Introduction to Pure Phenomenology*, 147–148.

39. Thomas Merton, *Zen and the Birds of Appetite* (New York: New Directions, 1968), 23–24.

40. Maslow makes a similar distinction between a plateau experience and a peak experience. See *Religious Values*, xiv–xvi.

41. James, *Varieties of Religious Experience*, Lecture 1, 33.

42. Ibid., Lecture 9, 167.

43. Fenggang Yang and Andrew Stuart Abel, "Sociology of Religious Conversion" in *The Oxford Handbook of Religious Conversion*, eds. Lewis R. Rambo and Charles E. Farhadian (Oxford Handbooks Online, 2014), 140–151 at 143.

44. Giordano et al., "A Life Course Perspective on Spirituality and Desistance," 27–28.

45. Clear et al, "The Value of Religion in Prison," 58.

46. A. D. Nock, *Conversion* (London: Oxford University Press, 1933), 5–7. In a historical overview, Marc David Beir broadens Nock's use of adhesion to include forced

allegiance or acculturation and syncretic religious expressions. See "Historical and Religious Conversion" in *The Oxford Handbook of Religious Conversion*, 25–37 at 25.

47. Arthur Greil, "Previous Dispositions and Conversion to Perspectives of Social and Religious Movements," *Sociological Analysis* 38 (1977): 115–125 at 123. See also V. Bailey Gillespie, *Religious Conversion and Personal Identity: How and Why People Change* (Birmingham, AL: Religious Education Press, 1979); Henri Paul Pierre Gooren, *Religious Conversion and Disaffiliation: Tracing Patters of Change in Faith Practice* (New York: Palgrave Macmillan, 2010); Theodore E. Long and Jeffrey K. Hadden, "Religious Conversion and the Concept of Socialization," *Journal for the Scientific Study of Religion* 22 (1983): 1–14.

48. Lofland and Stark, "Becoming a World-Saver: A Theory of Conversion to a Deviant Perspective," *American Sociological Review* 30 (1965): 862–875 at 862.

49. Rodney Stark, *Why God? Explaining Religious Phenomena* (Conshohocken, PA: Templeton, 2017), 103–104.

50. Ibid., 106.

51. David A. Snow and Richard Machalek, "The Sociology of Conversion," *Annual Review of Sociology* 10 (1984): 167–190 at 185. Ray Pawson speaks of the "capriciousness" of program outcomes since "evaluation research has failed to deliver a clear enough knowledge base on what we know and can know about how programmes work . . . Perhaps the time has come to blame the messenger." See "Evaluation Methodology: Back to Basics" in *Evaluating the Effectiveness of Community Penalties*, ed. George Meir (Aldershot: Avebury, 1997), 151–173 at 151.

52. Johnson, *More God, Less Crime*, 159–160.

53. William Bainbridge, "The Religious Ecology of Deviance," *American Sociological Review* 54 (1989): 288–295; Steven R. Burkett and David A. Ward, "A Note on Perceptual Deterrence, Religiously Based Moral Condemnation, and Social Control," *Criminology* 31 (1993): 119–134; Giordano et al., "A Life Course Perspective on Spirituality and Desistance"; Travis Hirschi and Rodney Stark, "Hellfire and Delinquency," *Social Problems* 17 (1969): 202–213.

54. Snow and Machalek, "Sociology of Conversion," 171–172.

55. Byron Johnson, "Religious Participation and Criminal Behavior" in *Effective Interventions in the Lives of Criminal Offenders*, eds. J. A. Humphrey and P. Cordella (New York: Springer, 2014), 3–18 at 13.

56. Snow and Machalek, "The Sociology of Conversion," 175. Lofland and Stark state the necessity of distinguishing between "verbal converts and total converts." See "Becoming a World-Saver," 864.

57. I am referring here to the watershed article by Robert Martinson that initially all but sank the rehabilitative vessel and, subsequently, led to a host of studies seeking to find a rehabilitative strategy that "works." Robert Martinson, "What Works? Questions and Answers About Prison Reform," *Public Interest* 35 (1974): 352–384.

58. Byron Johnson, "The Faith-Based Prison" in *The American Prison: Imagining a Different Future*, eds. Francis T. Cullen, Cheryl Leo Johnson, and Mary K. Stohr (Los Angeles: SAGE, 2014), 36–60 at 37.

59. Lewis Rambo speaks of the elements in conversion as "a sequence of processes, although there is sometimes a spiraling effect—a going back and forth between stages." See *Understanding Religious Conversion* (New Haven, CT: Yale University Press, 1991), 16–17. There are any number of authors who have charted and systematized the conversion experience. Most, as noted, take any fundamental change in life course as a conversion. Kerley gives four characteristics: timing, emotion, a new faith-based identity, and a new journey. See *Religious Faith*, 64. Rambo and Farhadian have seven stages: context, crisis, quest, encounter, interaction, commitment, and the cumulative quality of the various stages. See "Converting," 23–24. Kohlberg does not speak of conversion but stage transition from pre-conventional morality to conventional to post-conventional (autonomous and principled). See *The Philosophy of Moral Development*, 17–19.

60. Matthew Crawford writes of the "attentional economy." *The World Beyond Your Head* (New York: Farrar, Straus, and Giroux, 2014), 3–8.

61. William R. Miller and Stephen Rollnick, *Motivational Interviewing* 2nd ed. (New York: Guilford Press, 2002), 22.

62. Ibid. Turner speaks of "fixed and floating worlds." Despite all attempts to keep chaos at bay, life creates liminal spaces when the stable boundaries erected by the self or society are disrupted. Ancient religions built this chaotic element into their ritual practice to echo the permeability of all structures and, more importantly, the natural growth of communal bonds in the experience of liminality. See *The Ritual Practice* (Ithaca, NY: Cornell University Press, 1969), vii, Ch. 3.

63. Lonergan, *Method*, 235.

64. James, *Varieties of Religious Experience*, Lecture 8, 150.

65. Ibid., Lectures 6 and 7, 116.

66. D. A. Andrews and James Bonta, *The Psychology of Criminal Conduct*, 5th ed. (New Providence, NJ: LexisNexis, 2010), 193.

67. Reinhold Niebuhr, *The Nature and Experience of Man II* (New York: Charles Scriber's Sons, 1943), 109.

68. Lofland and Stark, "Becoming a World-Saver," 870.

69. Kerley, *Religious Faith in Correctional Contexts*, 56.

70. St. John of the Cross developed the metaphor of the dark night when he was in prison in Toledo, Spain. The basic idea is that the soul or transcendent self is incarcerated in the worldview and epistemology that the ego fashions out of its sense experiences. It habitually, and destructively, repeats its responses in much the same way that neuroscientists tell us that the synapses of the brain react to stimuli in an automatic fashion unless disrupted. Only by entering into meditation/contemplation, that is, a non-cognitive, non-judgmental, and compassionate presence to the present moment, can the inner and true self be set free from its captivity.

The result is a joyful uplifting of the spirit. See "The Ascent of Mount Carmel" and "The Dark Night of the Soul" in *The Collected Works of St. John of the Cross*, trans. Kieran Kavanaugh and Odilio Rodriguez (Washington, DC: ICS, 1979). On the relation between contemplation and reconfiguring the neural network, see James Austin, *Zen and the Brain* (Cambridge, MA: MIT Press, 1998); Patrick McNamara, *The Neuroscience of Religious Experience* (Cambridge: Cambridge University Press, 2009).

71. *Twelve Steps and Twelve Traditions* (New York: Alcoholics Anonymous World Services, 1952).

72. James, *Varieties of Religious Experience*, Lecture 9, 172–174.

73. Jon 1: 1–17. Jonah refused to heed the call of God to sail to Nineveh to preach a message of conversion and instead fled in the opposite direction. In the ensuing storm, he told the terrified crew members that he was the cause of the calamity and that they should thrust him into the sea. No sooner had they done this, a whale swallowed Jonah for three days and nights, after which, it vomited him onto the shore of Nineveh. Jack Abbot's famous memoir hinted at many of the above themes. *In the Belly of the Beast* (New York: Vintage, 1991).

74. Greil, "Previous Dispositions and Conversion to Perspectives of Social and Religious Movements," 120.

75. Frank K. Flinn, "Conversion: Up from Evangelicalism or the Pentecostal and Charismatic Experience" in *Religious Conversion: Contemporary Practices and Controversies*, eds. Christopher Lamb and M. Darrol Bryant (London: Cassell, 1999), 51–72 at 54.

76. James, *Varieties of Religious Experience*, 174.

77. Kerley, *Religious Faith*, 52.

78. Erzen, *God in Captivity*, 21–22.

79. Barnhart, *The New Birth*, 128.

80. Acts 9: 3–5. "I believe that almost all of the great themes of Paul's teaching emerged pivotally around his conversion experience. Something happened to this man that utterly redefined his life. Like all true converts (*con-vertere* means to turn around) there was a clear before and after. Unless you understand that the world was utterly realigned and redefined for Paul, you cannot appreciate the radicalism of his new vision. Jesus' choice of words, 'Why are you persecuting me?' (Acts 9: 4) is key. Later, during Paul's retreat in Arabia, he must surely have pondered this question: 'Why does he say I was persecuting him, when I was persecuting others?' . . . This enlightening experience taught Paul non-dual consciousness, which is the same mystical mind that had allowed Jesus to say things like 'Whatever you do to the least, you do to me' (Matthew 25: 40)." Richard Rohr, "Daily Meditation" March 7, 2016, available at https://cac.org/category/daily-meditations.

81. Massimo Leone, "Religious Conversion and Semiotic Analysis" in Ramdo and Farhadian, *The Oxford Handbook of Religious Conversion*, 369–385 at 370.

82. Nock, *Conversion*, 83, 188–189.

83. Robert J. Sampson and John H. Laub, *Crime in the Making* (Cambridge, MA: Harvard University Press, 1992), 179, 240.

84. Buddha means the "awakened one." The Buddhist practice of mindfulness is at the core of coming to full consciousness of the fiction of the separate self (the ego) and of recognizing one's full interdependence with all matter. Jesus develops the idea of mindfulness repeatedly in the gospels and uses the term "stay awake" in almost mantric-like fashion. Similar to the Buddha, he sought to deconstruct the ego as the precondition for a life of compassion: "If you love your life, you must lose it; and if you lose your life . . . you will find it" (Mk 8: 35).

85. Maruna et al, "Why God is Often Found," 171.

86. James, *Varieties of Religious Experience*, Lecture 9, 165. Mead is referenced in Snow and Machalek, "The Sociology of Conversion," 171.

87. Barnhart, *The New Birth*, 97.

88. Paul Ricoeur, "Life: A Story in Search of a Narrative" in *A Ricoeur Reader: Reflection and Imagination*, ed. Mario J. Valdez (Toronto: University of Toronto Press, 1991, 425–437 at 434.

89. Ibid., 436–437.

90. Leone, "Religious Conversion and Semiotic Analysis," 372; Nock, *Conversion*, 8.

91. Lonergan, *Method*, 131.

92. Emil Brunner, *Making Stories: Law, Literature, Life* (New York: Farrar, Straus, & Giroux, 2002), 4–5, 15; Bruce Hindmarsh, "Religious Conversions as Narrative Autobiography" in *The Oxford Handbook of Religious Conversion*, 344–361 at 345–347.

93. Brunner, *Making Stories*, 27–28.

94. Stanley Hauerwas, *Truthfulness and Tragedy* (South Bend, IN: University of Notre Dame Press, 1977), 35.

95. Brunner, *Making Stories*, 8.

96. Ricoeur, "Life: A Story in Search of a Narrative," 426.

97. Ibid., 435.

98. Ibid., 428.

99. Maruna, *Making Good*, 7.

100. Ibid., 87. Mordechai Rotenberg writes that "if you scratch the surface of any norm regulating psychology or psychotherapy, you will find behind it a theology or a theosophy that manifests itself in various secularized norms and forms of ontology." *Re-Biographing and Deviance* (New York: Praeger, 1987), 2–3.

101. Erzen, *God in Captivity*, 22.

102. Lonergan writes that "although the conversion is intensely personal, it is not purely private. While individuals contribute elements to horizons, it is only within the social group that the elements accumulate." *Method*, 269.

103. Ludwig Wittgenstein, *Philosophical Investigations*, trans. G. E. M. Anscombe (Oxford: Basil Blackwell, 1968), Section 243 ff.

104. Leone, "Religious Conversion and Semiotic Analysis," 373.

105. Huston Smith writes that the defining characteristic of religious metanarratives is they help believers understand that "you cannot understand anything unless you understand everything." *Why Religion Matters* (New York: Harper, 2001), 25.

106. Brunner, *Making Stories*, 93.

107. Ibid., 25. Ricoeur states that "the narrative schema has a history of its own, and that . . . history possesses all the characteristics of a tradition as a living passing-on of innovation which can always be reactivated by a return to the most creative moments of the poetic composition." See "Life," 429.

108. Milbank, *Theology and Social Theory*, 385–386.

109. Mauna et al., "Why God Is Often Found Behind Bars," 167.

110. Snow and Machalek, "The Sociology of Conversion," 173–174.

111. Lewis Rambo, *Understanding Religious Conversion*, 103; Lofland and Stark, "Becoming a World-Saver," 809–810.

112. Max Heirich, "Change of Heart: A Test of Some Widely Held Theories About Religious Conversion," *American Journal of Sociology* 83 (1977): 653–680 at 673; Lofland and Stark, "Becoming a World-Saver," 873.

113. Barnhart, *The New Birth*, 97.

114. David E. Jenkins, "Possible Theological Responses to Apparent Criminological Confusion" in *The Coming Penal Crisis*, eds. A. E. Bottoms and R. H. Preston (Edinburgh: Scottish Academic Press, 1980), 173–213 at 189.

115. Kerley, *Religious Faith*, 128.

116. Hauerwas, *Truthfulness and Tragedy*, 21.

117. Ibid., 104.

118. Ibid., 136.

119. Stanley Hauerwas develops this theme in an essay on Christian discipleship. See "How We Lay Bricks and Make Disciples" in *After Christendom* (Nashville: Abingdon, 1991), 93–111.

120. Lindbeck, *The Nature of Doctrine*, 35.

121. MacIntyre, *After Virtue*, 115, 202.

122. Barth, *Church Dogmatics*, IV/2, 566.

123. In discussing the theological notion of atonement (why Jesus had to die such a cruel death), Jerome Miller writes: "If the logic of sacrificial atonement nevertheless strikes a deep chord in us, it's because we know in our heart of hearts—and perhaps only there—that we ourselves have committed little murders." "The Cry of Abel's Blood," *Commonweal* 122 (April 14, 2017).

124. Heidegger, *Being and Time*, 322–332.

125. Ibid., 343–344, 349.

126. Maruna, *Making Good*, 121.

127. Nock, *Conversion*, 179.

128. Pieper, *Leisure*, 31.

129. Heidegger, *Being and Time*, 206–208.

130. Teilhard de Chardin, *The Divine Milieu*, 48.

131. In his song, "Anthem," Cohen writes: "There is a crack in everything. That's how the light gets in."

132. Rodney Stark, Lori Kent, and Daniel P. Doyle, "Religion and Delinquency: The Ecology of a 'Lost' Relationship," *Journal of Research in Crime and Delinquency* 19 (1982): 4–24 at 20–21.

133. Ibid., 73.

134. Johnson, *More God, Less Crime*, 157.

135. Lonergan, *Method*, 243.

136. Ibid.

137. Maslow, *Religions*, xiv; James, *Varieties*, Lecture 10, 209.

138. James, *Varieties*, Lecture 10, 209.

139. James spends much of his first lecture in *The Varieties of Religious Experience* describing the prejudice of "medical materialists" who reduce the ecstatic and life-altering behavior associated with religious experience and conversion to neurological and biological abnormality.

140. Becci, *Imprisoned Religion*, 139.

141. Kerley, *Religious Faith*, 69.

142. Erving Goffman, "Characteristics of Total Institutions" in *Asylums* (Garden City, NY: Anchor, 1961), 1–124 at 69–70. Hans Toch, similarly, speaks of "niches" or "oases" that perform the same function. See *Corrections: A Humanistic Approach* (Guilderland, NY: Harrow and Heston, 1997), 62–63.

143. Snow and Machalek, "The Sociology of Conversion," 169.

144. "A key element in many religious traditions is the idea of spiritual growth as an ongoing, developmental phenomenon." Ibid., 179.

145. Straus, "Religious Conversion," 163.

146. Alfred North Whitehead, *Process and Reality*, Corrected ed., eds. David Ray Griffin and Donald W. Sherburne (New York: Free Press, 1978), 40–41.

147. Berger and Luckmann, *The Social Construction of Reality*, 102–103, 65.

148. Gehlen, *Man in the Age of Technology*, 13.

149. Kohlberg, *Philosophy of Moral Development*, 57.

150. Conn, *Christian Conversion*, 117; Lonergan, *Method*, 238. Husserl states that "the material thing and my experience of the thing are two different matters." See *Ideas*, 116–117. For Heidegger, the "appearance 'of something' does *not* mean showing itself; it means rather the announcing-itself by something which does not show itself." See *Being and Time*, 52.

151. Cover, "Nomos and Narrative," 53.

152. Conn, *Christian Conversion*, 125.

153. Ibid., 131; Kohlberg, *Philosophy of Moral Development*, 19.

154. Lonergan, *Method*, 239.

155. Ibid.

156. Ibid., 239–240.

157. Kant, *Religion Within the Boundaries of Mere Reason*, 6: 47.

158. Sigmund Freud, *The Ego and the Id*, trans. Joan Riviere (New York: Norton, 1960), 15.

159. Lonergan, *Method*, 269.

160. Ibid., 240.

161. Niebuhr, *Nature and Destiny*, II, 108.

162. Lonergan, *Method*, 240.

163. Conn, *Christian Conversion*, 135.

164. Lawrence Kohlberg and Daniel Effenbein, "The Development of Moral Judgments Concerning Capital Punishment," *American Journal of Orthopsychiatry* 45 (1975): 614–640 at 635–637.

165. Levinas, *Entre Nous*, 17.

166. Richard Rohr, Daily Meditation, March 8, 2016. Available at https://cac.org/category/daily-meditations.

167. Rambo and Farhadian, "Converting," 58.

168. Ricoeur, *The Symbolism of Evil*, 351–353; Husserl, *Ideas*, 101.

169. Lindbeck, *Nature of Doctrine*, 65.

170. Ibid.

171. Wink, *Naming the Powers*, 107.

172. Peggy Giordano and her colleagues note that those with "a strong spiritual orientation" are aided beneficially in relation to "angry emotions." See "A Life Course Perspective," 21.

173. Heidegger, *Being and Time*, 296, 157.

174. Miller, "Quantum Change," 457.

175. On the positive approach to crises, see Andrew P. Tix and Patricia A. Frazier, "The Uses of Religious Coping During Stressful Life Events," *Journal of Counseling and Clinical Psychology* 66 (1998): 411–422 at 411. On the sense of well-being, see Willits and Crider, "Religion and Well-Being," 282, 291.

176. Rambo and Farhadian claim that conversion leads to "new ideals, new codes of behavior, new spiritual disciplines such as prayer, fasting and meditation, works of charity and evangelization." See "Converting," 61.

177. C. G. Jung, "Aion: Phenomenology of the Self" in *The Portable Jung*, trans. R. F. C. Hull (New York: Viking, 1971), 139–162.

178. Whitman, *Harsh Justice*, 9.

179. Lofland and Stark, "Becoming a World-Saver," 811.

180. Dorothee Soelle, *The Silent Cry* (Minneapolis: Fortress, 2001), 11.

181. Ibid., 62.

182. Ibid.

183. Ibid., 73.

184. Maruna, *Making Good*, 26–27. Most of the men and women interviewed by Kerley claimed "that self-agency was not enough to help them go straight." See *Religious Faith*, 160.

CHAPTER 4

1. I take some solace that well-known criminologists find that the term creates as much ambiguity as clarity: "Too often, rehabilitation is spoken about by criminologists in a sort of code language: Offenders should receive 'appropriate treatment' that is 'clinically relevant' and 'psychologically informed.' Yet often we are not told what this actually means in enough detail to judge the practices." Tony Ward and Shadd Maruna, *Rehabilitation: Beyond the Risk Paradigm* (London: Routledge, 2007), 28. Fergus McNeill makes a similar point. See "Four Forms of 'Offender' Rehabilitation: Towards an Interdisciplinary Perspective," *Legal and Criminological Psychology* 17 (2012): 18–38 at 18–19.

2. For a brief and helpful overview of the shifts in thought about rehabilitation since the 1960s, see Francis Cullen, "Taking Rehabilitation Seriously: Creativity, Science, and the Challenge of Offender Change," *Punishment and Society* 14 (2012): 94–114.

3. Andrews and Bonta magnify the importance of risk factors. *The Psychology of Criminal Conduct*, 131. Gottfredson and Hirschi emphasize the lack of self-discipline. See *A General Theory of Crime* (Palo Alto, CA: Stanford University Press, 1990). Sutherland pioneered differential association theory. See *Criminology*, 80–82. H. S. Becker helped establish the relevance of labelling theory. See *Outsiders: Studies in the Sociology of Deviance* (New York: Free Press, 1963).

4. Ann Chin Lin, *Reform in the Making* (Princeton, NJ: Princeton University Press, 2000), 5.

5. Giordano et al., "Gender, Crime, and Desistance," 1028.

6. Ibid., 1001.

7. Sam Lewis, "Rehabilitation: Headline of Footnote in the New Penal Policy," *Probation Journal* 52 (2005): 119–135 at 122; Rotman, *Beyond Punishment*, 3.

8. Lin, *Reform in the Making*, 4; Rotman, *Beyond Punishment*, 7.

9. Clare-Ann Fortune, Tony Ward, and Gwenda M. Willis, "The Rehabilitation of Offenders: Reducing Risk and Promoting Better Lives," *Psychiatry, Psychology, and Law* 19 (2012): 646–661 at 647.

10. Ward and Maruna, *Rehabilitation: Beyond the Risk Paradigm*, 15.

11. Tony Ward, "Prediction and Agency: The Role of Protective Factors in Correctional Rehabilitation and Desistance," *Aggression and Violent Behavior* 32 (2017): 19–28 at 25.

12. Rotman, *Beyond Punishment*, 118–119.

13. Hans Toch, *Corrections: A Humanistic Approach*, 4–5. See also Rothman, *Conscience and Convenience*.

14. Gwen Robinson, "Late-Modern Rehabilitation: The Evolution of a Penal Strategy," *Punishment and Society* 10 (2008): 429–445 at 430–434.

15. Ibid., 437.

16. McNeill, "Four Forms of 'Offender' Rehabilitation," 26. See Andrews and Bonta, *Psychology of Criminal Conduct*; D. A. Andrews, James Bonta, and J. Stephen Wormith, "The Risk-Need-Responsivity (RNR) Model: Does Adding the Good Lives Model Contribute to Effective Crime Prevention?," *Criminal Justice and Behavior* 38 (2011): 735–755: Ward and Maruna, *Rehabilitation: Beyond the Risk Paradigm*.

17. Ward and Maruna, *Rehabilitation: Beyond the Risk Paradigm*, 75.

18. Andrews and Bonta, *Psychology of Criminal Conduct*, 11.

19. Ibid., 19.

20. Ibid., 450–451.

21. Ibid., 451.

22. Ibid., 434.

23. Ibid., 438.

24. Ibid., 431.

25. Ibid., 446.

26. Ibid., 443–445.

27. Ibid., 449, 427.

28. B. F. Skinner, *Beyond Freedom and Dignity* (New York: Knopf, 1971); *Walden Two* (New York: McMillan, 1962) [orig. pub. 1948]. So, for Andrews and Bonta, the answer to the question, who am I? is met with Skinner's behaviorism and a sort of Platonic idealism: "if we say we are nervous or kind to others, then we act this way most of the time and with most people." Andrews and Bonta, *Psychology of Criminal Conduct*, 193.

29. Andrews and Bonta, *Psychology of Criminal Conduct*, 141.

30. Ibid., 131. Aside from these "core four" risks, there are four others: substance abuse, family, school/work, leisure/recreation. See Andrews, Bonta, and Wormith, "The Risk, Need, Responsivity (RNR) Model," 738.

31. For a brief summary of the intricate set of principles underlying RNR, see Andrews, Bonta, and Wormith, "The Risk-Need-Responsivity (RNR) Model," 738. For an even-handed and informative review of RNR, see Devon R. Polashek, "An Appraisal of the Risk-Need-Responsivity (RNR) Model of Offender Rehabilitation and Its Application in Correctional Treatment," *Legal and Criminal Psychology* 17 (2012): 1–17.

32. Ward and Maruna, *Rehabilitation* 104.

33. Polashek, "An Appraisal," 1.

34. Cullen "Taking Rehabilitation Seriously," 104–106.

35. "The prevailing American ideology was less purely rehabilitative than positivist . . . Its aim was to prevent further crimes by convicted offenders. When those crimes might be forestalled through rehabilitative efforts, treatment programs should be tried. But to the extent that the success of such programs was uncertain, the offenders who were bad risks could always be restrained." Von Hirsch, *Past of Future Crimes*, 5.

36. Gustave De Beaumont and Alexis De Tocqueville, *On the Penitentiary System in the United States and Its Application to France*, trans. Francis Lieber (Philadelphia: Carey, Lea, and Blanchard, 1833), 60; Polashek, "An Appraisal," 1.

37. On jail statistics see, Amy L. Solomon, Jenny Osborne, Stefan F. LoBuglio, Jeff Mellow, and Debbie Mukamal, *Life After Lockup: Improving Reentry from Jail to the Community* (Washington, DC: Urban Institute, 2008), xv.

38. Marie Gottschalk, "Razing the Carceral State." *Social Justice* 42 (2015): 31–51 at 32.

39. In the seminal article on the new penology, any risk assessment based upon the criminogenic tendencies of a given offender merely duplicates a prior risk assessment that has already been provided by the systems management approach of virtually all large institutions, including criminal justice, that evaluates "instances of the population" in terms of their capacity to meet the social, educational, and economic standards of those considered to be low risk. Those who are high risk are destined for a life outside the prodigal system of rewards given to the qualified and must find contentment in a hand-to-mouth existence or, failing that, life in a penal institution. See Malcolm M. Feeley and Jonathan Simon, "The New Penology: Notes on the Emerging Strategy of Corrections and Its Implications," *Criminology* 30 (1992): 449–474. Loic Wacquant makes a similar point, accompanied by his analysis of neoliberalism. See *Punishing the Poor*, Ch. 1.

40. Haney, *Reforming Punishment*, 174, 162.

41. Doris L. Mackenzie and David P. Farrington, "Preventing Future Offending of Delinquents and Offenders: What Have We Learned from Experiments and Meta-analyses?," *Journal of Experimental Criminology* 11 (2005), 565–595. Cullen thinks that Robert Martinson's striking essay, "Nothing Works," so galvanized retributivists and rehabilitative naysayers that the entire post-history of rehabilitation since that 1974 publication has been dominated by the need to empirically prove that some programs do indeed work. See "Taking Rehabilitation Seriously," 95–96. Marie Gottschalk laments the emphasis on the "evidence-based research agenda about 'what works,'" stating that it "will inevitably be highly constrained and politically vulnerable." Furthermore, it "has a poor track record when it comes to engineering important shifts both in penal policy and in all kinds of public policy." See "Razing the Carceral State," 39.

42. Mark Brown, "Calculations of Risk in Contemporary Penal Practice" in *Dangerous Offenders: Punishment and Social Order*, eds. Mark Brown and John Pratt (London: Routledge, 2000), 93–108 at 94–95, 102.

43. Andrews, Bonta, and Wormith, "The Risk, Need, Responsivity (RNR) Model," 745; Carl Rogers, *On Becoming a Person* (Boston: Houghton Miflin, 1961).

44. Andrews et al., "The Risk, Need, Responsivity (RNR) Model," 738.

45. Ward and Maruna, *Rehabilitation*, 17.

46. Quoted in Gottschalk, *Caught*, 26.

47. Ibid., 26.

48. Polashek, "An Appraisal," 8, 3.

49. Garland, *Punishment and Modern Society*, 186. In their work of mapping the evolution of conservative Republicans from ardent retributivists to proponents of decarceration for nonviolent offenders, David Dagan and Stephen Teles emphasize the influence of the technocratic approach to criminal justice favored by the Council on State Governments and the Pew Research Center. See *Prison Break: Why Conservatives Turned Against Mass Incarceration* (New York: Oxford University Press, 2016), Ch. 5.

50. Cullen, "Taking Rehabilitation Seriously," 108.

51. Ward and Maruna, *Rehabilitation*, 67.

52. Ibid., 24.

53. McNeill, "Four Forms," 30.

54. Maruna, *Making Good*, 96.

55. Rotman, *Beyond Punishment*, 7.

56. Ward and Maruna, *Rehabilitation*, 108.

57. Maruna, *Making Good*, 87.

58. Ibid.

59. Ward and Maruna, *Rehabilitation*, 117.

60. Ibid., 119. Ward, "Prediction and Agency," 23.

61. Ibid., 132.

62. Ibid., 123.

63. Ibid., 107.

64. Fortune et al., "The Rehabilitation of Offenders," 648.

65. Aristotle, *Ethics*, trans. J. A. K. Thompson (Harmondsworth: Penguin, 1963), I, vii.

66. Ibid.

67. Ibid., I, ix.

68. Ibid., I, xii; II, i.

69. Ibid., I, x; X, vii.

70. Ward and Maruna, *Rehabilitation*, 115.

71. Fortune et al., "The Rehabilitation of Offenders," 647.

72. Milbank, *Theology and Social Theory*, 33.

73. "[P]ersons in the segments of society whose behavior patterns are not represented in formulating and applying criminal definitions are more likely to act in ways that will be defined as criminal than those in the segments that formulate and apply criminal definitions." Richard Quinney, *The Social Reality of Crime* (Boston: Little, Brown, 1970), 21.

74. Francis T. Cullen, Jody Sundt, and John Wozniak, "The Virtuous Prison: Toward a Restorative Rehabilitation" in *Contemporary Issues in Crime and Criminal Justice: Essays in Honor of Gilbert Geis*, eds. Henry N. Pontell and David Shichor (Saddle River, NJ: Prentice Hall, 2001), 265–286. Also found in *The American Prison: Imagining a Different Future*, eds. Francis T. Cullen, Cheryl Leo Jones, and Mary K. Stohr (Los Angeles: SAGE, 2014), 62–84 at 65.

75. Cullen et al., "The Virtuous Prison" in *The American Prison*, 66.

76. Goffman, "Characteristics of Total Institutions," 69–70. On encapsulation, see Rambo, *Understanding Religious Conversion*, 103; Lofland and Stark, "Becoming a World-Saver," 809–810.

77. Hans Toch, similarly, speaks of "niches" or "oases" that perform the same function. See *Corrections: A Humanistic Approach*, 62–63.

78. St. John Climacus, *The Ladder of Divine Ascent*, trans. Archimandrite Lazarus Moore (New York: Harper, 1959), Step 5, 15.

79. Brockway, *Fifty Years of Prison Service*, 173.

80. Ibid., 308–309.

81. St. John Climacus, *The Ladder*, Step 5, 1.

82. Brockway, *Fifty Years*, 278.

83. Ibid., 320.

84. I am using ideology in its positive definition as a theoretical construct, not in its pejorative Marxist interpretation. On the notion of disciplinary constraints, I recently spoke in a criminal justice doctoral seminar and shared comments not unlike those in this section. The professor then said, in substance, that she and most of her students know that what I was saying is correct but the canons of investigation under the current hyper-quantitative paradigm would not permit them to voice it in a professional forum.

85. Cullen et al., "The Virtuous Prison," 74.

86. The contract model "obligates the state to care for an offender's needs and welfare" in exchange for legal compliance, thus disproving "the conservative claim that repression, as opposed to treatment reduces crime." Francis T. Cullen and Karen E. Gilbert, *Reaffirming Rehabilitation* (Cincinnati: Anderson, 1982), 34.

87. Lewis, "Rehabilitation: Headline of Footnote," 123.

88. Ignatieff, *A Just Measure of Pain*, 74.

89. There is a large and growing bibliography on the topic that I will leave the reader to investigate. The basic strategy of advocating a restorative "lens" to view the offense as opposed to a retributive one is, perhaps, most indebted to Howard Zehr. See *Changing Lenses* (Scottdale, PA: Herald Press, 1990).

90. Cohen, *Visions of Social Control*, 256.

91. Cullen et al., "The Virtuous Prison," 75.

92. Maruna, *Making Good*, 24.

93. Braithwaite, *Restorative Justice and Responsible Regulation*, 32–33.

94. McNeill, "Four Forms," 26.

95. Sampson and Laub, *Crime in the Making*, 8. Gottfredson and Hirschi, *A General Theory of Crime*.

96. Giordano et al., "Gender, Crime, and Desistance."

97. Ibid., 1000; Miller and Rollnick, *Motivational Interviewing*, 22.

98. Giordano et al., "Gender, Crime, and Desistance," 1000–1001.

99. Ibid., 1001.

100. Ibid., 1002.

101. Ward, "Prediction and Agency," 20.

102. Ibid., 24, 25.

103. Ibid., 25.

104. Sampson and Laub, *Crime in the Making*, 140.

105. Giordano et al., "Gender, Crime, and Desistance," 992, 1033.

106. Ward, "Prediction and Agency," 25.

107. Stark, *Why God?*, 81.

108. Ibid., 71–72, 73.

109. McNeill, "Four Forms," 19.

110. Ward, "Prediction and Agency," 27.

111. Rotman, *Beyond Punishment*, 117.

112. David Berreby, *Us and Them* (New York: Little, Brown, 2005).

113. "The juridic subject . . . is but a persona, an ideological construct. The subject entering the juridic arena appears initially as a multi-faceted, desiring person, but is offered a circumscribed discursive subject-position within which to take up residence in order to engage in acceptable juridic narrative constructions and to participate in juridic communication." Dragan Milovanovic, *Postmodern Law and Disorder* (Liverpool: Deborah Charles, 1992), 34.

CHAPTER 5

1. The term "socially embodied argument" is from Alasdair MacIntyre. See *After Virtue*, 207.

2. Lois Presser, "The Restorative Prison" in Cullen et al., *The American Prison*, 20–32 at 26.

3. Sykes, *Society of Captives*, xxxi.

4. Ibid., xxxii. Max Weber maintained that the foremost expression of power is found in law and bureaucracy. See *Economy and Society*, trans. Guenther Roth and Clauss Wittich (Berkeley: University of California Press, 1978), 956–1005.

5. Lin, *Reform in the Making*, 30.

6. James Beckford and Sophie Gilliat, *Religion in Prison: Equal Rites in a Multi-Faith Society* (Cambridge: Cambridge University Press, 1998), 16.

7. Douglas, *How Institutions Think*, 92.

8. Berger and Luckmann, *Social Construction of Reality*, 21. See also Garland, *Punishment and Modern Society*, 261.

9. Wink, *Naming the Powers*, 5.

10. Jean Dunbabin, *Captivity and Imprisonment in Medieval Europe 1000–1300* (Houndmills: Palgrave Macmillan, 2002), 2–3.

11. Sykes, *Society of Captives*, 4, 90.

12. Gershom Powers, a judge and first warden of the Auburn penitentiary, as quoted in W. D. Lewis, *From Newgate to Dannemora*, 114–115.

13. Donald F. Logan, *Runaway Religious in Medieval Europe* (Cambridge: Cambridge University Press, 1996); Skotnicki, *Criminal Justice and the Catholic Church*, 81–82.

14. William Bright, "The Council of Chalcedon" in *The First Four General Councils* (Oxford: Clarendon, 1892), canon 4.

15. Teresa of Avila, *The Letters of Teresa of Avila*, 2 vols. (London: Burns, Oates, & Washbourne, 1966), I, 26; Therese of Avila, *Story of a Soul*, trans. John Clarke (Washington, DC: ICS, 1975), 175.

16. The rules of monastic and, later, specific religious orders frequently mandated "life sentences" for crimes that would have merited death in secular courts, for example, murder. The term "life" was, however, more linguistic than literal, denoting the highest of three gradations of fault (grave, graver, gravest). A "poena gravissima" usually meant seven years, or even less, if the offender showed signs of metanoia or if the sentence was revoked by an abbot or general council. For the constitutions of many Catholic religious orders, see Johannes Dominicus Mansi, *Sacrorum Conciliorum* (Paris and Leipzig, 1901) [orig. pub. 1762]. See also Skotnicki, *Criminal Justice and the Catholic Church*, 89–92.

17. "The Catholic Church was the first institution to use imprisonment consistently for any avowed purpose other than detention." Norman Johnston, *Forms of Constraint* (Urbana: University of Illinois Press, 2000). Cf. Peters, "Prison Before The Prison," 27–30.

18. See, e.g., Richard Bauman, *Crime and Punishment in Ancient Rome* (London: Routledge, 1996); Peter Garnsey, *Social Status and Legal Privilege in the Roman Empire* (Oxford: Clarendon, 1970); Wayne Meeks, *The Origins of Christian Morality* (New Haven, CT: Yale University Press, 1993); Herbert Musurillo, ed. and trans. *The Acts of the Christian Martyrs* (Oxford: Clarendon, 1972).

19. Meeks, *Origins of Christian Morality*, 67–69; Cyril Vogel, "Sin and Penance" in *Pastoral Treatment of Sin*, ed. Philippe Delhaye (New York: Desclee, 1968), 177–282 at 182.

20. "A variety of lighter everyday sins of Christians were dismissed by mere open acknowledgment in their assemblies." See John T. McNeill and Helena M. Gamer, *Medieval Handbooks of Penance* (New York: Columbia University Press, 1938), 6.

21. The period of public penance lasted until the sixth century. See Paul Palmer, S.J., ed., *Sacraments and Forgiveness* (Westminster, MD: Newman, 1959), 139–140.

22. McNeill and Gamer, *Medieval Handbooks of Penance*, 5.

23. Joseph Favazza, *The Order of Penitents* (Collegeville, MN: Liturgical Press, 1988), 70–71; Karl Rahner, "Penance in the Early Church" in *Theological Investigations*, Vol. XV, trans. Lionel Swain (New York: Crossroad, 1982), 5–6.

24. "Constitutions of the Holy Apostles" in *The Ante-Nicene Fathers*, Vol. VII, trans. Rev. Alexander Roberts and John Donaldson (New York: Scribner's, 1925), II, xiv. Another early authoritative text featured a series of visions. In one, the angel reveals that "repentance is open until the last day." See "The Shepherd of Hermas"

in *Apostolic Fathers*, Vol. II, trans. Kirsopp Lake (London: William Heinemann, 1959), Vison II, ii, 5.

25. Favazza, *The Order of Penitents*, 241–243; Vogel, "Sin and Penance," 193.

26. Bernhard Poschmann, *Penance and the Anointing of the Sick*, trans. Francis Courtney (New York: Herder & Herder, 1964), 86–88.

27. Ibid., 91; McNeill and Gamer, *Medieval Handbooks of Penance*, 7–8.

28. Poschmann, *Penance and the Anointing of the Sick*, 47; Vogel, "Sin and Penance," 193.

29. Logan, *Runaway Religious*, 146.

30. Ibid., 243. See also, Rahner, "Penance in the Early Church," 4.

31. Vogel, "Sin and Penance," 194.

32. Tertullian, "On Penitence" in *Treatises on Penance*, trans. William P. Le Saint, S.J. (Westminster, MD: Newman Press, 1959), Ch. 9.

33. St. Benedict, *Rule*, Chs. 23, 24. Tal Asad, for one, sees no betrayal in this somewhat fractured portrait as he insists that some degree of force is necessary in all social arrangements. The pertinent question is the broader ethos of the monastic life into which the novice is to be socialized: "A remarkable feature of monastic discipline is that it explicitly aims to create, through a program of communal living, the will to obey. The Christian monk who learns to will obedience is not merely someone who submits to another's will by force of argument or by the threat of force . . . The obedient monk is a person for whom obedience is *his* virtue . . . force is a crucial element in a particular transformation of disciplines, not merely in keeping order among inmates." See Asad, *Genealogies of Religion* (Baltimore: Johns Hopkins University Press, 1993), 125.

34. Benedict, *Rule*, Chs. 25, 27.

35. Dom Jean Mabillon, a seventeenth-century Benedictine historian, writes of a meeting of Benedictine abbots in Aix-la-Chapelle in 817 to address abuses in imprisonment and to establish humane regulatory guidelines, among which were heated cells in winter and work for the confined. See Thorsten Sellin, "Dom Jean Mabillon: A Prison Reformer of the Seventeenth Century," *Journal of the American Institute of Criminal Law and Criminology* 17 (1927): 581–602 at 583.

36. Quoted in Taylor, *A Secular Age*, 263.

37. Sutherland and Cressey, *Criminology*, 308.

38. Braithwaite, *Restorative Justice and Responsive Regulation*, 33.

39. R. A. Duff, "Penal Communications: Recent Works in the Philosophy of Punishment" in *Crime and Justice: A Review of Research*, Vol. 20, ed. Michael Tonry (Chicago: University of Chicago Press, 1996), 1–97 at 53. He writes in another venue: "Criminal punishment . . . should ideally become self-punishment, the proper aim of inflicting punishment on a criminal is to persuade her to accept her punishment, to will it for herself, as a penance for her crime." See "Punishment and Penance—A Reply to Harrison," *The Aristotelian Society*, Supplementary Vol. 62 (1988), 153–167 at 159.

40. Mary Douglas makes the point on the "thought world" of institutions and the way they shape moral vision. See *How Institutions Think*, 128.

41. Alasdair MacIntyre, *After Virtue*, 241. See also *Whose Justice? Which Rationality?* (South Bend, IN: University of Notre Dame Press, 1988); *Three Rival Versions of Moral Inquiry* (South Bend, IN: University of Notre Dame Press, 1990).

42. "Rehabilitation is perverted when it is invoked to curtail rights and to coerce." See Rotman, *Beyond Punishment*, 146. Lewis argues similarly. See "Rehabilitation," 124.

43. Rotman, *Beyond Punishment*, 8, 21.

44. Ibid., 3.

45. Ibid., 9; Lewis, "Rehabilitation," 123.

46. Paula Smith and Myrinda Schweitzer, "The Therapeutic Prison," in Cullen et al., *The American Prison*, 3–18 at 13.

47. Ibid.

48. Garland, *Culture of Control*, 176; Becket, *Making Criminals Pay*, 9.

49. Kohlberg, *Philosophy of Moral Development*, 106.

50. Erving Goffman, *The Presentation of the Self in Everyday Life* (New York: Anchor, 1959), 9.

51. Ibid., 8.

52. Ibid., 13.

53. MacIntyre, *After Virtue*, 31.

54. Rotman, *Beyond Punishment*, 21.

55. John Braithwaite and Philip Petit, *Not Just Deserts* (Oxford: Clarendon, 1990), 45.

56. Ibid., 42–45.

57. Ibid., 42–45, 130–131.

58. Ibid., 37.

59. "[P]enal culture is the loose amalgam of penological theory, stored-up experience, institutional wisdom, and professional common sense which frames the action of penal agents and which lends meaning to what they do . . . any external force or determinant which seeks to transform penal practice . . . must first transform this penal culture if it is to become effective." Garland, *Punishment and Modern Society*, 209–210.

60. Braithwaite and Petit, *Not Just Deserts*, 42.

61. Albert Camus, *The Plague*, trans. Stuart Gilbert (New York: Knopf, 1993), 226, 228.

62. Ibid., 230–231.

63. Eschatology is the theological reflection that ensues from a focus upon the end of history. For an insightful employment of eschatology in service to a commitment to nonviolence, see John Howard Yoder, *The Original Revolution* (Scottdale, PA: Herald Press, 1971), 55–90.

64. Taylor, *Sources of the Self*, 517, 520.

65. Auguste Comte, *A General View of Positivism*, trans. J. H. Bridges (New York: Robert Speller, 1975), Ch. I; see also, Lasch, *The True and Only Heaven*.

66. Nowhere is this affinity between religion and science more apparent than in quantum mechanics. There are numerous volumes describing such phenomena as the superposition of electrons, the EPR effect of togetherness in separation, string theory, and Grand Unified Theory. For an overview of developments in physics since Einstein and their relation to theology, see John Polkinghorne, *Quantum Physics and Theology* (New Haven, CT: Yale University Press, 2007).

67. Alan Watts, *Behold the Spirit: A Study in the Necessity of Mystical Religion* (New York: Pantheon, 1971), xiii.

68. Clear et al., "The Value of Religion in Prison," 54.

69. Shadd Maruna, "Reintegration as a Right and Rites of Reintegration: A Comparative Review of De-Stigmatization Practices" in *Effective Interventions in the Lives of Criminal Offenders*, eds. J. A. Humphrey and P. Cordella (New York: Springer, 2014), 121–138 at 131, 125. R. A. Duff's work continually highlights the centrality not only of repentance and apology in his communicative ethic but the need to frame it in ritual fashion. See "Restorative Punishment and Punitive Restoration" in *Restorative Justice and the Law*, ed. Lode Walgrave (Cullompton, UK: Willan, 2002), 82–100.

70. Braithwaite, *Crime, Shame, and Reintegration*, Ch. 4.

71. Mathiesen, *Prison on Trial*, 21–22.

72. Aside from the host of socioeconomic and psychological challenges faced by those exiting penal institutions, some authors point to the "learned helplessness" that results from a prolonged period in which the prisoner is incapable of initiating virtually any action. This leads many to become "traumatized by the unstructured and unpredictable nature of the free world settings to which they return." See Haney, *Reforming Punishment*, 176. Becci reports that some released persons she worked with forgot about job interviews because there was no one to tell them to go. See *Imprisoned Religion*, 88.

73. I am thinking of the work of James Gilligan and Rene Girard in employing the element of narcissism. They would argue in different ways that violence is often produced by mutual rivalry for desired persons or objects (Girard) or as a result of feeling that one's self-worth or pride has been insulted by acts of disrespect either in interpersonal situations or as a result of social policy (Gilligan). See Girard, "Mimesis and Violence"; James Gilligan, *Preventing Violence* (London: Thames and Hudson, 2001), 29–45.

74. Cohen, *Visions of Social Control*, 256.

75. Howard Zehr, *The Little Book of Restorative Justice* (Intercourse, PA: Good Books, 2002), 37.

76. Carolyn Hoyle, "The Case for Restorative Justice" in Chris Cunneen and Carolyn Hoyle, *Debating Restorative Justice* (Oxford and Portland, OR: Hart, 2006), 1–100 at 45.

77. "Some schools aim to integrate restorative principles into most of their day-to-day activity, whilst others use family group conferencing only to deal with specific,

and sometimes more serious, incidents. The techniques used to conference youths who have been accused of bullying, being very disruptive or damaging property within the school are remarkably similar to restorative conferences between victims and offenders within the criminal justice process. Research has shown that such processes promote harmonious relationships in school, and typically bring about the successful resolution of conflict and harm." Ibid., 46.

78. Ibid., 8, 13.

79. Rather than providing a critical challenge to the status quo, restorative justice may simply serve an ideological function of reinforcing the dominant view of crime as individual pathology . . . [It] demonstrates a strong tendency to work within traditional criminal justice systems and, whilst doing so, fails to challenge the exclusionary processes of criminalization." Chris Cunnenn, The Limitations of Restorative Justice" in Cunneen and Hoyle, *Debating Restorative Justice*, 101–187 at 105–106.

80. This feeling of helplessness and hopelessness, however deficient in its interior logic, has been explored in texts such as the following: Elijah Anderson, *Code of the Street* (New York: W. W. Norton, 1999); James Gilligan, *Preventing Violence*; Robert J. Sampson, "Urban Black Violence: The Effect of Male Joblessness and Family Disruption," *The American Journal of Sociology* 92 (1987): 348–382; Loic Wacquant, *Punishing the Poor*.

81. Levinas, *Entre Nous*, 131.

82. Thomas Merton, *New Seeds of Contemplation* (Boston: Shambala, 2003), 36–37. "The Self of everyday Dasein is the *they-self*, which we distinguish from the *authentic self*." Heidegger, *Being and Time*, 167.

83. "What is real is what you have to deal with, what won't just go away just because it doesn't fit with your prejudices. By this token, what you can't help having recourse to in life is real, or as near to reality as you can get a grasp of at present." Taylor, *Sources of the Self*, 59. For Husserl, the real is the phenomenological starting point, it is "the experience as given to us." See *General Introduction to Pure Phenomenology*, 112.

84. Watts, *Behold the Spirit*, xxiii.

85. James H. Austin has done a neuroscientific study on the effects of Zen meditation on brain patterns and, specifically, the reconfiguring of synapses that leads to peaceful responses to stimuli of any sort: "Slowly, the aspirant who follows the Zen Buddhist path learns to merge the practices of meditative concentration with restraint and insight. The triad functions as an interactive unit, much as do lungs, heart, and brain. Reinforcing one another, they gradually bring their *coordinated* impact into thoughts, attitudes, and behavior. *Together they help one sort things out, observe which options work better, arrive at constructive solutions, keep one's best intentions on-line.* The result can be nothing less that spiritual renaissance." See *Zen and the Brain* (Cambridge, MA: MIT Press, 1998), 126.

86. Ibid. 3, 126. See also Patrick McNamara, *The Neuroscience of Religious Experience* (New York: Cambridge University Press, 2009).

87. Mohandas Gandhi, *Selections from His Writings*, 87.

88. This is expressed in Buddhism by the doctrine of non-self and in theistic religions by the aforementioned distinction between the true and false self. See, e.g., Sallie B. King, *Socially Engaged Buddhism* (Honolulu: University of Hawaii Press, 2009), 17–27, 149; Thich Nhat Hanh, *The Miracle of Mindfulness* (Boston: Beacon, 1987).

89. Mark Brown notes that the "dangerous offender . . . has taken on something of a routine appearance in contemporary penality" which has, in turn, led to "growth technologies in the penal sphere." See "Calculations of Risk," 93. Loic Wacquant speaks of a policy of *"confinement of differentiation"* that seeks to facilitate a "sub-traction" of entire groups of people from the social body. See "Suitable Enemies," *Punishment and Society* 1 (1999), 215–222 at 218.

90. Gilmore, *Golden Gulag*, 16.

91. "[A] small number of communities bear the disproportionate brunt of U.S. crime policy." Robert J. Sampson and Charles Loeffler, "Punishment's Place: The Local Concentration of Mass Incarceration," *Daedalus* 131 (2010): 20–31 at 20, 29.

92. The former Archbishop of Canterbury, Dr. Rowan Williams, speaks of contem-plation from a Christian perspective, but his conclusions regarding its effects can be expressed using any set of religious or secular metaphors: "[Contemplation] is very far from being just one kind of thing that Christians do: it is the key to prayer, liturgy, art and ethics, the key to the essence of a renewed humanity that is ca-pable of seeing the world and other subjects in the world with freedom—freedom from self-oriented, acquisitive habits and the distorted understanding that comes from them. To put it boldly, contemplation is the only ultimate answer to the un-real and insane world that our financial systems and our advertising culture and our chaotic and unexamined emotions encourage us to inhabit. To learn contem-plative practice is to learn what we need so as to live truthfully and honestly and lovingly. It is a deeply revolutionary matter." Rowan Williams, "Address to the Roman Synod of Bishops" (2012), 8. Available online at https://zenit.org/articles/archbishop-rowan-williams-address-to-the-synod-of-bishops/

93. Aldous Huxley, *The Perennial Philosophy* (New York: Harper & Brothers: 1945). See Thich Nhat Hanh, *Living Buddha, Living Christ* (New York: Riverhead Books: 1995); Mirabai Starr, *God of Love: A Guide to the Heart of Judaism, Christianity, and Islam* (Rheinbeck, NY: Monkfish Book Publishing Company, 2012); Watts, *Behold the Spirit*.

94. Berger and Luckmann, *The Social Construction*, 95.

95. "It is not the consciousness of men that determines their existence, but their social existence that determines their consciousness." Karl Marx, *A Contribution to the Critique of Political Economy*, trans. N. I. Stone (Chicago: Charles H. Kerr, 1904), 11–12. Wink makes the same point regarding the spirit of institutions. See *Naming the Powers*, 5.

96. Johnston, *Forms of Constraint*, 17–24.

97. See Lewis, *From Newgate to Dannemora*; Rothman, *Discovery of the Asylum*; Carl E. Schneider, "The Rise of Prisons and the Origins of the Rehabilitative Ideal," *Michigan Law Review* 77 (1979): 707–746; Negley K. Teeters and John D. Shearer, *The Prison at Philadelphia Cherry Hill* (New York: Columbia University Press, 1957). As the reader may know, the French government sent Alexis De Tocqueville and his colleague Gustave De Beaumont to study the two prototypical penitentiaries.

98. Wines, *Transactions of the National Penal Congress*, 566–567.

99. Erzen, *God in Captivity*; Byron Johnson, "Can a Faith-Based Prison Reduce Recidivism, *Corrections Today* 73 (2012): 60–62; Byron Johnson, "Religious Programs and Recidivism among Former Inmates in Prison Fellowship Programs: A Long-Term Follow-Up Study," *Justice Quarterly* 21 (2004): 329–354; Winnifred Fallers Sullivan, *Prison Religion, Faith-Based Reform and the Constitution* (Princeton, NJ: Princeton University Press, 2009).

100. Cullen at al., "The Virtuous Prison"; Garland, *Punishment*, 209–210; Lin, *Reform in the Making*, 4–6, 23, 30; Sykes, *Society of Captives*, 133–134.

101. Ronald Dworkin, *Life's Dominion* (New York: Knopf, 1993).

102. Robinson, "Late-Modern Rehabilitation: The Evolution of a Penal Strategy," 430.

103. Ward and Maruna, *Rehabilitation*, 17.

104. Robinson, "Late-Modern Rehabilitation, 437, 438.

105. Aristotle, *Ethics*, V, vii.

106. Aquinas, *Summa Theologica*, I–II. q. 94, a. 2.

107. James, *Varieties*, Lecture 9,167.

108. This approach receives a contemporary expression among a group of scholars and church leaders empowered to investigate the Scottish penal system. One of the committee members, Duncan Forrester, concluded that despite their long shelf life, the existent theories in the debate over the practice of criminal justice "often disguise, mystify, and subtly justify what is really happening." Instead, Forrester argued that reforming penal dynamics must begin with caring men and women whose primary concern is more phenomenological than theoretical; people who begin with the goal of looking "more deeply into the experience of being and surviving as a prisoner." Quoted in Hauerwas, "Punishing Christians," 188.

109. De Beaumont and De Tocqueville, *On the Penitentiary System*, 5. Jonas Hanway was an outspoken critic of solitary confinement. See, *Solitude in Imprisonment* (London: J. Bew, 1776).

110. Jeffrey Ian Ross, ed. *The Globalization of Supermax Prisons* (New Brunswick, NJ: Rutgers University Press, 2013).

111. De Beaumont and De Tocqueville, *On the Penitentiary System*, 5.

112. The literature on meditation/contemplation is virtually endless. Some of the sources that I have consulted are: Austin, *Zen and the Brain*; James Finley, *Christian Meditation* (San Francisco, Harper, 2014); Laird, *A Sunlit Absence*;

Thomas Merton, *New Seeds of Contemplation*; Watts, *Behold the Spirit*; Ken Wilber, *Integral Meditation* (Boulder, CO: Shambhala, 2016).

113. Miller, *In the Throe of Wonder*, 7.

114. Levinas, *Entre Nous*, 15.

115. "Overall, our study demonstrates that religion can reduce negative behavior, even in an exceptionally negative context such as a prison facility." Kent R. Kerley, Todd L. Matthews, and Troy C. Blanchard, "Religiosity, Religious Participation, and Negative Prison Behaviors," *Journal for the Scientific Study of Religion* 44 (2005): 443–457 at 455.

116. Miller, *In the Throe of Wonder*, 6.

117. Miller and Rollnick, *Motivational Interviewing*, 4, 9.

118. Bonita M. Veysey, Johanna Christian, and Damian J. Martinez, "Identity Transformation and Offender Change" in *How Offenders Transform Their Lives*, eds. Bonita M. Veysey, Johanna Christian, and Damian J. Martinez, eds. (Cullompton, UK: Willan, 2009), 1–11 at 5.

119. Charles Colson, *Justice That Restores* (Wheaton, IL: Tyndale House, 2001), 106–107. For more detail on the Humaita prison and the APAC Methodology that it is based upon, see Mario Ottoboni, *Kill the Criminal, Save the Person* (Washington, DC: Prison Fellowship International, 2000).

120. Quoted in Sykes, *Society of Captives*, 36. Mary Douglas's anthropological investigations revealed the regularity with which altruism is augmented in small communal associations. See *How Institutions Think*, 21.

121. Duff, "Penal Communications," 53.

122. Hampton, "The Moral Education Theory of Punishment," 236.

123. Ibid., 234–235.

124. Graeme Newman, *Just and Painful* (New York: Harrow and Heston, 1995), 82.

125. Ibid.

126. The Quakers have a long-standing commitment to penal reform beginning most notably in the Eastern State Penitentiary and, more recently, in an influential monograph from the early 1970s that helped seal the fate of traditional rehabilitative theory. See American Friends Service Committee, *Struggle for Justice* (New York: Hill & Wang, 1971).

127. Magnani and Wray, *Beyond Prisons*, 155.

128. Sykes, *Society of Captives*, 65–66.

129. Meyer, *The Justice of Mercy*, 4.

130. Ibid., 4–5.

131. He states that "Roman Christianity . . . overdetermines all language of law, of politics . . . No alleged disenchantment, nor secularization comes to interrupt it." Jacques Derrida, "On Forgiveness" in *On Cosmopolitanism and Forgiveness* (Abingdon and New York: Routledge, 2001), 27–59 at 32.

132. Ibid.

133. Ibid., 29.

134. Ibid., 49.

135. Ibid., 31.

136. On the comparison of a first-century worldview based upon purity with one based upon compassion, see Marcus Borg, *Meeting Jesus Again for the First Time* (San Francisco: Harper, 1994), 46–58.

137. Paul Tillich, *The New Being* (New York: Charles Scribner's Sons, 1955), 7.

138. L. Gregory Jones, *Embodying Forgiveness* (Grand Rapids, MI: Eerdmans, 1995), 136.

139. Ibid., 145–146.

140. Taylor, *Sources of the Self*, 151.

141. Kerley et al., "Religiosity, Religious Participation, and Negative Prison Behaviors," 455; Sykes, *Society of Captives*, 65–66.

142. Johnson, "Can a Faith-Based Prison Reduce Recidivism?", 60–62.

143. Johnson, "The Faith-Based Prison," 42.

144. Erzen, *God in Captivity*, 4.

145. Johnson, "The Faith-Based Prison," 43, 47.

146. Maruna et al., "Why God Is Often Found," 163.

147. See Giordano et al., "Gender, Crime, and Desistance," 1001.

148. Johnson notes that the faith-based prison as a specifically Christian exercise could not, and should not, be implemented throughout the entire institution. Ibid., 57–58.

149. Colson, *Justice That Restores*, 90–94, 94.

150. Sullivan, *Prison Religion: Faith-Based Reform and the Constitution*, 48.

151. Becci, *Imprisoned Religion*, 132.

152. Alexander Shalom, "Bail Reform as a Mass Incarceration Reduction Technique," *Rutgers Law Review* 66 (2014): 921–930.

CONCLUSION

1. Lofland, *Deviance and Identity*, 12. Derrida also employs the term "crime against humanity" in his exposition on forgiveness. He employs the phrase to emphasize that we all have committed such crimes. There is thus no logic in singling out anyone for committing acts in which we have all taken part. See Derrida, "On Forgiveness," 32ff.

2. "Every scientific memoir in its record of the 'facts' is shot through and through with interpretation. The methodology of rational interpretation is the product of the fitful vagueness of consciousness. Elements which shine with immediate distinctness, in some circumstances, retire into penumbral shadow in other circumstances, and into black darkness on other occasions. Any yet all occasions proclaim themselves as actualities within the flux of a solid world, demanding a unity of interpretation." Whitehead, *Process and Reality*, 15.

3. Wink, *Engaging the Powers*, 69.

4. Sutherland, *Criminology*, 22.

5. Bauman, "Social Issues of Law and Order," 206.

6. Winter, *Elements for a Social Ethic*, 109.

7. The we-relation "is not accessible to scientific explication . . . [it is] the lived-experience of vivid simultaneity which can be brought to consciousness in reflection but has the character of immediacy." Ibid., 117.

8. Whitehead, *Process and Reality*, 21.

9. "There are, therefore, two minimum conditions necessary and sufficient for the existence of a legal system. On the one hand, those rules of behaviour which are valid according to the system's ultimate criteria of validity must be generally obeyed, and, on the other hand, its rules of recognition specifying the criteria of legal validity and its rules of change and adjudication must be effectively accepted as common public standards of official behaviour by its officials. The first condition is the only one which private citizens need satisfy . . . The second condition must also be satisfied by the officials of the system." H. L. A. Hart, *The Concept of Law* (Oxford: Clarendon, 1961), 116–117.

10. Cover, "Nomos and Narrative," 68.

11. Ronald H. Preston, "Social Theology and Penal Theory and Practice: The Collapse of the Rehabilitative Ideal and the Search for an Alternative" in Bottoms and Preston, *The Coming Penal Crisis*, 109–125 at 116.

12. Gauchet, *The Disenchantment of the World*, 6. Max Heirich, in his study of conversion, notes that conversion can be best be spoken of in a literature that treats religion less as a system of truth and more towards the discovery of "a ground of being that creates and orders experience more generally . . . it involves examination of core senses of reality, identifying aspects which must be responded to with the whole being." Heirich, "Change of Heart," 674.

13. Taylor, *Sources of the Self*, 47.

14. Teilhard de Chardin, *The Divine Milieu*, 35.

15. Derrida, "On Forgiveness," 30.

16. Meyer, *The Justice of Mercy*, 74, 81–85.

17. Miller and Rollnick, *Motivational Interviewing*, 5.

18. Simmel further adds that "the inner aspect of this outer reserve is not only indifference but, more often than we are aware, it is a slight aversion, a mutual strangeness and repulsion which will break into hatred and fight at the moment of closer contact, however caused." See Georg Simmel, "The Metropolis and Mental Life" in *The Sociology of Georg Simmel*, trans. Kurt H. Wolff (New York: Free Press, 1950), 409–424 at 410, 413–414, 415–416.

19. Quoted in Sellin, "Dom Jean Mabillon," 581–602 at 587.

Index